CONTEMPORARY ISSUES
IN THE
EARLY YEARS

CONTEMPORARY ISSUES IN THE EARLY YEARS:

Working Collaboratively for Children

Edited by
Gillian Pugh

Paul Chapman Publishing in association with the
National Children's Bureau

P·C·P
Paul Chapman
Publishing Ltd

NATIONAL
CHILDREN'S
BUREAU
Early Childhood Unit

Paul Chapman Publishing Ltd
144 Liverpool Road
London
N1 1LA

British Library Cataloguing in Publication Data

Contemporary issues in the early years: working collaboratively
for children
I. Pugh, Gillian
372.19

ISBN 1 85396 173 6

Typeset by Setrite Typesetters, Hong Kong
Printed in Great Britain by The Baskerville Press, Salisbury, Wiltshire

C   D   E   F   7   6   5   4

CONTENTS

LIST OF ABBREVIATIONS

AMA	Association of Metropolitan Authorities
BAECE	British Association for Early Childhood Education
CATE	Committee for the Accreditation of Teacher Education
CRE	Commission for Racial Equality
DE	Department of Employment
DES	Department of Education and Science
DH	Department of Health
EC	European Community
EOC	Equal Opportunities Commission
ERA	Education Reform Act
ESAC	Education, Science and Arts Committee
EYCG	Early Years Curriculum Group
HMI	Her Majesty's Inspectorate
IIU	Independent inspection unit
LA	Local authority
LEA	Local education authority
LMS	Local management of schools
MSC	Manpower Services Commission
NCB	National Children's Bureau
NCC	National Consumer Council
NCMA	National Childminding Association
NCVQ	National Council for Vocational Qualifications
NFER	National Foundation for Educational Research
NNEB	National Nursery Examination Board
NVQ	National Vocational Qualification
OMEP	World Organization for Early Childhood Education
PGCE	Postgraduate Certificate in Education
PPA	Pre-school Playgroups Association
SAT	Standard Assessment Task
SCDC	Schools Curriculum Development Committee
SEAC	Schools Evaluation and Assessment Council
VOLCUF	Voluntary Organizations Liaison Council for Under Fives

BIOGRAPHICAL DETAILS OF CONTRIBUTORS

Gillian Pugh is Director of the Early Childhood Unit at the National Children's Bureau. She has worked extensively with central and local government on the development of a policy for young children, and has published books and training materials on policy development, on co-ordination of services and on curriculum. She was a member of the Rumbold Committee on the education of children aged three to five, and of the AMA working party on services for young children. Previous work at the bureau has included national studies of parental involvement in pre-school services, of parent education and support, and of services for handicapped children and their families. Before joining the bureau she worked with the Schools Council Humanities Curriculum Project.

Peter Moss is Senior Research Officer at the Thomas Coram Research Unit and Co-ordinator of the European Commission Childcare Network. He has worked at Thomas Coram for twenty years, specializing in work on families with young children, services for them and work–family issues. He has co-ordinated the European Childcare Network since 1986.

Peter Elfer is Senior Development Officer at the Early Childhood Unit of the National Children's Bureau. He qualified as a field social worker in 1975 and since then has worked as a practitioner and manager in social services in the voluntary and statutory sectors. He joined the Early Childhood Unit in 1987 where he has been examining the implications of the Children Act for services for young children.

Dorothy Wedge is County Adviser, Services to Under Fives for Cambridgeshire. Originally qualified as a social worker, she has worked with young children and their families in a number of capacities – nursery teaching and pre-school home visiting in London, social services area adviser in Norfolk, and now in a challenging joint-funded post in Cambridgeshire.

Tricia David is Lecturer in Education at Warwick University. She has been a headteacher, a researcher, and a tutor in adult and community education. She currently holds a 1991–2 Kellmer Pringle Fellowship for multi-professional development work and she is Vice-Chair of the UK branch of the World Organization for Early Childhood Education (OMEP).

Mary Jane Drummond is Tutor in Primary Education at the Cambridge Institute of Education. She has taught in infant and primary schools in Hackney and Sheffield, and during the 1970s was a member of the Schools Council Communication Skills in Early Childhood Project led by Joan Tough. She joined the Cambridge Institute in 1985 where she works on in-service courses for teachers and early years educators in East Anglia. Her interests include personal, social and moral education, and the emotional dimensions of education, particularly assessment and staff relationships.

Cathy Nutbrown is Co-ordinator for Early Childhood Education with Sheffield Education Department, working with early childhood educators in statutory and voluntary services. She was recently a member of the research team in the Sheffield Early Literacy Development Project, and is currently developing work on early literacy and schema, and running multi-disciplinary courses on these and other early childhood issues.

Iram Siraj-Blatchford is Lecturer in Education (Early Years) at the University of Warwick. She has taught nursery, infant and junior children and has been in teacher education for five years. She has lectured nationally and internationally on quality early years education, and is engaged in research and writing as well as teaching.

Professor Sheila Wolfendale is Principal Lecturer and Course Tutor to the MSc Educational Psychology course at the Polytechnic of East London. She has worked as a primary and a remedial teacher, as an educational psychologist, and as a college of education lecturer and university tutor. She is author, co-author, editor and co-editor of books, pamphlets, training manuals and articles on a number of areas, including learning difficulties, special educational needs, educational psychology, parental involvement and early years.

Janine Wooster is Co-ordinator of the Pre-school Home Visiting Team for Children with Special Needs in the London Borough of Newham. She has been a teacher of children with special needs for the past ten years and co-ordinator of the pre-school team for three, working with the Newham Portage scheme and the national Portage Association.

Dorothy Rouse is Development Officer in the Early Childhood Unit at the National Children's Bureau. She has worked *with* children in nursery and infant schools, and *for* children as a consultant and as a tutor in training institutions, where she has trained educators from education, social service and voluntary sector settings. She has a special interest in how children learn, and in the curriculum for children from birth to eight years old.

Sue Griffin is Training Officer for the National Childminding Association (NCMA). She was previously Development Officer for the NCMA in south-west England, during which time she was seconded to the Working with Under Sevens Project to develop standards for National Vocational Qualifications. She has also had a long involvement with the playgroup movement, going from parent helper to chair of the Pre-school Playgroups Association.

Margy Whalley is Head of Pen Green Centre for Under Fives and Families in Corby. She taught in primary schools in this country before spending seven years as a pre-school/community development worker in the Amazon and Papua New Guinea. Since coming back to England, she has 'found out about community education, Freire, multi-disciplinary work and feminism, and become a parent' – and her daughter would like her to stop writing and cook some proper meals.

Dorit Braun is Assistant Director (Development) of the Community Education Development Centre in Coventry. Her background is in family and health education. She has worked on a number of development projects, including producing materials for parent groups, for preparation for parenthood and for training teachers around issues of child abuse.

Audrey Curtis is Senior Lecturer at the University of London Institute of Education. She has been a playgroup worker, has taught early years and special needs, and trained teachers in initial and in-service courses. She is currently involved with higher degree work at the Institute of Education, is a consultant to Unicef and the British Council, and is European President of the World Organization for Early Childhood Education (OMEP).

Dr Denise Hevey is Director of the Vocational Qualifications Development Centre at the Open University. She was previously involved in the development of courses on child abuse and neglect, and working with children and young people. During 1989 and 1990 she was seconded to the Local Government Management Board to develop national occupational standards for work with young children and their families in preparation for the introduction of National Vocational Qualifications. She is President of the National Childminding Association.

NATIONAL CHILDREN'S BUREAU

The National Children's Bureau was established as a registered charity in 1963. Its purpose is to identify and promote the interests of all children and young people and to improve their status in a diverse and multiracial society.

The Bureau works closely with professionals and policy-makers to improve the lives of all children but especially children under five, those affected by family instability and children with special needs or disabilities.

The Bureau collects and disseminates information about children and promotes good practice in children's services through research, policy and practice development, publications, seminars, training and an extensive library and information service.

The Early Childhood Unit was established in 1986 as a national centre for advice, consultancy, training and information on current practice, thinking and research in the early years field. It aims:

(1) to raise awareness of the needs of young children;
(2) to improve policy and service provision for children across social services, health, education and the voluntary sector;
(3) to support the raising of professional standards of practice.

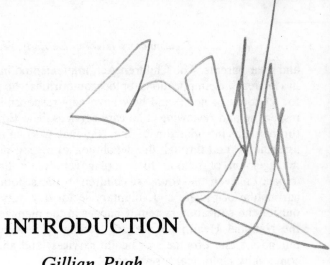

INTRODUCTION

Gillian Pugh

A willingness to devote adequate resources to the care of children is the hallmark of a civilized society, as well as an investment in our future.

(Mia Kellmer Pringle, 1975, p. 148)

The best preparation for being a happy or useful man or woman is to live fully as a child.

(Plowden Report, CACE, 1967, para. 506)

This is a book about meeting the needs of young children: children who are powerless and vulnerable, but children who are intensely curious, energetic, and instinctive and enthusiastic learners. And it is about the environment and the experiences that we offer to children: about equality of opportunity for all children, about respecting and valuing children, about carefully observing children and planning how to meet their needs as individuals now and in the future. It is also about the relationships between adults and children, and between the adults – parents and educators – who work with and care for children. It is about working across boundaries, boundaries between parents and professionals, and between 'carers' and 'educators', and finding time to care for each other as well as for our children.

But because how we view childhood and treat children is a reflection of the values of the society we live in, the book is also about the context and the systems within which we live and work in the 1990s.

The book is written at a time of considerable change in welfare services in the United Kingdom. Major legislation in health, education and social services is changing both professional practice and its impact on children and their parents. The Children Act, implemented in the autumn of 1991, has far-reaching implications for local authorities who must provide services for 'children in need' and now have new responsibilities for registering, inspecting and reviewing child care services. The Education Reform Act, through the introduction of the National Curriculum and processes of assessment, and through the devolution of responsibility for the financial management of schools to school governors, is having a considerable impact on even the youngest children in the school system, and on the curriculum of private and voluntary sector day nurseries and playgroups outside the education system. Changes in the management and funding of the National Health Service are leading to new relationships between purchasers and providers of health services, and an uncertain future for community child health services.

In all these areas the enterprise culture and a market-forces approach to service provision are leading to new roles for local authorities, as they become regulators and inspectors of private and voluntary sector provision as well as, and sometimes instead of, providers of services themselves. Issues of 'quality assurance', 'performance criteria', 'consumer rights' and 'value for money' are on many agendas, but there are different agendas, and the rights and needs of children are not always the first consideration. For this is also a decade in which an increasing number of families with children in the UK have been living in poverty, without access to a basic standard of living that most citizens have come to expect as of right (Bradshaw, 1990).

Since it was established in 1986, the Early Childhood Unit has been involved with many of these changes at central and local government level. Focusing as it does on the needs of children across the boundaries of health, care and education, and working at the interface between research, policy and practice, the Unit has been very busy during this period. The legislation has led to intense debate amongst politicians, managers and practitioners, and the increasing demand from employers for women to return to work has led to unprecedented interest in the national press about the shortage of child care. The establishment of the DES committee of inquiry into the education of three- to five-year-olds chaired by Angela Rumbold and the development of national guidelines on good practice in day care, playgroups, out-of-school clubs and child-minding have fed into the Department of Health's consultation process on the Guidance accompanying the Children Act. The extensive work programme set up by the Care Sector Consortium in preparation for the implementation of a system of National Vocational Qualifications has involved hundreds of early childhood workers in defining their skills and competences and contributing to the publication of national standards for child care workers. All these national developments have taken place in a context of growing understanding of how early childhood services are developing in Europe, and how governments elsewhere are responding to the needs of families to be able to balance work and family responsibilities.

The work of the Early Childhood Unit is underpinned by a number of basic principles that reflect the rights of all children to good quality services that support their overall development within the context of their family. Four of these principles form the starting point for *A Policy for Young Children: A Framework for Action*, a policy statement subscribed to by all the main agencies – statutory and voluntary – who work with or are concerned about the health, welfare and education of young children in Britain, and it is perhaps fitting that a book that reflects so many current developments in the early years field should start with these principles:

> – that young children are important in their own right, and as a resource for the future;
> – that young children are valued and their full development is possible only if they live in an environment which reflects and respects their individual identity, culture and heritage;
> – that parents are primarily responsible for nurturing and supporting the development of their children and that this important role should be more highly valued by society;
> – that central and local government have a duty, working in partnership with parents, to ensure that services and support are available for families; services that encourage children's cognitive, social, emotional and physical development; and meet parents' needs for support for themselves and day care for their children.
>
> (National Children's Bureau, 1990, p. 1)

Embedded in these statements are values and principles that are central to all the chapters in this book. The new legislation and a resurgence of interest in day care and early education bring challenges as well as opportunities for those who work with young children. The contributors to this volume have been invited to explore some of the key issues that face early childhood practitioners, managers and policy-makers in the early 1990s, as they attempt to keep their sights clearly on the needs of our youngest children. Central to almost every chapter is a clear value position, and a call for establishing explicit principles to underpin our work.

Just as the Under Fives Unit changed its name to Early Childhood Unit during 1991 to reflect these changes, so the contributors have taken an overall 'early years' brief (usually seen as the years 0—8) whilst concentrating on the years 0—5. Contributors have also taken the view that care and education for young children should be inseparable, and most support the view of the Rumbold Committee that

> Education for the under fives can happen in a wide variety of settings and can be supplied by a wide range of people. Some will be professional teachers; many will not...we have therefore used the term 'educator' throughout to describe an adult working with the under fives, unless our meaning is more limited.

> (DES, 1990a, Introduction)

The renewed emphasis on integration or co-ordination is welcome, but is not without its dangers. Within the education system, nursery education is seen as the first stage in a continuous process of learning, and nursery teachers in the UK — unlike almost anywhere else in the world — are accorded similar status to other teachers. One of the dilemmas reflected in this book is that of horizontal versus vertical co-ordination: if the pull towards co-ordination of all under-fives services becomes too great, is there .a corresponding weakening of the continuity between education before five and education after five? In striving to 'upgrade' all non-education nursery provision, is there a danger that all non-statutory services — including nursery education — will instead be downgraded? This is thrown into relief most vividly in Chapter 11 on training.

The book is in three parts — Policy, Practice and Training — all three of which are informed by the implications of recent research. The first three chapters are concerned principally with policy. Gillian Pugh reviews early childhood care and education in the UK within the context of recent legislation and developments at local level and, despite some encouraging trends, finds a continuing lack of coherence, commitment, and resources. Peter Moss draws on his experience as co-ordinator of the European Childcare Network to examine policy and recent trends in Europe and outlines a proposed European Commission Recommendation on Childcare. Peter Elfer and Dorothy Wedge examine the concept of quality, looking at the importance of the values inherent in any definitions of quality and questioning whether the framework provided by the Children Act is adequate for monitoring and supporting quality services.

Part 2 on practice in the early years includes five chapters on the quality of the experiences that we offer young children. Tricia David asks what we mean by curriculum in the early years, looking at the context and process of learning, at breadth and balance, and at continuity and progression within early years settings and in relation to the National Curriculum.

Mary Jane Drummond and Cathy Nutbrown identify and discuss the key questions that face educators as they observe and assess children, a process that should always be central to planning for children's learning.

Although the central tenet of each chapter is that of equality of opportunity and a quality service that meets individual needs, three chapters look at specific issues. Iram Siraj-Blatchford looks at the impact of racism on children's identity and attitudes, at the potential offered by the Children Act for combating racism, and concludes with some specific suggestions for promoting racial equality, arguing that understanding cultural differences is not enough on its own. Sheila Wolfendale and Janine Wooster review developments in relation to young children with special needs in the context of legislation, research and practice, including a case study of practice in one London borough, and conclude that special needs in the early years is currently in receipt of more attention, resources and provision than at any other time, albeit in a somewhat haphazard way. Dorothy Rouse and Sue Griffin look at the particular needs of children under three, concentrating on children's needs for relationships with significant responsive adults, and for developmentally appropriate learning experiences.

Two chapters focus on relationships between adults who work with children. Margy Whalley describes the process of developing and supporting a multi-professional staff team, working with parents, volunteers and workers from other agencies. Dorit Braun examines why working with parents should be an integral part of early years provision and argues for training to support the development of appropriate skills and attitudes.

In the final chapter, Audrey Curtis and Denise Hevey confront the complex issue of training to work in the early years, looking at the skills, knowledge and understanding that are required and at recent developments in teacher training and in preparation for National Vocational Qualifications, and conclude with a number of alternative scenarios to take training forward.

Early childhood care and education are indeed at the crossroads. New directions in research, in practice and in legislation offer early years educators the opportunity to build on their skills, their commitment and their enthusiasm and to ensure that all children have access to services that meet their individual needs. Young children, however, are not a national priority, and politicians may have other priorities and make other choices. Educators, too, have choices – about how they assess children and plan the curriculum, about how they exercise their power over children, about how they work with parents and other educators. If we are to seize the opportunities offered today, then surely we must work collaboratively, travel together and speak loudly and with one voice.

PART 1
POLICY

1

A POLICY FOR EARLY CHILDHOOD SERVICES?

Gillian Pugh

Within the context of developments outlined briefly in the Introduction, this chapter seeks to assess what progress, if any, has been made in the last five years in developing a national policy on child care and early education to meet the needs of young children and their families. It will outline eight areas that such a policy should address:

(1) a co-ordinated approach, ensuring equal access to services and supported by legislation and resources;
(2) structures and systems to support a co-ordinated policy;
(3) a range of services to meet the needs of children and their parents;
(4) information for parents;
(5) setting standards and monitoring quality;
(6) an appropriate curriculum;
(7) a rational system of training and support;
(8) adequate pay and conditions and improved status for early years educators.

The first three of these will be dealt with in most detail, as the rest are covered by other chapters in the book.

The Early Childhood Unit's initial review of services for under fives looked specifically at attempts to co-ordinate services traditionally provided by education, social services, health and the voluntary sector. The report reviewed the historical development of provision for under fives, and found a patchwork of fragmented and uncoordinated services, showing wide variations between one part of the country and another, within the context of a 'low national commitment to developing and resourcing pre-school services, and the absence of a national policy on what services should be provided, for whom and by whom' (Pugh, 1988, p. 80).

The Unit survey revealed a 'groundswell of interest amongst local authorities in rethinking provision, and in looking again at structures for planning and organizing services, but this in the face of low resourcing, seemingly intractable problems over vested interests between departments, and often no clear sense of direction as to the best way forward' (p. 81). The report concluded that 'The challenge now is for central government to provide an overall framework within which services can be developed flexibly at local level' (p. 81). Some of the issues that such a policy should include have been outlined in further articles (Pugh, 1987, 1990), and formed the basis for the collaborative policy framework publication noted in the Introduction (National Children's Bureau, 1990).

A CO-ORDINATED POLICY, ENSURING EQUAL ACCESS TO QUALITY SERVICES, SUPPORTED BY LEGISLATION AND APPROPRIATE RESOURCES

Co-ordination?

Whilst there is some value in a diversity which can be sensitive to local needs, the current divisions between one form of service and another owe more to history and the professional jealousies of providers than to the needs of children and their families. It is now broadly accepted that in the early years in particular children's needs have to be seen as a whole and that services must respond to their social, emotional, physical and intellectual development. The starting point of a policy must therefore ensure that the underpinning principles, the aims and objectives, and the mechanisms for planning, delivering and managing services are developed in a co-ordinated way, drawing on the skills and expertise of parents and of all those who come to work with children from different professional backgrounds. If this were an easy challenge we would have made a great deal more progress than we have over the last thirty years. The obstacles have been well documented, and will be familiar to all early years practitioners who have tried to work across the traditional barriers. There will be different priorities between service providers, different ideologies, different boundaries — territorial and geographic, different training, different management and accounting systems, and even different languages. We should not underestimate the difficulties of co-ordinating our approach, but in the interests of providing children with continuity and coherence and in making the most efficient use of scarce resources, then a co-ordinated policy, with mechanisms for joint planning, management and review, must surely be a first priority.

Trends in levels of provision

The commitment in the 1972 White Paper to expand nursery education to accommodate 50 per cent of three-year-olds and 90 per cent of four-year-olds was reiterated by the more recent report of the House of Commons Select Committee (1989) which recommended that nursery education should be expanded until it is available to all three- and four-year-olds whose parents want it. More recently, reports have also recognized the need for a dramatic increase in day care. Current statistics, however, show how far short we still fall. As can be seen from Table 1.1, there is still a very limited amount of full day care, particularly for children under three, and public investment in nursery education and day care remains limited. The figures show increases in the percentage of children in private nurseries (numbers of places grew from 25,000 to 58,000 between 1985 and 1990) and with childminders; some increases in nursery education; and a slight decrease in playgroups. Comparisons with Europe show that we are still at the bottom of the league table in publicly funded day care and education (*see* Table 2.1, Chapter 2).

These trends reflect both demographic changes and government policy. The number of children under five is likely to increase by about 7 per cent in the next ten years and considerable expansion will be required just to retain current levels of provision. With rather more publicity, we have also seen what has been described as the demographic time bomb. A reduction in the number of school-leavers, and an increase in the number of women with children already joining the work-force to fill this gap, has finally put child care on the agenda, albeit with the needs of the economy rather than the child in mind.

The government response on day care and on nursery education has been to emphasize the role of the private and voluntary sectors. 'The government believes that there is scope for substantial private and voluntary sector involvement in this field, and will seek ways of maximizing the contribution which such provision can make to the fulfilment of demand for high quality nursery education' (House of Commons 1989). This has been followed by a comment by Kenneth Clark on BBC television

Table 1.1   Under fives in England: population and use of services 1975, 1985 and 1990

	1975	1985	1990
Population 0–4	3,227,900	2,973,400	3,189,400
Places per 100 children 0–4:			
LA day nurseries	0.8	1.0	0.9
Private registered nurseries	0.8	0.8	1.8
Childminders	2.6	4.7	6.4
Places per 100 children 3–4:			
Playgroups	23.3	33.8	33.2
Pupils as % of 3- and 4-year-olds:			
Nursery schools and classes	10.0	22.5	24.5
Under fives in infant classes	18.9	20.7	21.6
Independent schools	2.1	2.5	3.2

Source: Early Childhood Unit Statistics 1991, compiled from government sources.

(22 January 1991) that 'nursery education for all children is not a realistic prospect'.

With regard to day care, 'the government believe that in the first instance it is the responsibility of parents to make arrangements, including financial arrangements, for the day care of pre-school children' (Department of Health evidence to House of Commons, 1989). The role of employers is seen as critical and was stressed in an interview that John Patten, Home Office Minister and chair of The Ministerial Group on Women's Issues, gave to the *Independent* (12 January 1989): 'Employers must realize that the only way to defuse this demographic time bomb ticking away underneath them is by taking the initiative themselves to support family life and to support mothers who want to work'. This view has not been welcomed by employers. In the words of Business in the Community:

> Such an approach will give rise to patchy provision, excluding many groups and individuals from access...a better approach would be an equal partnership between central government, local authorities and employers. [Our] experience is that private and public partnership are most successful when they add value to mainstream provision, rather than acting as a substitute for it.
>
> (BIC, 1991)

This emphasis on employers providing for the needs of working parents, together with an emphasis on public funding only being for children in need (*see* below), is leading to a three-tier service: children of working parents in private sector provision; children in need in local authority nurseries; and children for whose parents part-time provision is convenient in nursery schools in some areas and in playgroups in others.

Equal access?

As the Rumbold Report acknowledged, 'access to services is still largely determined by where a child lives, when his or her birthday is, whether the parents have access to information about services, and whether they can afford fees where there is no public provision' (DES, 1990a, pp. 27–8). Clark's review of research (1988) pointed out that access to education has already become unequal for young children by the time they reach the statutory age for starting school.

For some children early education is particularly important. The House of Commons Select Committee report (1989) concluded that good quality pre-school education is of benefit to all children but particularly those with special needs, from socially or economically deprived backgrounds, and for those whose first language is not English. Yet evidence shows that many of those most in need are those least likely to have had any pre-school experience (Osborn and Milbank, 1987), and many children who would particularly benefit from nursery education are unable to take up places because the short hours do not suit the needs of working parents.

For children with special needs, the sooner assessment takes place, the better the chance of them being placed in an appropriate nursery setting. Once formal statements have been made, children will have access to ancillary help, special equipment or support teaching. The 1981 Education Act stipulated that children with special needs should be integrated into mainstream provision wherever possible, but in areas where there is little provision, nurseries and playgroups often have difficulty in meeting the needs of such children.

A policy that leaves service development to market forces tends to disadvantage those who are already disadvantaged, and, as is now evident in the United States, is vulnerable to changes in the economy. The patchwork of provision also makes it difficult to ensure continuity between one service and another. Because of the paucity of services, some children may use two or three different services a day – perhaps starting with a childminder, going to a morning playgroup, then back to the childminder before going on to a nursery class, then back to the childminder before going home. Although parents are always the key figures in these transitions, for those who are working it is not easy to ensure that the needs of the child are met, and as Rumbold points out, the achievement of desirable educational continuity and progression may be at risk.

In contrast to the rest of Europe, day care in the UK is seen as a private matter to be resolved by parents who are either expected to make their own arrangements with a relative or buy in services in the market-place. The EC Childcare Network reports (EC, 1988, 1990) show that the UK has one of the fastest growing employment rates for women with a child under five, but the poorest arrangements for maternity leave, and the lowest rates of publicly funded child care, though a substantial amount of private and voluntary sector provision (*see also* Chapter 2).

Legislation to support a co-ordinated policy?

Will the Children Act 1989 and the Education Reform Act 1988 create a more co-ordinated approach to an early years policy? They are each, in their respective fields, having a considerable impact not just on services for children, but also on the role of local authorities, and on the relationship between central and local government, between departments within local government, and between families and service providers. Consideration of a third major piece of legislation − the NHS and Community Care Act 1989 − is beyond the scope of this chapter, but there are concerns that the health needs of children have not been fully addressed in this latest reorganization of the health service (Woodruffe and Kurtz, 1989). The split between purchasers and providers and the creation of separate trusts within health authorities are already making a co-ordinated approach to policy development and planning very difficult.

The Children Act will perhaps have the greatest impact including as it does new regulations to replace the Nurseries and Child-Minders Regulation Act 1948. The scope of the new Act is considerable, and although a substantial part is concerned with family support and child protection, those sections dealing with children under eight are likely to have far-reaching consequences. The principles underpinning the Act are all central to good practice in the early years: these are that the welfare of the child is paramount, that the concept of parental rights should be replaced by one of parental responsibility, that professionals should work in partnership with parents and with each other, and that sensitivity to values, beliefs and practices in relation to race, language, culture and religion should become an integral part of all provision.

With regard to services for children under eight, the Act envisages three main roles for local authorities:

(1) the duty to provide for children 'in need...as is appropriate', and in making such arrangements to have regard to the different racial groups in the area to which children in need belong. The concept of 'children in need' is widely defined as those whose health and development is unlikely to be achieved or maintained, or may be significantly impaired, without the provision of services, or those who are disabled. The Act also empowers local authorities to make provision for children who are not in need, although the Guidance (DH, 1991) makes it clear that public funds are unlikely to be sufficient to provide for all parents who require services.

(2) The duty to register all day care provision for children under eight that is in operation for two hours or more, including out-of-school clubs, and keep a register of provision. The registration process has to check that the persons offering care, and the premises, are 'fit', and registration may be cancelled if the person or premises is judged to be 'seriously inadequate'. This would include failure to have regard to a child's religion, race, culture and language. Nurseries and child-minders must be inspected at least once a year, and social services may seek the help of the education authority in registering and inspecting.

(3) The duty to review the level, pattern and range of provision of childminding and day care, taking account of nursery and primary education, every three years. The review must be undertaken jointly with the LEA and in consultation with health authorities, voluntary organizations and others, and a report must be published.

The recognition of the importance of minimizing the effect upon children of their disabilities and of giving them the opportunity for access to mainstream services is to be welcomed. So too is the emphasis throughout the Act on children's 'racial origin, religious persuasion and cultural and linguistic background'. But there is concern that to separate 'children in need' from other children will become a self-fulfilling prophecy. If children are categorized in this way, it will surely continue to support the existence of a stigmatized underclass of families who are failing.

All young children have needs, and research has shown both the immediate and the lasting value to all children of good quality early childhood care and education. But even given a limited view of need, there is a very real danger that local authorities will begin to define children according to the resources available, as had already happened in preparing Statements for children with special educational need, rather than in response to the actual needs of individual children. As a substantial plank in a potential policy for young children, the Children Act fails to accept, as other European governments do, that all children have a right to a good quality, affordable service that will promote their all-round development.

With regard to the review, the Guidance makes it clear that this cannot be a snapshot taken once every three years but should be part of an overall policy on service development, supported by a co-ordinated committee structure (DH, 1991, para. 9.10). The Guidance urges co-ordination between day care and education services (para. 1.16) and looks at how co-ordination can be effected. However, it does not take the step of facilitating co-ordination or encouraging integration by repealing those elements of existing legislation which prohibit real movement at local level.

Whilst the Children Act urges co-ordination, the Education Reform Act (ERA) and the Education (Schools) Bill reduces the role of the local education authority and in effect makes co-ordination more difficult.

The impact of the ERA on children under five is less direct than the Children Act, but is nevertheless being felt in nurseries and playgroups all over the country. The introduction of the National Curriculum with its associated subject-based programmes of study for children of five and upwards, and assessment for all children at seven, has put considerable pressure on some early years practitioners to alter the way in which they work in order to 'feed into' the National Curriculum and prepare children for base-line assessment at five. We return to this issue under the section on curriculum below.

One other aspect of the ERA is beginning to have an impact on nursery education: local management of schools (LMS) and delegated budgets. As governors take over many of the responsibilities of the LEA in relation to the running of a school, it is becoming increasingly difficult for local authorities to implement policies in relation to nursery provision in general and co-ordinated provision in particular. Because nursery education is discretionary, it is perfectly feasible for governors to create their own policies on under fives, and, for example, to decide to employ a nursery nurse rather than a nursery teacher, or to employ teachers in reception and nursery classes with no early years experience, or to create very large reception classes. Centres jointly funded by education and social services present particular problems, unless the governors are willing to pass funding over to a separate management committee.

It is perhaps worth reflecting on the evidence given by the Association of County Councils to the House of Commons Select Committee (1989):

'Educational research has consistently indicated that the most important single step towards the improvement of the quality of education in this country would be to provide a coherent and comprehensive system of pre-school education for all'. It is ironic that an Act born out of concern for standards and quality should have failed to make any contribution at all to the development of a programme of nursery education.

The Children Act, the Education Reform Act — and indeed the NHS and Community Care Act — all have a clear focus on monitoring, regulating and reviewing services, on quality control and on making information available to consumers/parents. But as the Cornish have it, you can't fatten a pig for market by continually weighing it. Inspection on its own will neither create new services, nor produce quality in those that exist. The legislation fails to provide a lead in creating a co-ordinated framework for the development of services, and the resources to take that development forward. (See also postscript to Chapter 3)

What about resources?

Despite a very limited expansion in nursery education, it is clear that in terms of a national policy there is no overall commitment to resourcing services for young children. The question of what it would cost to expand services to the point where they met demand, and how such an expansion would be costed and paid for, has been the focus of a follow-up study to the Unit's policy framework. The report estimates that it would cost £1 billion to upgrade current services to the point where they were able to provide a quality service (much of this going to playgroups) and that a further one million places will be needed for children under five in the next ten years (Holtermann, 1992). However, a complex equation of how this money is to be found shows that a combination of parental fees (based on income), employers' contributions and government subsidy will actually bring more back to the Exchequer in income tax and national insurance contributions than will be paid out. It remains to be seen whether this equation is acceptable to government.

There has, then, been no shortage of government initiatives and new legislation, but can they, taken together, be seen as a co-ordinated approach to child care and early child education within a clear policy framework? The evidence suggests that the answer has to be no. There are many issues that have not been addressed, and the education and health legislation are in fact moving towards fragmentation rather than co-ordination. There is a pressing need for an integrated approach from central government, for a commitment to additional public expenditure and a common approach to funding services, for a review of training and staffing for early years services, and for a consideration of early education and child care in the context of a wider debate about the interrelationship between work, family responsibilities and child care (Moss, 1990).

There have, however, been some developments at local level, and it is to an interplay between central and local government in addressing some of these issues that we now turn.

ESTABLISHING STRUCTURES AND SYSTEMS TO SUPPORT A CO-ORDINATED POLICY

The integration of responsibility for services within a single government department has been the subject of countless recommendations in reports over the last fifteen years, but very little has been achieved in practice. The Unit policy framework, representing the views of twenty-one national organizations and mindful of the sensitivities of different views held by those organizations, compromised in its recommendation that

> one government department should take a 'lead' on under fives and their families. Until such time as this is resolved, an Inter-Departmental Committee, at senior level within government and consulting with statutory and voluntary providers, should be charged with formulating such a policy, and planning and monitoring its implementation.
>
> (National Children's Bureau, 1990, p.4)

The Rumbold Committee, chaired as it was by a Minister at the Department of Education and Science, was even more vague, commenting that 'We believe that the achievement of better co-ordination would be greatly helped if central government gave a clear lead, setting a national framework within which local developments could take place' (DES, 1990a, para. 215).

Others have been more bold, and have called for the DES to be given the lead role, on the grounds that education is universal and 'non-stigmatized', that the main focus is on the development of the child, and that there can then be greater continuity between pre-school and school. Labour Party policy, *The Best Start* (1990), heralds an intention to establish the Department of Education and Science as the 'lead' department for under-fives education and care, charged with developing a coherent policy on services for young children and their families, whilst the Equal Opportunities Commission in *The Key to Real Choice* (1990) calls for the creation of a National Childcare Development Agency under the aegis of the DES.

Other reports (e.g. Association of Metropolitan Authorities, 1991;

National Consumer Council, 1991) acknowledge that although the DES has little experience of policy for very young children or welfare issues, on balance the DES is the most logical location for the lead department. The requirements of the Children Act, however, would make it important to keep the separate identity of services for young children within the Department, and for expertise to be developed in those areas where there is little at present. Moves to unify services within education would reflect similar developments elsewhere in the world, for example in New Zealand and Spain, both of which now see 0–5/6 as the first stage in their education system.

Structures at local level

At local level, the Unit's work with over seventy local authorities over the last five years has shown how difficult it is to develop clear policies and structures without a clear lead from the centre. However, the impetus of the Children Act, with the requirement that the review of services should be undertaken jointly, and within the context of a development plan and a co-ordinated structure, is already leading local authorities to review their collaborative procedures. Three main strategies appear to be evolving:

(1) The most common is to establish an under-fives/under-eights sub-committee of education and social services committees. In order to ensure collaboration with other agencies, this committee co-opts representatives from the health authority/ies, from other authority departments such as leisure services, housing and planning, and from the voluntary and private sectors. Although the AMA working party (1991) commented that to co-ordinate within existing frameworks is not a viable option, it is at least a start.

(2) An alternative approach is to establish a committee (with the same co-options) as a subcommittee of the policy and resources committee, with delegation of general duties as above from education and social services. This approach has been favoured in Leeds and Humberside, and is being considered by a number of other authorities. Officer support, sometimes in the form of a separate Under-Fives/Eights Unit, may well be based in the Chief Executive's Department.

(3) A third alternative, which begins to move from co-ordination to integration, has been to delegate responsibility for all under-fives services to the education committee, and to delegate management responsibility to the education department. Strathclyde was the first

authority to do this, and decisions to move in this direction have subsequently been taken by Sheffield, Manchester, Islington, Southwark, Newham, etc.

Which structure is adopted will clearly need to reflect local patterns of decision-making. What is more important than the kind of structure established, is that it should work. Attempts to co-ordinate or integrate services by setting up such committees over the last fifteen years have invariably failed because they have not been given any 'teeth'. They have simply been talking shops, rubber-stamping decisions made elsewhere. In our experience, a number of points should be taken into consideration if a co-ordinating/integrating structure is to be effective:

(1) There needs to be a clear policy agreed by all the main providers of services within the local authority, setting out the principles upon which services should be based, the aims and objectives for the service, a development plan, and a clear process for implementation and review.

(2) The committee structure and departmental/administrative structure must support an integrated approach to the planning of services.

(3) A committee or subcommittee will function best where it has delegated responsibility for policy development and resource deployment, and is not merely a forum for discussion.

(4) There is a need for clear support from senior elected members and the council as a whole, and from chief officers. This is particularly important. As services for under fives are largely discretionary, they are frequently at risk when public expenditure is cut back.

(5) There needs to be clarity about roles, and about management responsibility, and clear lines of communication both within departments (between senior management, middle management and practitioners) and between departments.

(6) Relationships with the health authority need to be established and nurtured. This has proved particularly difficult over the years. The frequent reforms to which the NHS has been subjected have removed most of the posts that were at one time responsible for creating links with local authorities, and it has not been easy to know with what level of the health system to connect, nor how to work closely with both the 'purchasers' and the 'providers', and with representatives of individual trusts. The vagaries of different boundaries − such that

Surrey, for example, has to involve seven different health authorities on its planning committees – have also impeded progress in involving health professionals in local authority planning. There are, however, some good examples of collaborative work, particularly in relation to child protection, and children with special needs.

(7) Involvement of the voluntary and private sectors: local authorities have not traditionally involved the voluntary sector in planning services, and yet in many authorities families are almost entirely dependent on playgroups and childminders, and increasingly employers and private nurseries are meeting the needs of working parents. In relation to the process of planning and review, it is important to establish systems whereby all voluntary groups can be represented, and not just the Pre-school Playgroups Association, which is often the only one the local authority knows. This may be most effectively managed through a voluntary sector forum, which can provide a mandate for a representative to the under-eights committee (*see* Ball and Stone, 1991).

(8) One of the most effective ways of ensuring the involvement of practitioners is through the establishment of local liaison groups. This model is now being widely adopted, and provides both a forum for multi-disciplinary co-operation and training, and a means of consulting on and implementing policy.

(9) The value of under-fives/under-eights development posts in supporting a co-ordinated approach to service delivery has also been widely recognized and there are now such posts in many local authorities, albeit mainly established on a short-term basis.

PROVIDING A RANGE OF SERVICES TO MEET THE NEEDS OF CHILDREN AND THEIR PARENTS

What parents want or what children need?

The concept of 'need' has been touched on in relation to the Children Act requirements that local authorities should provide day care for children who are deemed to be 'in need'. But is it actually possible – or at least desirable – to distinguish between the 'needs' of children and the wishes or demands of parents? How are local authorities to define need? Will they base it on the needs of individual children, or on a wider assessment, targeting resources on an area of need? Will they just include children 'being looked after' by the local authority, children on the child protection register and perhaps children in bed and breakfast accommodation? Or will it be extended to children whose parents are unemployed, or who receive housing benefit or poll tax rebate? What about different perceptions of need – how possible will it be to devise a common register for children so defined by social services, health and education, and including children with disabilities? From the family's point of view, are these needs so very different from those of a single parent, for whom a job will mean he or she can stop being dependent on income support, but who cannot work without reliable and affordable child care? There has always been a tension between 'professionally defined need' and 'consumer demand' and Smith (1990, p. 58) argues that it is absurd to restrict publicly provided day care to 'professional definitions' of need targeting 'problem families'. 'Provision is a necessary response to parents' (usually the mothers') decisions to seek employment – it is a fact that children of working parents *need* day care, irrespective of any moral argument about whether women are right to *want* to work or not.'

If we look at what parents are asking for, we find that demand greatly outstrips supply and that surveys over many years show a continuing preference for nursery education over playgroups and for day nurseries over childminders (for details of consumer surveys, *see* Early Childhood Unit reading list). However, there is considerable variation between surveys, reflecting different local circumstances and expectations. For example, the tight-knit community in Sunderland, with high levels of nursery education and where most young families have access to the extended family, brought a lower than usual demand for further day care (Statham, 1991). It is hard to infer preferences from surveys – in areas where provision is poor or patchy, parents may have very low expectations, and articulate their preferences in terms of what exists, rather than what they would like (National Consumer Council, 1991). However, where they are given the option of new and extended provision, they have shown a preference for multi-purpose centres, offering both nursery education and day care (*see* Scott, 1989).

In consulting parents, as with involving voluntary groups in planning, it is important to ensure that the mechanisms are in place to support that consultation, if it is not to be just a token gesture. As an extensive consultation exercise in Gloucestershire found (Webster, 1990), parents often do not understand the channels which they can use to express their views and make their voices heard, despite the council's best efforts. Finding out parents' views and involving them in the process of planning and reviewing services requires resources, particularly staff time.

A range of services to meet local need?

The need for flexibility in the provision of services in order to meet the needs of children and their parents has been well documented (*see* Pugh, 1988), and the value of combined nursery centres and community nurseries offering day care and nursery education, and often drop-in facilities, health surveillance and a range of support services for parents as well, was reinforced by the Rumbold Committee.

However, the last two or three years has seen a growth in new kinds of facilities – for example, private and employer-based nurseries – and a new role emerging for the local authority as an enabler and facilitator and regulator, rather than simply a provider of services. It would seem that these private nurseries, although an important part of the day-care jigsaw, are unlikely to provide more than a limited answer to the shortfall in provision. With regard to employer-funded provision, with the exception of a few large companies such as the Midland Bank, there is evidence of only very limited investment in nursery provision, and a preference on the part of parents, local authorities and employers for partnership nurseries based in the community rather than in factories and offices.

The private-for-profit sector is also unlikely to be able to increase its share of the market very dramatically, given the charges that parents have to bear (around £150 per week for children under two in London) to support the costs of a nursery of reasonable quality. A recent review of seventy private nurseries found very little money available for investment, poor premises, untrained staff, few teachers, lack of access to in-service training, high staff turnover and little evidence of equal opportunities (Penn, in press).

The range of services in any one area is also likely to include a substantial number of playgroups and childminders, currently providing for the largest number of children in sessional and all-day care. The playgroup movement has grown and changed substantially in recent years, and a recent review suggested four possible scenarios for playgroups in the years ahead: as a stopgap whilst nursery education is being developed; as a substitute for nursery education; as a preparation for nursery education; and as an alternative to nursery education (Moss, 1990). The playgroup movement sees its role as providing parents with an alternative, but research has shown that in fact parents have very little choice, and that there are few parts of the country where both playgroups and nursery education exist. For those areas that are dependent on playgroup provision there is thus a very real challenge to provide adequate levels of funding, so that they really can provide a quality service. As the Bureau study found (Holtermann, 1992), a well-resourced playgroup will cost little less than nursery education.

Childminders too are offering a more professional service, and in many authorities registration is linked to at least some training. But are childminders offering a public or a private service, and how can their private role as a home-based parent substitute be publicly monitored and regulated? A recent study (Ferri, 1992) looking at the impact of childminder training found that this dichotomy created considerable tensions, and recommended that these could best be resolved if childminders were employed by the local authority.

In looking at a balanced local service, which gives both diversity and choice, two issues are emerging. The first is to ask how, if most parents want nursery education for their children, this is to fit into the patchwork of private and voluntary sector provision. The second issue, which will perhaps ultimately help to resolve the first, is to point to the new role that many authorities are taking on as development agencies, establishing partnerships with the voluntary sector and with employers in developing nurseries, consultancies and consortia in tandem with their own role as providers of services (*see*, for example, Oxfordshire, Fife, Leeds, North Tyneside). A proactive approach to partnership within an integrated policy framework may well help to prevent the two-tier or even three-tier system suggested above.

CONSULTING WITH AND INFORMING PARENTS

It is often easier for professionals to provide services that they think parents and children ought to have, than to take time to talk to and listen to parents. The concept of partnership that is central to the Children Act is to be welcomed, but partnership is an elusive concept (*see* Pugh and De'Ath, 1989) and the new emphasis on consultation will require new skills and a change of attitude on the part of many managers and practitioners (*see also* Chapters 9 and 10).

Both the Children Act and the Education Reform Act oblige local authorities and schools respectively to provide parents with information which will inform their decisions when chosing child care or education. This requirement is long overdue, and should ultimately help puzzled parents to distinguish between the many different types of pre-school provision. For local authorities to provide information on their services would seem to be a reasonably simple task, but the Unit has been surprised at how difficult this information has been to unearth, particularly in authorities that have decentralized their services. A recent survey of

Welsh authorities, for example, (Hanney, 1991) found that there were no booklets for parents in Wales, and even in areas where such information does exist, it is very soon out of date.

A new approach has been to establish authority-wide computerized systems to provide up-to-date information for parents, such as that run by the Sheffield Under Fives Information Service, or to set up services that combine an information with a child care development function, such as that operated by North Tyneside or the Childcare Links projects in Brighton and elsewhere.

SETTING STANDARDS AND MONITORING QUALITY

One of the main concerns in an uncoordinated system which depends so heavily for service provision on the voluntary and private sectors, is how quality is to be established and maintained. The Rumbold Report commented on the 'need to raise the quality of a good deal of existing provision' and referred back to concerns raised by the Education Select Committee on the educational component of playgroups and day nurseries. Clark (1988, p. 268) had expressed particular concern at failure to meet the needs of many children in day nurseries who she felt needed to have access to stimulating and varied experiences if 'their own characteristics and home circumstances are [not] to lead to very early failure in the educational system'. On the strength of this concern, the Select Committee called on the DES and DH to issue guidelines of good practice for use in day nurseries, and encouraged social service advisers to call on HMI and LEA advisers for advice (House of Commons, 1989).

The Children Act and its accompanying Guidance (DH, 1991) respond to both these issues. They provide a baseline below which standards must not fall, and a structure for registration, inspection and review, although still within an uncoordinated system. The Guidance sets standards on ratios (though these were weakened at the eleventh hour), room size and space, record-keeping, health and safety and discipline, and, drawing on the Rumbold Report, goes further than previous government guidance in looking at curriculum issues and equal opportunities as well as the number of toilets and amount of floor space.

Whilst the Children Act provides the bottom line, guidelines for 'good practice', aspiring towards rather better quality services, have also been published. The National Children's Bureau's *Young Children in Group Day Care* (Cowley, 1991) is being widely used across all sectors, and other voluntary groups such as the Pre-school Playgroups Association

(1990), Kids Clubs Network (1989) and the National Childminding Association (1991) have also produced guidelines.

Establishing national standards is one thing; turning the words on the page into better quality services is quite another. Whilst the potential offered by the inspection and review procedures is to be welcomed, particularly if they involve both education and social services advisers, the work-loads on both departments' advisory services, and the uncertainty over the future role of LEA advisers and inspectors, does leave the implementation of this area of the Act in some doubt. It is also important to see the whole issue of quality within the wider context of other policy issues addressed in this chapter (*see* European Commission, 1990, and Chapter 3 in this book).

MEETING THE NEEDS OF CHILDREN THROUGH AN APPROPRIATE CURRICULUM

One of the most positive features of the National Curriculum is that it has encouraged early years educators, who have sometimes been reluctant to speak out, to articulate more clearly the way in which young children learn, and their role as adults in supporting and extending that learning. Many have feared that the introduction of the National Curriculum will lead to pressure to formalize education at the earliest opportunity and follow a narrow and more rigid curriculum which will not be in the child's best interests. This is of particular concern for the substantial number of four-year-olds who are now going early into primary school, often into classes where teachers are inappropriately trained and the curriculum is not well suited to the needs of such young children. Clark (1988) speaks of the importance of a public relations exercise to ensure that parents and other teachers (and, one might add, governors and the general public) see pre-school education as of value in its own right, rather than simply as a preparation for school. One such response has been *Early Childhood Education: The Early Years Curriculum and the National Curriculum* (EYCG, 1989), put together by a group of practitioners and teacher trainers to illustrate how much of the best practice in nursery and infant classrooms is already providing a foundation upon which the National Curriculum can be built (*see also* Chapter 4).

The Rumbold Committee was able to resist the suggestion that there should be a national subject-based curriculum for under fives, and focused instead on the principles upon which early education should be built:

> The educator working with under fives must pay careful attention, not just to the content of the child's learning, but also to the way in which that learning is

offered to and experienced by the child, and the role of all those involved in the process. Children are affected by the *context* in which learning takes place, the *people* involved in it, and the *values and beliefs* which are embedded in it. For the early years educator, therefore, the process of education − *how* children are encouraged to learn − is as important as, and inseparable from, the content − *what* they learn. We believe that this principle must underlie all curriculum planning for the under fives.

(DES, 1990a, paras. 67−8, original emphasis)

The central focus of the Early Childhood Unit's work − and indeed of this book − is the need to ensure that all children have access to good quality learning experiences, which respond to their individual needs, in whatever setting they find themselves. This is as important for children from black and minority ethnic families who may find the curriculum does not value and reflect their own culture, as for disabled children who may not have access to mainstream services; as important for children of eighteen months old who may be in day care for the first time, as for children who are just four and find themselves in a group of thirty-five children in a primary school. It calls for skilled educators whose understanding of child development, and ability to observe and assess the progress of individual children, enables them to structure and support children in their learning. These issues are taken up in more detail in Chapters 4−8.

The publication of reports and guidelines that point to the needs of our youngest children are no doubt helpful, but we should not underestimate the pressure that early years educators are under from some parents and from teachers of older children to subscribe to other principles and other approaches. It is perhaps particularly important that parents understand how young children learn for, as Watt (1990, p. 130) argues, 'if the child-centred curriculum is to survive within National Curriculum guidelines, then not only must teachers be seen to be committed to it, but parents must identify with it'. This poses a particular challenge in those parts of the country where there is little or no good quality pre-school education.

PAY, CONDITIONS AND STATUS
TRAINING AND SUPPORT

High-quality work in early childhood education is only possible with sufficient staff of high calibre and with appropriate training. In the UK, as indeed in many other countries, those who teach the youngest children are lowest in the pecking order. It is often assumed that anyone can teach young children. Pascal's research (1990) found that only half of reception class teachers had been trained in early years education, and yet as many primary heads will argue, four-year-olds are the pupils who demand the greatest skill, the most organization, and the most energy. There is a chronic shortage of trained early years teachers and a move by some local authorities to employ nursery nurses instead of teachers. In the private and voluntary sectors, well over half of all workers are not formally qualified.

Whilst the status and pay of nursery and infant teachers may not match that of teachers of older children, it is considerably better than that of all other early years workers. The experience of combined nursery centres (*see*, for example, Chapter 9) shows just how difficult it is to agree a common scale of pay and conditions for staff from different backgrounds, and the recommendation in the recent AMA report (1991) for a national working party to resolve this issue is to be welcomed.

The main issues in relation to training are discussed by Curtis and Hevey in Chapter 11. Concerns about the appropriateness of current training for early years teachers, about the implementation of National Vocational Qualifications, and about the links between professional and vocational training suggest that critical policy decisions need to be made in the training world. The potential for an integrated approach to training, and a training that meets the needs of educators working in all settings with children from birth to eight, is very real, but only time will tell if there is the political will and the resources to realize this potential.

CONCLUSION

Developments over the last decade have created a number of building blocks in an early years policy, and the chapters in this book celebrate many of them. The concern for quality and for quality assurance is to be welcomed, as is the continuing focus on a child-centred early years curriculum, and the emphasis that the Children Act places on co-ordination and review, and on responding to children's cultural and linguistic background. The demand for day care is forging some imaginative partnerships, and the need for further expansion is generally more widely understood. But we are still far from developing a national policy that reflects the eight areas outlined in this chapter, or the broader issues of work and family responsibility. Fragmentation, lack of resources and lack of vision persist in preventing all children having access to the start in life they so richly deserve.

2

PERSPECTIVES FROM EUROPE

Peter Moss

INTRODUCTION

This chapter is an attempt to put a quart into a pint pot. In the space of a few pages, I shall try to give an overview of early childhood services, and related policies, in the European Community (EC); to discuss some general problem areas; to introduce some innovative developments; and to consider the content and significance of a growing 'European dimension' in services and policies. The process of condensation is inevitably at the expense of nuance and qualification, and several important issues are entirely omitted. For example, any attempt to discuss quality has been defeated by shortage of space, compounded by the lack of information available about quality in services and more conceptual problems about defining 'quality' which would require a substantial preamble.

Having acknowledged the problems in the task set, I am encouraged to proceed for a number of reasons. Readers can get lost in long and detailed accounts comparing different countries; a brief overview, presenting a few broad features, may be a better way in (readers whose appetites are whetted may like to consult European Commission (1988, 1990) and Melhuish and Moss (1990) for more detailed accounts of services and policies in EC countries). Above all, it is important that those interested in issues to do with children and their welfare and with women and gender equality (or both) should understand both the potential and the limitations of the European Community with respect to early childhood services, and the possibilities for influencing the direction of

European policy and initiatives in this area. A democratic Europe cries out for the participation of concerned individuals and organizations, rather than leaving developments to politicians and bureaucrats however well intentioned.

Finally, I refer in this chapter to 'early childhood services', by which I mean services often referred to in Britain under the headings of 'day care', 'child care' and 'pre-school or nursery education'. I have used the term 'early childhood services' not only as a convenient umbrella, but also because, as I shall discuss later, the more specific and common terms seem to me to be problematic, reflecting and encouraging a fragmented way of thinking about provision for young children and their carers.

EARLY CHILDHOOD SERVICES IN EUROPE: A BRIEF OVERVIEW

The infrastructure of early childhood services

By making some broad generalizations and ignoring some important exceptions, it is possible to describe a pattern of early childhood services found in most countries in the European Community (*see* Table 2.1 for a league table of levels of publicly funded provision). The upper age limit, if 'early childhood' is defined as ending when compulsory schooling begins, is normally six. Preceding this, countries provide nursery education or kindergarten for most children from three upwards; in some cases (France, Italy, Belgium) provision is almost universal, while in others (Spain and Portugal), there is an active policy to expand services. In most cases, too, this provision is available for at least the equivalent of the English school day.

For children under three, the picture is rather different. Most children in this youngest age group attend services because parents are at work, and the extent of this (or rather maternal employment) varies considerably (*see* Table 2.2). Use of services for children under one is also influenced by leave provision, first maternity leave (universally available, on average for about three months after birth), then parental leave. Maternity leave protects and promotes the health and well-being of the mother and her new-born child and is, by definition, only for women; by contrast, parental leave provides parents with an opportunity to care for a very young child and should be equally available to mothers and fathers (hence employer-provided 'career break' schemes are not the same as parental leave, being only available to one parent unless both parents happen to work for the same employer).

Table 2.1 Places in publicly funded early childhood services as percentage of all children in the age group

	Date to which data refer	For children under 3	For children from 3 to compulsory school age	Age when compulsory schooling begins	Length of school day (including midday break)	Outside school hours care for primary school children
Germany	1987	3%	65–70%	6–7 years	4–5 hours (a)	4%
France	1988	20%	95%+	6 years	8 hours	?
Italy	1986	5%	85%+	6 years	4 hours	?
Netherlands	1989	2%	50–55%	5 years	6–7 hours	1%
Belgium	1988	20%	95%+	6 years	7 hours	?
Luxembourg	1989	2%	55–60%	5 years	4–8 hours (a)	1%
United Kingdom	1988	2%	35–40%	5 years	6½ hours	(–)
Ireland	1988	2%	55%	6 years	4½–6½ hours (b)	(–)
Denmark	1989	48%	85%	7 years	3–5½ hours (a,b)	29%
Greece	1988	4%	65–70%	5½ years	4–5 hours (b)	(–)
Portugal	1988	6%	35%	6 years	6½ hours	6%
Spain	1988	?	65–70%	6 years	8 hours	(–)

Key: ? = no information; (–) = less than 0.5%; (a) = school hours vary from day to day; (b) = school hours increase as children get older.

Notes: The table shows the number of places in publicly funded services as a percentage of the child population; the percentage of children attending may be higher because some places are used on a part-time basis. Provision at playgroups in the Netherlands has not been included, although 10 per cent of children under 3 and 25 per cent of children aged 3–4 attend and most playgroups receive public funds. Average hours of attendance – 5–6 hours per week – are so much shorter than for other services, that it would be difficult and potentially misleading to include them on the same basis as other services; however, playgroups should not be forgotten when considering publicly funded provision in the Netherlands.

Source: European Commission 1990.

Table 2.2 Parental employment, 1988

	% employed – women with child under 10	% employed – men with child under 10	% employed – women aged 20–39, without children	Change in % employed, 1985–8 – women with child under 10	% unemployed – women with child under 10	% unemployed – men with child under 10
Germany	38 (21)	94 (1)	75 (15)	+2.6 (+2.5)	6	3
France	56 (16)	93 (1)	75 (11)	+1.3 (+1.9)	10	5
Italy	42 (5)	95 (2)	55 (4)	+3.6 (+0.7)	8	3
Netherlands	32 (27)	91 (9)	68 (30)	+8.2 (+7.7)	8	5
Belgium	54 (16)	92 (1)	68 (13)	+2.8 (+2.4)	12	5
Luxembourg	38 (10)	98 (–)	69 (5)	+3.7 (0.6)	2	1
United Kingdom	46 (32)	88 (1)	83 (20)	+7.5 (+6)	8	8
Ireland	23 (7)	79 (1)	67 (6)	+5.1 (+1.5)	8	17
Denmark	79 (32)	95 (2)	79 (6)	+2.6 (−1.5)	8	3
Greece	41 (5)	95 (1)	52 (3)	+3.8 (−0.2)	6	3
Portugal	62 (4)	95 (1)	69 (6)	No information	6	2
Spain	28 (4)	89 (1)	44 (5)	No information	10	8
European Community	44 (17)	92 (2)	71 (13)	No information	8	5

Key: Figures in brackets = percentage employed part-time

Source: European Commission 1990.

Every country in mainland Europe (except Luxembourg) now offers some form of parental leave, lasting from a few weeks to two or more years. However, the leave period (unlike maternity leave) is usually unpaid or paid only at a low flat rate, and is taken almost entirely by mothers. It is also rather inflexible, not giving parents the right to decide how they will take it; for example, part time or full time, in one block or several. (The contrast is striking with parental leave in Sweden, which offers twelve months' leave at 90 per cent of earnings, with a further three months at a low flat rate, with parents given the right to take it full time or part time, and in one continuous leave period or as several shorter periods of leave. The development of this leave provision means that few children under twelve months in Sweden are now found in any form of early childhood service.)

Most children under three using services are provided for privately (that is, both the provision *and* its funding are private, an important distinction to which I shall return), mainly by relatives (grannies remain a vast and publicly neglected source of care), childminders or 'babysitters'; childminders are rare in Spain, Italy and Greece, where individual care is more commonly provided by 'babysitters' looking after children in the children's own home. Some form of publicly funded service is also available for this age group, but levels of provision are generally low, in most cases available for 5 per cent or less of the age group (Table 2.1). Publicly funded provision is mostly in group care (usually nurseries), though a few countries also have systems of 'organized childminding', where childminders are recruited, paid and supported by local authorities or publicly funded private organizations.

Organized childminding systems operate in France and Belgium, which have relatively high levels of publicly funded services for children under three. This is partly because they have more extensive provision specifically for this age group, but also because they have adopted the practice of admitting two-year-olds to nursery school systems which mainly cater for children over three. Indeed in France, nearly half of all two-year-olds are in nursery schools.

Four exceptions

This is the broad pattern in most countries in the EC. Four countries, however, are significantly different. Denmark is in every respect exceptional. Employment rates for women with children are the highest in Europe; over 90 per cent are in the labour force. Compulsory school (as in the rest of Scandinavia) begins at seven, prior to which the great majority of children over three attend some form of publicly funded service; most go to kindergartens or similar services offering full-time provision, with nearly all six-year-olds also attending part-time pre-school classes in primary school. The main distinguishing feature of Denmark, however, is the high level of publicly funded services for children under three. These services (either group care or organized childminding, though it is also possible for a small group of parents to combine to employ a shared nanny and claim public funds) provide for nearly half of all under threes, and Denmark is the only EC country where publicly funded provision accounts for most of the children in this age group who attend some form of early childhood service.

These features of Denmark – high levels of maternal employment and extensive publicly funded services which are generally considered to offer a high standard of service to children and parents – are not a long-standing tradition. They have developed over the space of only thirty years. Faced by a growth of employment among women with children in the 1960s, Danish society (the political decision had all-party support) decided to ensure the availability of good quality, local services for children with parents at work, and backed that decision up with substantial and sustained public investment. It remains an impressive example of combining the needs of the labour market, children and parents.

The other three exceptions are very different from Denmark. Ireland, the Netherlands and Britain have had low levels of maternal employment (although Britain has begun to show clear signs in the last five years of a significant increase); moreover, in the case of the Netherlands and Britain, there has been a high level of part-time jobs among those mothers who are employed (Table 2.2). (Denmark also has substantial part-time employment, but the hours worked by Danish part-timers are much higher on average than those worked by British or Dutch part-timers.) Publicly funded services for children under three are at a low level, though not that much different in quantity from many other countries. What marks out Britain and Ireland is the absence of any parental leave (the Netherlands introduced a scheme in 1990), and the exclusion of parental employment (except where the parent is a lone mother or father) as a priority reason for admission to what little publicly funded day care exists.

The most striking differences, however, are for over threes. Compulsory schooling begins at five in both Britain and the Netherlands, and at six in Ireland, but these countries have limited (in the case of Britain) or no nursery education. Britain is also the only country which operates a part-time shift system as a matter of deliberate policy in its nursery education provision. All three countries have responded to this gap in provision in a similar manner; many children are admitted to primary school before compulsory school age and extensive playgroup provision has developed. There are many similarities between the playgroup movements in these three countries (which are the only ones in Europe where playgroups have such a significant presence); for example, children attend playgroup on average for only five or six hours a week, far less than even part-time nursery education. There are also some important differences. For example, playgroups in the Netherlands provide for two- and three-year-olds, while nearly all four-year-olds are in primary school (on a non-compulsory basis); moreover, most playgroups in the Netherlands receive some public funds. By contrast, playgroups in the UK and Ireland have fewer two-year-olds and more four-year-olds, and only a minority get any public funds. (For a fuller comparison of playgroups in the three countries, *see* Statham *et al.*, 1989.)

Contrast between Britain and rest of Europe

This brief overview highlights a number of broad and widespread features of early childhood services in the European Community, including the introduction of parental leave, a recognition of some public responsibility for the children of employed parents (though in most cases, with a large shortfall in the supply of publicly funded services), and a recognition of the need to develop nursery education as a generally available service for children over three (and here, the shortfall in supply is generally far less). In all three respects, Britain differs: no parental leave; an explicit rejection of any public responsibility to support working parents and their children; and an earlier acceptance of the principle of nursery education, in the 1972 White Paper, subsequently abandoned. The situation in Britain has been strongly influenced by the view that care and education of young children is mainly a private matter (the main exception being where child, parent or family are deemed to have some inadequacy or disability). The approach in mainland Europe has been more influenced by concepts of social solidarity, emphasizing the importance of providing support to adults in the parenting phase of their life course, which is recognized to be (like childhood) of wider social significance.

Some specific features

The overview above outlines the basic infrastructure of early childhood provision. Some other, more specific common features should also be noted. First, in most countries there is a divide at three between different types of publicly funded services. Three is often the upper age limit for publicly funded nurseries and childminding, after which children enter nursery schooling or kindergartens. Services for children under three are usually the responsibility of local and regional government welfare or health departments, while nursery schooling is usually provided by national or regional government as part of the schooling service. Where kindergarten systems operate, however, responsibility usually continues to rest with local welfare authorities (though kindergartens may offer a very similar experience to nursery education, they are outside the school system).

Second, there is considerable diversity in how publicly funded services are delivered. In some countries (for example, Italy), publicly funded services for children under three are almost entirely provided directly by local authorities (though nursery education, while publicly funded, is delivered by a mixture of central government, local authorities and church and lay organizations). In other countries (for example, Ireland or the Netherlands), publicly funded services are provided almost entirely by private, non-profit organizations. In other cases, there is a mix. Denmark, for example, has very extensive publicly funded services which may be provided by local authorities or private organizations; however provided, there is a high level of autonomy for individual centres.

Third, most European countries operate some form of regulation of private sector nurseries, but no country regulates 'babysitters' and there is considerable variation in the extent to which childminding is regulated. Moreover, even where registration of childminders is required, there is considerable variation in actual coverage achieved. While most childminders are probably registered in Britain, in Germany the opposite is true. France requires registration of childminders, but is unique in attempting to use this system to ensure not only that certain basic standards are met, but also that certain basic benefits are provided. A 1977 law gave registered childminders a special status and certain legal entitlements, including a minimum wage, social insurance and paid holidays. While this established an important principle, the practice has not been entirely satisfactory; since 1977, the proportion of unregistered childminders has increased, and the government is currently looking at further ways to improve the position of registered childminders and to increase their numbers.

Fourth, while all countries in the Community fund services directly (to a greater or lesser extent), four − France, Belgium, Portugal and Luxembourg − at present also subsidize parents' costs through tax relief. In each case, however, there is also a policy of increasing publicly funded services; tax relief therefore is a supplement to, rather than a substitute for, the direct funding of services. In addition to tax relief, employed parents in France are entitled to an allowance if they use a babysitter or a childminder. This allowance is specifically intended to cover parents' social insurance contributions as employers of a babysitter or childminder, and is part of the general policy intended to improve the status and position of these workers. However, as with other measures discussed above, this has encountered problems. The allowance is claimed by only a minority of parents using childminders; most parents appear to be ill informed about the benefit, while many childminders are not interested in social security cover and are more worried about being caught in the tax net.

Finally, the pay, conditions and training of many workers with young children is poor. The worst conditions occur among those working with the youngest age group, children under three, and particularly among those who provide services privately (childminders, relatives, babysitters). In general, the situation is better for workers in nursery education and kindergarten, although often their position remains inferior to teachers working with older children in the compulsory school system.

SOME COMMON PROBLEMS IN EARLY CHILDHOOD SERVICES

As well as common features, we can identify a number of common problems in the systems of early childhood services in the European Community. In this section, I want to pay attention to five 'problem areas' which seem particularly important.

Local inequalities in provision

Considerable variations exist in levels of publicly funded provision between member states (*see* Table 2.1). However, variations also exist within every country. In France, for example, nearly half the places in nurseries are in the Ile-de-France area, although this area accounts for less than a fifth of the population. In Italy, there are large regional variations for children under three; regions in the north provide for over 8 per cent of children (with nearly 20 per cent coverage in the Emilia-Romagna region centred on Bologna) compared to 1 per cent in the south. In Denmark, the highest levels of provision are found in the two largest cities (Copenhagen and Århus), the lowest levels in small urban and rural local authorities. Overall, levels of services are highest in large urban areas, lowest in rural areas and smaller towns, though even within these broad groupings there are large differences. Variations are also most common for children under three; nursery education is more evenly spread, especially where overall levels of provision are high.

Some of these variations may be put down to differences in need or demand, but most can only be fully accounted for in terms of the priorities of local or regional authorities and the commitment of politicians in these authorities to the needs of young children and their families. The underlying problem, however, arises from the provision of many services, especially those for children under three, being left the subject of local discretion. No member state sets targets, at national level, for services. The inevitable consequence is that access to services becomes a lottery, depending on where children live rather than what their needs are.

Costs and funding

While some member states have managed to fund virtually universal nursery education, none has yet managed to fund services for under threes that meet demand (there is a shortfall even in Denmark) or parental leave that provides proper compensation for lost earnings. The consequences include parental leave that is structured in such a way as to ensure that it is unlikely to be taken by fathers; major inconsistencies in the cost of services to parents (parents paying far more for services for children under three than over three); and the continuing poor pay, conditions and training of many workers in early childhood services, an inevitable consequence of being dependent on what parents can pay.

All EC countries face a similar and profound problem. As long as women have provided care and education for young children on an unpaid basis (as mothers or relatives) or a low-paid basis (as childminders or babysitters), the costs of providing this service have been carried by women, particularly in the form of forgone earnings and lost benefits (such as pension rights); the costs have been real and heavy but also invisible, in the sense that politicians have either not recognized them or felt able to ignore them, taking it for granted that women would and should continue to carry them. However, as the labour market demand, and employment opportunities, for these women carers increase, the question of cost becomes visible and pressing. Children need more non-parental care and education; traditional non-parental carers prove harder to recruit on the previous low-cost basis; there is likely to be a growing concern with quality of children's experience, and evidence suggests that quality requires certain material conditions (for example, in terms of pay and training for workers, staff/child ratios and so on) (Clarke-Stewart, 1991).

Add to this a similar set of issues concerning other types of care (for example, for elderly people) and it is clear that the cost of caring and how that cost is to be allocated represents a central political, social and economic issue. However, it is also clear that no EC state has really confronted the issue. Instead, there have been a series of *ad hoc* responses – small increases in public expenditure here, an interest in employers paying for services there, small-scale support for parents' costs through tax relief in some countries, unpaid or low-paid leave measures and so on.

Within this broad failure to confront and consider a fundamental issue, we can discern several possible future strategies. Denmark has tackled the issue head on, through funding services directly from taxation, together with a substantial parental contribution; in 1990, public expenditure on early childhood services for children under five was proportionately six times higher in Denmark than in Britain. France has sought to fund services through general taxes (including the whole cost of three years nursery education), but supplemented by an employer levy. All French employers contribute to regional funds, from which are paid cash benefits to families and subsidies to local authorities to support and develop services for young children. In Britain, the strategy is to limit tax-based funding to a minority of children, leaving parents to meet most costs with, in some cases, the support of individual employers where they deem this is necessary to ensure an adequate supply of labour.

Fragmentation and incoherence

Early childhood services are, in most cases, conceptually fragmented and incoherent in practice. The division between 'care' and 'education' continues to be widespread, in particular between services for children under and over three. In some countries (Britain, Portugal and Greece) this division is also apparent in divisions between different services for children over three. Services for the under threes continue to be seen primarily as meeting the needs of children of working parents for care while parents are at work (with the additional function of providing a preventive and support service to children or families with major problems). For the over threes, services are primarily seen as part of a general education system, which often takes little note of the care needs of children and parents.

Lack of coherence in practice is pervasive, and flows in large measure from the conceptual fragmentation of services. The availability of services varies (more shortfall for under threes), as do hours of opening (under-threes services have longer hours and are open for more weeks in the year); administrative responsibility differs, involving not only different departments (health, welfare, education) but also often different levels of government (local, regional, national); funding arrangements and the cost to parents are quite different (thus nursery education is free of charge, while parents pay for publicly funded nurseries); and the pay, conditions and training of workers are related to children's ages and the responsible system, rather than to the actual needs of children and the value of the work undertaken.

An inadequate policy framework

The development of early childhood services requires clear and coherent policies on children and gender equality (since early childhood has such major implications for women, and women are so centrally involved in the care and education of young children). No member state, however, has clear and co-ordinated policies spanning these two areas, to provide a framework within which specific policies on early childhood services for children and the reconciliation of the care of children and parental employment could be effectively and coherently developed. In some countries, services, especially for children under three, have developed in the context of 'family policy'. In France, for example, the support of nursery and other services for young children, tax relief for parents' child care costs and parental leave are all seen as part of a family policy, one of whose objectives is to offer parents choice in their way of life, including between employment or being at home. In practice, however, there is little choice:

> If no [day care] place is made available, there is no choice, only chance or luck. With no qualifications and a saturated labour market, there is no choice, only the possibility to stay at home. When a single income is insufficient to meet the needs of a family there is no choice − a working mother has to carry on working if she has a job....In the end, real choice is only available to a minority of women at the top end of the social scale.
>
> (CNAF, 1980, p. xx)

This quotation draws attention to the distinction between the rhetoric of choice and the reality it disguises; it also emphasizes that a situation of real choice involves ensuring a number of major and expensive conditions. The French example illustrates the risks to women of developing early childhood policies without a clear equal opportunity dimension.

Responding to ethnic diversity

Many European countries have substantial minority ethnic populations, and most have begun to respond to this in their thinking about early childhood services. The main response, however, has been either assimilationist or multi-cultural. In this respect, Britain is unique in the relative prominence given to anti-racism as a basis for service development.

TOWARDS A NEW APPROACH TO SERVICES

In recent years, and since the publication of the EC Childcare Network's reports on child care in Europe (European Commission, 1988, 1990), the 'league table' approach to Europe has become particularly influential in Britain, by which I mean the constant emphasis on quantitative aspects of services and, in particular, levels of publicly funded services. This approach may have served some purpose, in raising awareness in Britain about the relatively low priority given in public expenditure to early childhood services. To the extent that this level of expenditure has reflected a government view about the boundaries between public and private responsibility for the care and education of young children, it has revealed an important difference in orientation between Britain and many other European countries.

However, the 'league table' approach may have helped to conceal some other important parts of the overall picture. The situation in Britain contains some real strengths: there are many individual centres of excellence; nursery education, where it exists, is of a high standard, with nursery teachers enjoying the same training and pay as primary school teachers; the Children Act promises important improvements in the regulation and review of services; and important and often innovative work has been undertaken in areas such as curriculum for pre-school education, quality and anti-racism. Standards in some European services are lower than many people in Britain would consider adequate. But above all, the 'league table' approach has led people to ignore some important developments emerging in parts of Europe and the ideas behind them. I want in this section to highlight three innovations which seem to me to be of particular significance.

Towards coherent early childhood services

There is an increasing questioning in parts of Europe of the fragmentation and incoherence underlying many early childhood services. Since the

1970s, there has been a strong movement in parts of northern Italy to emphasize the educative role of nurseries, and nursery and nursery school provision is integrated into education departments in a number of local authorities. More recently in Spain, there has been a similar movement to emphasize the educative as well as care role of services for children under three, with the recent (1990) Education Law recognizing 0–6 as the first stage of the education system and teacher training courses increasingly providing an 'under threes' option. A number of local authorities in Britain have also made significant moves to integrate responsibility for early childhood services (*see* Chapter 1).

The process has been taken furthest in Denmark. The Danish system for children under seven is totally integrated. Services are recognized as having a dual care and pedagogical function. The pay, conditions and training of workers is the same (although workers may specialize in their training in work with different age groups). Responsibility rests with one department at local and national level. In this case (as in other Scandinavian countries), responsibility rests with social welfare rather than education. However, care and education services for children under seven (and outside school hours provision for children over seven, which is part of the same system) dominate the work of these welfare departments, while there is a strong pedagogical tradition (reflected in high standards of training) in this area of work.

The Danes' integrated system has also enabled them to question approaches to the age grouping of children in services. Originally, services were strongly age segregated: nurseries for under threes, kindergartens from three to school, and centres providing outside school hours care for primary school for children from three to seven. In recent years, there has been an increasing concern to provide wider age groupings, in the interests of children's relationships and experience. Most services developed in recent years have been 'age integrated insitutions', providing for children from babies up to seven and, in some cases, up to ten or older. Examples of similar approaches, combining services for children under and over three, are also to be found in some other countries, although age segregation remains the norm (the problem of developing an integrated approach when under threes are a local welfare responsibility and over threes a national educational responsibility should again be emphasized).

The questioning of old divisions, especially between care and education, has also been reflected in the language used to describe services. The Danes refer to pedagogical services (with workers called pedagogues). In Spain, the word for nurseries (*guaderia*) is being replaced by the term *escuela infantile.* The earlier French term for care (*garde*) has generally been replaced by the word *acceuil*, which means literally 'welcoming', while the term *acceuil educatif* introduces an educative orientation. In English, however, terms such as 'day care', 'child care' and 'nursery education' remain common, without an adequate alternative ('educare' may carry the meaning, but is a clumsy term; the generic term 'educator' used in the Rumbold Report (DES, 1990a) for workers in early childhood services provides another contribution to the search for a new English-language terminology); in this case, terminology both reflects divisions and reinforces them.

Towards multi-functional early childhood services

Northern Italy has early childhood services that are both extensive in quantity and widely recognized to be of high quality. However, this area of Europe has undergone a series of important developments in thinking about the purpose of these services. Following the passing of a law in the late 1960s, which transferred responsibility for nursery services for children under three to local and regional government, a number of more vigorous and committed local and regional authorities in the north took the opportunity to develop the number of places available. From the beginning, these services were seen as providing care for young children while parents were at work. However, as already mentioned, in the early 1980s there was a period of re-assessment leading to a new emphasis on the educative as well as caring role of nurseries, with measures (for example, in training and support) taken to develop this broader role. Most recently, there has been a further process of evaluation. A diversification of services has begun, to enable them to meet the needs of a wider range of children and their carers. This means, for example, providing part-time services for parents with part-time jobs, drop-in sessions, playgroups and playgrounds and so on.

This process of diversification is not at the expense of the original function of nurseries; good quality provision for children with full-time working parents remains a central task. Diversification means extending nurseries to become multi-functional centres for all children and carers in their area. This approach breaks down not only the care–education divide, but the tendency to fragment services, conceptually and in practice, so that one service provides 'child care for working parents', another 'day care for children in need', a third support for mothers at home and so on.

Examples of multi-functional services are also emerging in other countries (Pen Green Centre in Corby is an exemplary case in Britain – *see*

Chapter 9). However, unlike some family centres in Britain, most of these multi-functional services do not have a 'therapeutic' or 'community work' orientation. They develop from a perspective which regards early childhood services as a need and right of all communities and families, and as an expression of social solidarity with children and parents which recognizes the needs of both employed and non-employed parents and their children.

Parental involvement

There are a number of examples of services which place emphasis on parental involvement in management, for example in the nursery services of many parts of northern Italy where parents play an active part in the system of social management, and in Danish services. An example of a service actually run by parents is the system of *crèches parentales* in France. The number of these parent-run nurseries has increased from 30 in 1982 to 700 in 1991, providing for 12,000 children (many in rural areas and small towns). They provide services for children under three, including all-day care; parents set up and run the service, and there is a national organization (ACEP) with regional branches. Parents who use the service have to commit themselves to working with the children (for example, half a day a week) and to participating in management.

An important feature about this service (and one of several ways in which the *crèche parentale* differs from the 'community playgroup' in Britain, which is another example of a parent-run service) is that it is publicly and substantially funded and employs full-time workers who receive the same pay and conditions as workers in more traditional nurseries. Finally, it should be noted that the *crèche parentale* is one of a range of publicly funded services; most provision for children under three is provided in ordinary nurseries or 'organized childminding'. This means that parents who want to run the service attended by their children can have the opportunity to do so, but that playing such an active role is not an expectation of all parents wanting services.

THE 'EUROPEAN DIMENSION' IN EARLY CHILDHOOD SERVICES

This chapter has dealt mainly at the level of individual European countries. In conclusion, though, I want to consider developments at a European (or more specifically European Community) level. The Community's interest in aspects of early childhood services goes back to the Treaty of

Rome and Article 119 which commits the Community to seek equal treatment for men and women in the labour market. The European Commission, in its attempt to promote such equal treatment, has identified the 'reconciliation of employment and family responsibilities' as one of the conditions required – and this in turn has led the Commission to take an increasing interest in issues concerning the care of children as an essential part of the solution to this reconciliation condition.

In 1983, as part of the Community's First Equal Opportunity Programme, the Commission initiated a Directive on Parental Leave and Leave for Family Reasons. A Directive is legally enforceable in member states, and the Commission's proposal envisaged setting minimum standards for these two types of leave throughout the Community, including each worker having an entitlement to at least three months of parental leave, with the entitlement to be non-transferable (in other words, if fathers did not take leave, their entitlement could not be transferred to their partners). To come into force, Directives must be adopted by the Council of Ministers, representing the governments of each member state (the Commission initiates Directives, the Council decides whether to adopt them). Unfortunately, mainly because of opposition from the British Government, the proposed Directive was not adopted, and remains 'on ice', possibly to be brought forward again by the Commission.

In 1986, as part of its Second Equal Opportunities Programme, the Commission established a Childcare Network, consisting of an expert from each member state. During the remaining four years of the Programme, this Network undertook a range of work, publishing a number of reports, reviewing policies and services in general, and analysing a number of specific issues (for example, rural families, workers in services and men as carers).

In 1990 the Community Charter of Basic Social Rights for Workers, under the heading of 'the Right of Men and Women to Equal Treatment', called for 'the development of amenities enabling those concerned to reconcile their occupational and family obligations more easily' (Eurospeak for services and other measures to support employed parents). The Action Programme for Implementing the Charter, and the Community's Third Equal Opportunities Programme which began in 1991, called for the Commission to prepare a Recommendation on Childcare. A Recommendation, like a Directive, is a Community measure; unlike a Directive it is not legally binding, being confined to recommending action to member states. Both the Childcare Network and the European Parliament in a Resolution on Childcare and Equality of Opportunity (April 1991) have argued for a Directive, and while the Commission has determined on a Recommendation, a Directive remains on the agenda for future discussion;

the call for it will get stronger should member states not respond positively to the Recommendation.

Currently, the Recommendation has been adopted by the Commission (July 1991), but now goes to the Council of Ministers, who will decide whether or not to adopt it (a Recommendation can come from the Commission or the Council of Ministers; a Council Recommendation carries more political clout, since it has been approved by the representatives of all governments, but for the same reason may be subject to more dilution if the proposal put forward by the Commission is unacceptable to certain member states).

The proposed Recommendation, adopted by the Commission and now put forward to the Council of Ministers, envisages measures in four areas 'to enable women and men to reconcile their occupational and family obligations, arising from the care and upbringing of children'. These areas include services providing care for children; leave arrangements for employed parents; making the environment, structure and organization of the work-place responsive to the needs of workers with children; and the encouragement of increased participation by men in the care of children to ensure a more equal sharing of family responsibilities between men and women.

On services providing care for children, member states are recommended to 'take measures designed to ensure all parents in or seeking employment, education or training have access to locally based and good quality services...[that] are affordable [and] combine safe and secure care with a broad education or pedagogical approach'. Flexibility and diversity of services should be encouraged, combined with coherence between different services. Member states should seek to improve training (both initial and continuous) of workers, so that training becomes 'appropriate to the great importance and social and educative value of their work'. Particularly important, the proposed Recommendation recognizes that public funding has 'an essential contribution [to make] to the development of affordable, good quality, coherent services which offer choice to parents'.

Once adopted (and it must be stressed that the version adopted by the Council may differ from the version submitted by the Commission), the Recommendation is due to be followed by a guide to good practice from the Commission, which will supplement the broad objectives and principles stated in the Recommendation with more detailed guidance. In these measures, as well as the blocked Parental Leave Directive, we can see emerging gradually a Community policy affecting children. However, it is important to understand the limits of the EC's present involvement with children. To take initiatives, the Commission must have competence, in other words it must have a legal basis for action, which can only come from the Community's treaties. At present the Commission has competence to deal with equality issues, but not with issues concerning children *per se*. Hence, for example, the Recommendation cannot include children whose parents are not employed or in training nor can it recommend that services for children with employed parents should not be developed in isolation from services for other children.

In whatever form it is adopted by the Council of Ministers, the Recommendation is unlikely to lead to major, immediate changes. It does, however, mark an important milestone in the development of a European policy in the area of early childhood services. This policy development process is gradual and incremental, but will increasingly influence national policy and services. Another example of this process is the gradual involvement of the Structural Funds — the Community's own resources — in the area of early childhood services. The first report of the Childcare Network, recognizing that member states varied in their national resources, recommended that the 'Commission should examine, as soon as possible, what existing funds within the Community might be used to provide financial assistance to member states with lower levels of national income to support the development of child care services' (European Commission, 1988, p. 300). This was followed up by a report from the Network which specifically examined the potential contribution of the Structural Funds to the development of child care services. It seems that the Funds, as they stand, can be used to fund services, though further work is needed to increase awareness at all levels of this potential. In 1991, however, the Commission introduced a specific child care component as part of a Programme funded by the Structural Funds to promote the vocational training and employment of women. The sums involved were small and short-term, but again the significance must be viewed in a longer-term perspective.

What the eventual scope and shape of European policy will look like will not become clear for several years and will depend on a number of factors, not least the ability of organizations concerned with children and early childhood services to develop a co-ordinated and effective lobbying capability aimed at the European political process. Unfortunately, the Recommendation has not had the benefit of such a lobby to press for a strong and effective measure; indeed, combined with media disinterest and a general ignorance of the workings of the Community, the Recommendation (like many other social measures) has received little attention in Britain.

This formal development of policy and initiatives at Community level is not, however, the only 'European dimension' in the development of services and policies. Perhaps as important in the long run is the framework provided by the Community for the exchange of ideas, experience and knowledge between member states, regional and local authorities, organizations, projects and individual workers. Such exchanges will not lead to some uniform set of European services. What they can do, however, is contribute to the spread of good practice and ideas, a raising of expectations and greater understanding of the assumptions and context which have influenced the developments in each member state.

This is written in expectation and with a certain degree of wishful thinking. There are risks. Dragging back advanced services to a lowest common denominator might occur rather than a process of levelling up to the best. Cheap and dubious practices in one country may attract the attention of the government in another country. Perhaps, above all, balancing the interests of economies with those of women and children may not be achieved. The need to extend the Community's competence to include citizens outside the labour force and to develop a Community that has strong social objectives, as well as economic ones, is essential if this balance is to be attained. Finally, all organizations with interests in children and their carers must inform themselves of European Community processes, initiatives and structures, to fit themselves to play an active role at a European as well as a national level.

Postscript

The Commission's proposal for a Recommendation on Childcare, was sent to the Economic and Social Committee (ECOSOC) of the European Communities and to the European Parliament for their opinions. These were given in November 1991. They supported the Commission proposal, but included some proposed amendments which would have strengthened the Recommendation. The Council of Ministers subsequently agreed a Recommendation in December, to be officially published in Spring 1992. The Council Recommendation still recognises the need for action in four areas (services, leave arrangements, the workplace and more equal sharing between men and women), but in a number of important respects, especially in relation to services, the final Recommendation is substantially weaker than the original Commission proposal. None of the proposed amendments from ECOSOC or the Parliament have been included. As the proceedings of the Council take place in private, there is no way of telling why the final Recommendation has been weakened or the positions taken by individual Governments. It should be emphasised, however, that this is not the end of the Community's involvement in early childhood services; the episode of the Recommendation should be seen as part of a long-term process.

3

DEFINING, MEASURING AND SUPPORTING QUALITY

Peter Elfer and Dorothy Wedge

INTRODUCTION

It is important to define quality in relation to care and education provision for young children for at least two reasons.

First, although we have in the UK a wide range of types of service, offering very different experiences to children (including childminding, day nurseries, playgroups and nursery schools), they are sometimes grouped together under a single heading such as nursery education (Angela Rumbold, *Hansard*, 4 February 1991) as if they were one coherent service. When we are discussing the quality of a particular service, we need to be sure we do so on the basis of a clear common understanding of the objectives and underpinning philosophy and values of that service.

Second, the last decade has seen an emphasis on the economic value of commodities or services, particularly in the public sector. This too has reinforced the need to be able to define and describe clearly the objectives any service has for young children and the conditions and circumstances in which it will be possible (or very difficult) to achieve those objectives.

Partly because of these two factors, there have been a number of recent reports and initiatives aiming to describe the characteristics of high quality provision for children. These have sometimes been in the form of principles of good practice and sometimes entailed more detailed standards. We refer to these different ways of defining and describing quality collectively as quality frameworks.

We need to recognize that the care and education of any child happens primarily through a set of unique relationships. Part of the professionalism of early years workers is the ability to be able to acknowledge that they will, probably at the same time, be helping and sometimes hindering children's development, in the different ways that they interact with and respond to each child.

The workers' task is not only objectively to apply quality frameworks, however sophisticated, but also to acknowledge and appraise continually the unique contribution they make to the educative relationship. It is this unique subjective relationship that is perhaps the most influential and precious resource the child has. Yet somehow the effective educator has to find a way, without losing the uniqueness of each relationship with each child, of continually assessing and appraising that relationship.

One danger of the use of quality frameworks is that they focus attention on the framework itself rather than the quality of interaction with the child. An example of this is the intense debate in relation to the Children Act Guidance about staff/child ratios. Many care and education settings will claim that they reach required standards because they have engaged the correct number of staff, with little attention being paid to how the staff work with children.

None of this is to argue against the need for quality frameworks. The danger of not having a coherent set of standards is that many staff will simply feel they work in a vacuum and little will happen consistently (or at all) to assess quality and improve practice. In this respect, the considerable development work invested recently in the production of statements of quality and codes of practice is very much to be welcomed. However, we believe the key to the effectiveness of such frameworks is the extent to which they help workers continually evaluate their relationships with children.

The chapter is in three sections:

(1) issues in the definition and description of quality;

(2) the contribution of the Children Act and official Guidance to defining and supporting standards;

(3) three initiatives in Cambridgeshire which sought to support early years workers in developing their practice with young children through piloting the application and assessment of standards and the use of a team in individual and direct work with teachers.

ISSUES IN DEFINING AND DESCRIBING QUALITY
The pressure to define quality

(Or 'Looking for research to support what we happen to believe matters'.)

At the time the Children Bill was making its passage through Parliament, the Early Childhood Unit received a large number of requests, particularly from private, voluntary and social services settings, for a statement of quality and standards in work with young children. Of course, there had been concern about standards prior to the Children Bill with much research on the way children under five learn and develop (*see*, for example, Clark, 1988). In addition, two reports had recently been published (DES, 1989a; House of Commons, 1989) which addressed the conditions and circumstances in which young children most effectively learn and develop, and the need for this knowledge to be available to adults working with young children in an increasingly diverse range of settings.

It was, however, the imminence of a new legislative framework for the registration of early years provision other than that in formal education settings that led to the urgency of requests for an immediate and authoritative statement of quality and standards. It was not difficult to understand this urgency. There was an acute shortage of day care provision and an expectation by government that the shortage would be met through commercial day care. Under-fives advisers in social services departments, responsible for registering these new sources of day care, were in a particularly uncomfortable position, struggling to ensure at least minimum standards without restricting development. Their task was made more difficult by the frequent absence of any well-documented policy and standards statements.

Where these did exist, there were often wide variations between them undermining their credibility. The values and principles that underpinned the statements were frequently either not explicit or not accepted by potential providers who would be subject to them. There seemed therefore to be a feeling that many of the disputes that arose between the local authorities and providers could be resolved by invoking a national standard whose authority rested in formal research and which would, as a definitive statement of quality, command widespread consensus.

Limitations of research

(Or 'What the researchers thought mattered'.)

Some writers do suggest that there may be some general consensus, at least on the needs of children:

There is broad agreement about what children need in order to develop properly, and that first consideration should be given to the welfare of the child, whilst not interfering unnecessarily with the rights and wishes of the parents.

(Thoburn, 1986, p. 546)

Assumptions about what children need and how adults might provide it have varied widely even this century. Very generally, however, there is consensus in much of the current child development literature that children need to feel loved, respected and listened to.

(European Commission Childcare Network, 1991, p. 5)

However, these writers are quick to emphasize how limited this consensus is:

When it comes to individual cases, however, there may be disagreement about whether the care given in a child's own home is 'good enough', or about the respective weight to be given to different needs, especially if not all can be met.

(Thoburn, 1986, p. 546)

We can therefore make informed guesses about what young children need. But our understanding is relative and is coloured by our wider social perceptions and values. We recognize that in stating the needs of children we are also making a statement about our own beliefs.

(European Commission Childcare Network, 1991, p. 5)

It is striking that much recent work on approaches to quality emphasizes that it is a more complex notion than one that can be addressed by research alone. Four common ideas emerge as important to a fuller understanding of quality:

(1) the notion of quality is meaningless unless there is clarity about the *values and beliefs* that underpin a service;

(2) in the provision of any service there may be a number of '*stakeholders*' who could be considered as users and other groups who may have a key interest in the way the service is provided;

(3) review of quality needs to entail more than a review of the individual service and must include the *policy and organizational framework* within which a service operates;

(4) assessing quality must go *beyond the application of checklists* and frameworks.

Values and beliefs

(Or 'It all depends on what you think really matters'.)

Reference has already been made to the dependence on values and beliefs of any assertions about the needs of children. Other writers reinforce this:

> This raises the question of whether governments have any responsibility in this area and if so, whether the responsibility is primarily to protect children from possible harm through enforcing minimum standards for all services or to ensure good quality services for all children. In either case terms need defining. What harm do we wish to prevent? What do we mean by good quality? The answers to either question are bound to be value based.
>
> (Moss and Melhuish, 1991, p. 11)

> The context [for inspection] includes clear definitions and a clear understanding of:
>> the policies for each main area of service provision derived from the principles and values underpinning the social service department's philosophy of care.
>
> (DH, 1991, p. 10)

Any approach to assessing quality must be preceded by a working through of what we believe matters, what we are trying to achieve and how we will reconcile competing or conflicting goals. Within this process, research has a role to play but it has a supporting rather than a leading part. Our values and beliefs should be more openly informing our choices about the research areas we consider important rather than the other way round. Farquhar summarizes this well:

> In order for the definition and assessment of quality in early childhood centres to be appropriate and acceptable it is important that the way quality is defined and the methodological approach taken is developed from our knowledge and understanding of empirical research in the area, the philosophical base of the individual programme, and our current social and cultural values for early childhood education.
>
> (Farquhar, 1990, p. 73)

This has two key implications. First, the appeal for an 'off the shelf', authoritative statement of quality and standards in child care needs to be responded to with some caution. It is extremely important that there should be national statements of good practice, that is, statements which are government led, for example *Starting with Quality* (DES, 1990a) or official guidance (DH, 1991), as well as statements which are based on widespread consultation (codes of practice, for example Cowley, 1991; PPA, 1990; Kids Club Network, 1989; NCMA, 1991).

However, it is difficult for these documents to be explicit and detailed in the values, beliefs and standards laid down as they need to be acceptable to a very wide range of organizations and constituencies. Their main function is primarily as *source* documents to assist direct service providers in the process of determining their own specific value commitments and priorities:

> Our discussion of quality acknowledges a diversity of circumstances and a diversity of perspectives or values.... Indeed, we believe that the process involved in defining quality – with the opportunity it provides to explore and discuss values, objectives and priorities – is of the utmost importance, and can be lost where people simply adopt existing measures.
>
> (European Commission Childcare Network, 1991, p. 8)

In this sense national frameworks are an essential and valuable tool but their contribution is more to the process of defining quality than prescribing it directly.

Stakeholders in quality

(Or 'From whose point of view are we looking?')

The second idea in much recent writing on quality is that a focus on values and beliefs prompts recognition of the existence of other groups (parents, other carers, staff, local communities) who also have a legitimate interest in quality:

> Issues of who are the users of a service underlie the concept of quality in public services...
>
>   Who are the users of child care? The child, the parents or society at large?
>   Whose interests may be damaged by this service or the way we provide it?
>
> (Stewart and Walsh, 1989, p. 8)

Farquhar identifies four groups of 'user': 'In the social, educational and political context of New Zealand pre-compulsory education, there are four different ways of viewing how to ensure and promote quality' (Farquhar, 1990, p. 79), and she goes on to refer to the perspectives of parents, staff, cultural and child development, whilst Moss in the UK speaks of 'what we want or do not want for children, parents, workers and local communities' (Moss and Melhuish, 1991, p. 11).

The perspectives of local communities and differing cultures is perhaps one of the most important and neglected areas in considerations of quality. We live in a multi-cultural, multiracial society in which variations in patterns of parenting and the differing priorities held by parents for their children's development have largely been ignored (Maximé, 1986).

The Children Act 1989 should help to change this through its general requirement that needs arising from race, culture, religion and language must be taken into account by service providers. There is also the more specific power to cancel the registration of providers of childminding and day care where care is 'seriously inadequate' having regard to race, culture, religion and language. However, an approach is also needed which will enable judgements to be made about quality in relation to the extent to which the needs of children are positively identified and met rather than only when minimum standards are breached. That is something that can only be done by consultation with and involvement of local communities and these processes are very much in their infancy.

The policy and organizational context

(Or 'Are we looking at the individual service or the whole system?')

Not only do we have to consider different interest groups but also whether judgements about quality are made at the individual service level or in relation to the policy and organizational framework within which services are provided.

Farquhar seems to suggest that these two levels are alternatives: 'Definitions of quality may focus on the whole childhood service.... Alternatively, definitions of quality may be specific to individual early childhood programmes' (Farquhar, 1990, p. 75).

The implication is clear that any approach to assessing quality needs to be centred on the specific aims, objectives and operating conditions of an individual service although the assessment will be made in the context of the policy of the overall organization, for example the local authority.

The key point here would seem to be the need to establish an approach to evaluation that does not become too biased towards either the policy formation levels or the individual service levels of the organization.

Moss emphasizes the relationship between service and policy levels more strongly than Farquhar:

As a society we have yet to draw up the full policy agenda...which recognizes the profundity and inter-connectedness of the issues facing us concerning childhood and the upbringing of children, the relationship between employment, parenthood and gender equity and the allocation of work and cost across the whole field of caring work.

(Moss and Melhuish, 1991, p. 18)

Yet even within the limited scope of policy options at local authority level, the complexity of applying broad values set nationally to local areas and individual services has perhaps not been sufficiently recognized. The values that underpin parts of official guidance, for example that the *fact* of need rather than the *cause* is to be a prime feature of local service philosophy (DH, 1991, para. 1.9), will conflict with the values held by some local elected members. In addition, parents of children with disabilities may not wish their support services to be merged with those for children whose need arises because of family, emotional and social difficulties.

Beyond checklists and frameworks

(Or 'Can you measure relationships?')

A fourth idea in recent writing on defining and measuring quality is the extent to which the application of checklists and frameworks can offer an adequate approach to quality assurance. Two writers in particular refer to this:

> Some elements of quality proposed in the literature are easily articulated and enumerated. . . . However, if the only indexes of quality used during centre inspection and review are those that are measurable and required of every centre then this will limit the promotion of high quality education and care.
>
> (Farquhar, 1990, p. 77)

> Any system of quality control which tries to rely too heavily or exclusively on rules, flow charts and checklists of warning signs and to reduce the part played by the individual family, child, residential or field social worker in decision-making may be of limited relevance and value.
>
> (Thoburn, 1986, p. 550)

The view of both these writers is that measurables (ratios, qualifications, group size, training, etc. in the case of early years care and education and procedures, documentation and decision-making in the case of child protection) cannot alone provide an adequate analysis of quality. This appears to be in marked contrast to guidance from the Department of Health on the use of independent inspection units (IIUs): 'The inspection process should be rooted in explicit values and measurable standards' (DH: SSI, 1991, para. 4.6).

In relation to monitoring and evaluating the curriculum, the Rumbold Committee considered that:

> it should take place at three levels:
> within the individual class or group; within the institution (school, unit, day nursery, playgroup, etc.) and across all the services for under fives within a local authority
>
> (DES, 1990a, para. 134)

and the committee called for educators to build into the planning cycle a broad review of the effectiveness and value of the provision they make, extending beyond the immediate setting to include parent and community links and other factors (para. 95).

This begins to address the concern of Farquhar and Moss that the perspective of all 'stakeholders' should be taken into account in reviews of quality. However, whilst acknowledging the importance of appraisal of individual professional practice (para. 97), the committee make very little reference to how this is to be achieved in practice. Chapter 10 of their report on the Education, Training and Support of adults working with under fives refers mainly to the first two of these three elements. It seems a pity, especially given the spirit of a report that seeks to relate to 'a wide variety of settings', that it should not refer to the long tradition of professional supervision in social work practice and what this might have to offer to supporting staff self-appraisal in other disciplines.

Nevertheless, the report is crucial in the emphasis it gives to the appraisal of quality at every level and by implication that the assessment and development of quality cannot be limited to measurable standards only.

THE CONTRIBUTION OF THE CHILDREN ACT 1989
A strengthened legal framework

(Or 'The care of children is not a private matter between parents and carers'.)

The Children Act was implemented in October 1991 and gives regulatory and developmental responsibilities to local authorities in England and Wales in relation to standards of care. These standards were previously subject to the Nurseries and Child-Minders Regulation Act 1948.

Regulatory responsibilities revolve around the concept of 'fit person'. Local authorities have a duty to register providers of care for children under eight of two hours or more for reward in the provider's home or whether or not for reward elsewhere. The burden of proof of fitness is on the local authority and in this respect the Act is similar to the 1948 Act. However, the Children Act strengthens the regulatory powers of authorities, including new powers and duties to impose requirements (for example, on numbers of staff and children), to inspect and to cancel registration.

The main emphasis of the Act is on regulation but there are developmental responsibilities which relate to both individual services and to strategic planning. For individual services, whilst regulation should have a developmental effect, specific development powers are limited to:

(1) seeking help from education authorities in registration and inspection;

(2) the provision of training, advice, guidance and counselling;

(3) a duty, when making day care available, to have regard to the racial groups to which children in need belong.

The strategic responsibilities of authorities are quite new. They are enshrined in a specific duty to undertake, with the local education authority and at three-year intervals, a general review of all childminding and day care provision.

Issues in implementation

(Or 'Can the law require standards beyond child protection?')

The central concept of both the 1948 and 1989 Acts in relation to standards of care is that of a 'fit person'. New powers and duties and detailed guidance (DH, 1991) on standards and assessing fitness are very much to be welcomed. However, standards will only improve in practice if providers of care are able to co-operate with local authorities in an active and integrated implementation of the Act, if adequate resources are made available and if there are the necessary shifts in professional practice and public acceptance of standards.

The importance of these factors is illustrated in the case of the 1948 Act by the results of a recent survey (Elfer and Beasley, 1991). This showed widespread lack of confidence in the powers of that Act to enable local authorities to take effective action against providers of care who could not achieve minimum standards. Legal opinion, however, was that in many cases examined in the survey, the Act could have been used more effectively if professional, managerial and legal practice had been of a higher standard, each of course linked to resource availability.

In a recent speech to the Women's National Commission seminar on child care, Virginia Bottomley, Minister with responsibility in the Department of Health for implementation of the Children Act, stated that: 'the new system incorporates two new powers which should have a major impact in the key area of standards of service' (Bottomley, 1991), and she went on to refer to the power to seek help from local education authorities and the duty to inspect at least once a year. Our main point here, reflecting the theme of this chapter, is that the Children Act will not make a major impact on standards of service unless a realistic level of resources and professional and management support is devoted to its implementation. We have tried to illustrate this in relation to the two features of the Act identified by Mrs Bottomley.

Collaborating with the education authority on standards

(Or 'Care and education are not separable'.)

Such collaboration needs to address the development of skills in each of the three essential stages of setting, observation of and assessment of standards. This is important if the different areas of knowledge and experience held in social services and education are to inform each other for the benefit of children. In practice there are serious obstacles to collaboration and Gillian Pugh has described some of these in Chapter 1. However, an important step in supporting collaboration has been the issuing in the official Guidance of detailed advice on standards considered acceptable to both the Department of Health and the Department of Education and Science: 'These standards apply to all services – those managed by social services or education departments or other departments within a local authority and by independent providers and childminders' (DH, 1991, para. 6.1).

The Guidance goes much further than any previous official documents in setting out standards for the programme of activities offered to children and the involvement of parents. It also makes clear reference to the values that should underpin implementation of the Act, for example concerning equal opportunities:

> The values deriving from different backgrounds – racial, cultural, religious and linguistic – should be respected.
>
> (Para. 6.2)

> It is important that...practice enables young children to develop positive attitudes to differences of race, culture and language and differences of gender.
>
> (Para. 6.11)

> Children should have the right to be cared for as part of a community which values the religious, racial, cultural and linguistic identity of the child....The extent to which a day care setting fulfils rights may be used in defining the quality of care for that setting.
>
> (Para. 6.28)

In relation to the discussion at the beginning of this chapter about the importance of values and beliefs in any approach to defining quality, these references are cornerstones of quality. The principle that all services should combat discrimination and seek positively to promote the racial and cultural background of all children arises out of a value that is central to the Children Act 1989. It should underpin all services for children and might be part of what Peter Moss refers to as 'an area of shared values in British society, on which base we can build a core area of agreement about quality, while accepting diverse concepts of quality outside this core area' (Moss and Melhuish, 1991, p. 12).

The detailed references in the Guidance to values and principles, particularly concerning equal opportunities, represent a major step forward in supporting the development of quality services by supporting a definition of quality. It is disappointing that the Guidance is not more detailed on the translation into practice of values that are fundamental to the Act, in particular those that relate to equality of opportunity. It is recognized that the Guidance has to address a very wide range of services, organizations and local circumstances. There is also the argument that any quality framework must not be prescriptive but enable adults involved with individual services to develop their own detailed standards. However, where national quality frameworks leave scope for local services to work through the process of translating 'shared values' into practice, they also leave scope for those values to remain little more than fine words. If Mrs Bottomley's assertion, that the power to collaborate with local education authorities will have a major impact on standards, is to be fulfilled, local advisers will need a great deal of time and support to work with service providers. (But see footnote) That is demonstrated in the third part of this chapter by reference to work in Cambridgeshire.

The new inspection duty

(Or 'Assessing quality with a clipboard?')

The Children Act 1989 makes it a duty (previously a power) for local authorities to inspect all registered provision at least once a year. This duty is often referred to as the annual inspection but it was emphasized in Parliament (*Hansard*, 6 June 1989) that the duty is to ensure services are of an acceptable standard and we need to keep in mind this function rather than the legal minimum frequency.

There is much to commend this new emphasis on inspection, not least because it highlights the importance of clear standards. This is not only essential to any systematic approach to developing quality but a question of natural justice. Providers of care should only be inspected against criteria that they have been clearly informed about at the time of their registration.

Inspection needs to be used as a means to promote standards and not just to monitor them. It is very welcome that Mrs Bottomley has acknowledged this: 'It will be a positive instrument, used not just to detect low standards, but as a means of encouraging and advising on improvements' (Bottomley, 1991).

However, many concerns have been expressed about the implementation of the inspection duty. How will it be perceived by carers? Who will undertake it? Will they have the skills to assess interactions with children as well as more tangible measures of hygiene, safety and space requirements? The requirement under the National Health Services and Community Care Act 1989 to establish independent inspection units (IIUs) in relation to services for adults has been seen by some authorities as an opportunity to include within them their inspection responsibilities under the Children Act. This has been seen as a more cost-effective use of resources and an opportunity to apply the principle of impartial or 'arm's length inspection' to children's and adults' services.

Such an arrangement has risks as well as advantages. Regulation (registration and inspection) and development need to be undertaken and understood as parts of an integrated process. Regulation needs to be strong enough to protect children but implemented in a way that supports development. The experience of the Cambridgeshire teacher support team (and countless other experience) is that adults are best helped to reflect on and develop their practice when they feel supported and valued in that process rather than feeling 'regulated'.

Where IIUs are used, the emphasis is likely to be on inspection and the Guidance reinforces this:

> Where conflict may arise between the inspector role and the advisory and supportive role the inspector role must come first, and it must be clear when an inspector is conducting a formal inspection and when he/she is providing support.
>
> (DH: SSI, 1991, para. 4.25)

Again the question needs to be asked how the provision of advice and support can be maintained and integrated with inspection whilst protecting the impartiality of inspection. The Department of Health has addressed this in two respects.

First, it has commissioned the development of a specialist in-service training pack (NCB, 1991), specifically for staff responsible for registration, inspection, advice and support, which provides a common training course for all staff whether responsible for one or all of these functions.

Second, it makes the suggestion (DH: SSI, 1991, para. 5.10) that staff might be seconded into IIUs. This would not only support an integration of the primarily regulatory role within the unit and developmental role outside but would make available to the inspection role the knowledge and skills of experienced advisers.

Independent inspection units could have much to offer but again the

Minister's belief about their contribution to promoting standards depends critically on units developing an approach to quality that is not tightly restricted to measurable standards, on the skills of the staff they recruit and on the protection and development of training and support.

Strategic review

(Or 'Collaboration made mandatory'.)

One of the most promising features of the Children Act 1989 in relation to young children is that the call in previous guidance (LASSL(76)5 and LASSL(78)5) for co-ordination and collabroration is developed into a specific duty (section 19). The review must be conducted with the education authority and includes all registered provision for under eights, holiday and out-of-school provision for older children 'in need' and arrangements for the provision of advice and support. Review of provision for children in need does not apply in Scotland. The review must have regard to provision that is not registered, for example education facilities for young children.

The review will address issues about the way services link together which were identified at the beginning of this chapter as integral to any assessment of quality.

In introducing the review, the Guidance says that 'The review duty gives legislative support to government policy that the level, pattern and range of day care and related services for young children should be worked out at local level' (DH, 1991, para. 9.1). This highlights the importance of collaboration but two key issues are not addressed.

First, effective service delivery at local level depends on effective collaboration at central level: 'We believe that the achievement of better local co-ordination would be greatly helped if central government give a clearer lead, setting a national framework within which local development could take place' (DES, 1990a, para. 215).

Second, the words 'level, pattern and range' leave in doubt the extent to which the review should be addressing quality at service level. This is primarily the purpose of inspection but issues of quality at service and organizational levels are closely linked as we have discussed. The Guidance (DH, 1991) does refer to links with inspection (para. 9.13), to the identification of 'unusual or innovative schemes' (para. 9.14) and the analysis of issues including curriculum (9.14).

The implications of these references fit very well with the four ideas present in current debate about quality discussed at the beginning of the chapter. Local authorities will need to agree a policy on what they consider to constitute quality or excellence and how it will be recognized and assessed. Without this, the review will be extremely difficult to conduct in a coherent way. With it, and with the collaboration of the private and voluntary sectors, the review offers a major opportunity to define, measure and support quality.

SUPPORTING QUALITY IN CAMBRIDGESHIRE
Standards into practice

(Or 'Making a difference for children'.)

It is the purpose of regulation to require and register acceptable minimum standards, and the report of the three-year review will act as a regular monitor of progress and help to assess how standards are translated into practice. Effective standards will depend partly on whether the local authority has worked out a strategy for monitoring and is confident it can take action where it finds unacceptable practice. Local authorities will also need to have thought through how providers will be enabled to change practice for the better.

In this section we describe three different initiatives in Cambridgeshire. The first illustrates the kind of major areas of concern which may come to light in inspections, observed in this instance by college students and staff; the second examines the potential of the National Vocational Qualification for under-sevens workers; and the third demonstrates a practical approach to supporting change on an individual basis.

Falling below standards

(Or 'The answer is not just more regulation'.)

It is well known that our 'patchwork' of services is very variable in quality, some of it very good (usually the best resourced) and some very poor. In Cambridgeshire, tutors in the college teaching nursery nurses and advisers in social services are already discussing what they can contribute separately and together to improve some of the child care provision in a city area. They are concerned that too many practitioners are isolated from others, unchallenged and uncritical of themselves, with their provision based on old ideas and prejudices.

Financial constraints in both the private and public sectors mean that staff are rarely able to have time out for training (if it is provided in their area). They see the low motivation of child care workers as a reflection of the status given to care and education in our society. They are concerned that low-paid employees find it difficult to speak out about bad practice, recent examples of which have included:

(1) inappropriate use of discipline;
(2) flouting regulations and good practice with regard to health and safety;
(3) taking more children than are registered for;
(4) lack of stimulation and disinterest in the children by staff;
(5) private providers indifferent to the needs of children and staff;
(6) overcrowding in rooms and insufficient supervision.

These issues are not peculiar to Cambridgeshire but are the kind of examples of worst practice identified nationally (Elfer and Beasley, 1991). Some are clear breaches of tangible and specific registration requirements (and may constitute grounds for cancellation of registration under the Children Act) whilst others are more complex.

Both the college and the social services department are members of a multi-disciplinary group reviewing training for early years workers. Voluntary and private providers are represented too and all are prepared to be committed to an equal partnership of giving and receiving knowledge. They are working on a programme of study days, workshops and conferences which will be available to everyone working with young children in the area. Some of the private providers are very keen for their staff to attend courses but financial constraints prevent them from releasing them during the working day. It would also be difficult for them to pay their staff for evening or weekend attendances. One possibility is to require the providers of child care to close their establishments so that their staff could have 'INSET days' three times a year (as, for example, happens for half a day each week at Pen Green, *see* Chapter 9). Such an obligation would need to be written into contracts with parents, of course, requiring them to take time off work to enable the training to take place, but it seems the only way to break the vicious circle.

Testing standards

('The experience of the National Vocational Qualification.')

The Children Act is not the only current force for change in the field of care and education for young children. The establishment of a National Vocational Qualification (NVQ) system promises the possibility of a revolution, if it is given the resources which will be needed for its establishment (for a further discussion of NVQ, *see* Chapter 11).

The 'performance criteria' for NVQ have been carefully drafted after thorough consultation. Practitioners who ask to be assessed will be called candidates and 'competency' will be assessed as they work with children in playgroups, day nurseries, crèches, schools or homes.

Cambridgeshire was one of the ten areas asked to pilot the standards in 1990. It required hard thinking about the question of standardizing expectations across disciplines. It showed areas that needed support and training and it removed the 'them and us' feeling between voluntary and statutory agencies. The solidity of relationships were tested by the agencies verifying each other. This was very successful:

> One of the major advantages has been the cross-fertilization of ideas, interests and expertise, because it has given our area a good excuse to work across disciplines. It has been one of the major desires of most people working in the child care field and this has given us a push in the right direction.
>
> (Cambridgeshire Regional College, 1990)

Although it was difficult and somewhat stressful to establish a common notion of what the basic 'competent' practitioner level would be, it gave participants working in different settings confidence to think that they were being assessed to the same standard. Moreover, it gave a tremendous boost to multi-disciplinary work because it started a process of evaluation, both within and between services, which has great potential for encouraging and supporting quality provision.

Raising standards

(Or 'A practice-centred approach.')

The great strength of the National Vocational Qualification system is that it is based on practice and assessed in the work-place. It supports practitioners' motivation to gain validation and to confirm and deepen their learning. Their training will be in their own hands and they will be able to 'plan, do and review' (to borrow the language of High/Scope), which is at the heart of all learning. The impetus for change will come from the individual worker and will have more chance of success than any quality criteria imposed from above, whether by government or the hierarchy of the organization. Good provision will become better as managers and practitioners look together at their practice, questioning how, for example, they

> contribute to the planning, implementation and evaluation of structured activities for a child.
>
> (NVQ, standard C19)

Or:

> observe and assess the development and behaviour of children.
>
> (NVQ, standard C16, Working with Under Sevens Project, 1990)

It will cause them to look again at the children's care and education. Observation of children's play and problem-solving, together with listening to their talk, will rekindle their respect for children's thinking. It should also encourage them to look outside for stimulation for themselves and the children and to ask themselves whether the environment they provide might have become too predictable, a benign, secure routine without excitement.

Questions such as:

(1) are we expecting enough of ourselves and the children?
(2) are we engaged in on-going discussions with parents about their children's emergent abilities?

are positive and optimistic if we ask them of ourselves, but from an employer, inspector or parent they can be threatening.

As practitioners are relating to children and parents they will be assessed by their managers, tutors or inspectors in an interactive and open way. Such a potent mixture of ages and agencies will surely guarantee subjectivity and objectivity in ample measure!

Working with children, with colleagues and with parents is an emotional business, and defining, measuring and supporting quality must rely to some extent on feelings. To acknowledge this is important in terms of both honest assessment and professionalism. We can only 'know' good quality when we can articulate how we react to it. Intuitive responses and 'gut feelings' are fine as long as we can describe them and use them as evidence of our judgements.

As well as the recent experience of the NVQ pilot, Cambridgeshire has had the benefit of a substantial contribution by a Pre-school Support Team in the Education Department. Six advisory teachers have been working alongside teachers, nursery and general assistants and parents in schools and playgroups. For the past five years they have demonstrated good practice, taking ideas, equipment and an extra pair of hands to encourage appropriate provision for young children. Their practical play workshops demonstrating mathematics, science, creativity, pre-writing and reading in exciting and imaginative ways have succeeded with teachers, parents, headteachers and governors. By taking activities into schools they have achieved more than course lecturers or inspection visits. Their enthusiasm has been catching and many support groups meet after school to share problems and progress.

There are very few overnight successes. Learning, whether it be about children's development and thinking, parent's perceptions or oneself, is a slow individual process. To be effective it needs to be one to one at least part of the time. Care and education are indivisible components of adult learning as much as they are for children and the responsive relationships which went with the practical help were important factors in effecting change.

CONCLUSION

('A message repeated.')

Quality frameworks and lists are an essential part of developing quality provision. However, quality itself may be a misleading concept if it encourages the idea that we are all agreed on what we are looking for and want for children before we have actually gone through some process to ensure that. The translation of frameworks into practice is complex and demands time and resources. That is because working with children is primarily a matter of reflective and carefully managed relationships which take time to understand and change.

In the past, training has implied that experts hold the right messages which have to be passed down to other people. Surely we can look forward to seeing something more dynamic than that, based on mutual respect and understanding of skills and experiences across disciplines.

Postscript

The Education (Schools) Bill currently going through Parliament includes the privatisation of the school inspection service. If this Bill is enacted as it stands, collaboration between education and social services on planning, reviewing and monitoring services – a central provision of the Children Act – will be very much less likely to happen.

p.66-67

PART 2
PRACTICE

4

CURRICULUM IN THE EARLY YEARS

Tricia David

The children were sitting on the 'story mat', their legs crossed. 'That way everyone can fit on,' the nursery teacher had explained. It was springtime, the theme for many of the children's activities, with the emphasis on exploring, representing, re-creating and creating (transforming) their understandings of the experiences offered. As they had been talking about baby animals, especially baby birds, a parent had produced a disused nest, which Diana, the teacher, was now holding out for all to see. She explained in hushed tones about the Mummy and Daddy birds she had observed going in and out of the hedge by her kitchen window, and how she had crept out, not wishing to frighten the birds, for a closer look.

'Imagine my surprise, children, there were four baby birds in that tiny nest, and sometimes the Mummy and Daddy too. I wonder, however could' holding up fingers now to help with the concepts involved 'one, two, three, four baby birds, and a Mummy, and a Daddy, all fit into a little nest like this?' Diana had intended her last 'question' to be simply rhetorical, indicating wonder at different aspects of life, but John, having reflected on his own experiences of the world, attempting to make sense of what he had just been told, offered the sage advice: 'I expect they all cross their legs.'

Sarah, aged four, was making delicate fingertip patterns to represent flowers, describing as she did so what she was trying to create with the finger paints. She had gone through phases of using these experimentally, spreading, daubing, making squiggles, using lower arms and elbows as well as whole hands and fingertips. She had explored the characteristics of the paint, texture-wise, colour-wise, and the properties of different surfaces, such as a clear, vertical screen, as well as table-tops, paper, and so on. One could say that she had become an expert finger-painter, who had found lots of answers to the question, 'What does this do?' and had moved on to the question, 'What can I do with this?' The playgroup supervisor, Mary, a woman with many years of experience in work with young children, and sensitive to their emotional as well as their cognitive, social and physical needs, watched, ready to intervene, should a child need encouragement, or 'extension activities' to foster further learning. She held her breath as both Sarah's hands, palms outstretched, went forward to the two saucers of paint. Later, she told Sarah's Mum, 'I knew exactly what she was going to do, I almost stopped her, the flowers she'd painted were so lovely. But she did what was important for her, she had narrated the whole picture, how the flowers would grow, but because it's winter, they're all under the ground.' If Sarah had not verbalized during her totally engrossed finger-painting process, or Mary and Sarah's mother not taken interest in these concerns, maybe no one would have known that the swirls of paint covering the paper hid the delicately arranged flowers, nor understood the educational process this young child had experienced.

The above two examples of children in action in early years settings illustrate the ingredients Tina Bruce identified as the three elements required in the construction of an early childhood curriculum – the child and processes and structures within the child; knowledge the child already has; and knowledge the child will acquire competently but with imagination (Bruce, 1987, p. 65). Similarly, the examples illustrate how children try to 'make sense' of their experiences, how 'For the children themselves, the effective curriculum is what each child takes away. Schools and their teachers need ways of finding out what each child's experience is and how well they are learning what the school intends' (Schools Council, 1981, p. 1). If we, as a society, intend that all our young children have access to an appropriate early years curriculum for three- to five-year-olds, as a current entitlement and as a foundation for later learning, we need to explore what we mean by the term 'curriculum' for this age-group, why we so decide, and how such a curriculum may be available whatever type of setting a child may attend. However, we cannot take it for granted that opportunities for what we may consider 'worthwhile', appropriate, or positive learning will be available willy-nilly. Our children could be learning that one can be cruel to, or manipulate, those less powerful than oneself; that certain kinds of activity, people, abilities or attributes are accorded a higher value than others, despite the avowed intentions of the adults. For example, in one nursery, the staff realized that although their stated aims included 'developing independence, . . . creativity', they actually stultified both these through their own behaviours, pre-structuring the activities and environment to such an extent that children were not allowed, or able, to override aspects determined by the adults.

Additionally, if we wish to assert that an early years curriculum is an entitlement for the present and one which should provide children with a foundation for later learning (now, partly 'delivered', through the National Curriculum), how are children to be afforded continuity — how will the early years (birth to five) and the post-five curricula link together?

WHAT DOES 'CURRICULUM' MEAN?

Although there are still disagreements among curriculum theorists, generally speaking, people discussing curriculum manage their thoughts about the interrelated aspects of school life, by suggesting that the whole curriculum is made up of the aims and objectives; teaching and learning styles, including assessment and evaluation; content; resources available (people, space, equipment); use of resources; relationships; and rules.

In the introduction to her book *A Curriculum for the Pre-school Child*, Audrey Curtis writes:

> The main purpose of the book is to demonstrate that there is a recognizable curriculum for children under statutory school age based on skills and competencies to be developed in a flexible and child-centred environment, and that there is ample material with which to challenge and extend children without offering them a 'watered-down' reception class programme.
>
> (Curtis, 1986, pp. 2–3)

Curtis makes two significant points here: firstly, that a curriculum exists — something which, as David (1990, p. 72) asserts, many pre-school practitioners were loath to admit, because it 'smacked of subjects, set lessons, and a syllabus, rather than their own view of what was important in the lives of young children — holistic development through free and spontaneous play'; secondly, that a distinct curriculum, different from that in the infant school, and more appropriate to their developmental stage, is essential for children during this period of their, so far, brief lives. Put more bluntly, as Gwen Stubbs, formerly Staffordshire's Early Years

Inspector, used to say, to bring home the uniqueness of this age-group, 'They aren't five-year-olds with their legs cut off.'

In support of this view of the settings for, and therefore the curriculum for, our youngest children being special, research indicates that

> The contexts of the nursery school, nursery class, day nursery and playgroup may be said to share a common ideology. A nursery represents a recognizable social world which is clearly differentiated from the social worlds of the home and of the infant school. This social world of the nursery may be distinguished with reference to the ideas held by the nursery practitioners about the nature of young children and their learning processes....In the infant school the range of didactic methods is comparatively great, encompassing both formal instruction and discovery learning. In the nursery, although a certain element of structure may obtain, this tends to be covert; the emphasis is clearly upon play as the method of knowledge and skill acquisition.
>
> (Hutt *et al.*, 1989, pp. 227–8)

In more recent field work, Burgess, Hughes and Moxon (1991) have replicated these findings, although their observations were restricted to nurseries in the maintained sector of education, reception classes for four-year-olds, and combined nursery centres. The findings of this team suggest that there are indeed commonly held principles for the implementation of a suitable curriculum for under fives, but that the translation of these in practice varies according to the type of provision, and the social context in which the provision operates. Their report should raise our levels of concern that children in all settings experience coherence, continuity, and equality of opportunity — for these were aspects in which discrepancies were found.

The members of the Rumbold Committee stressed from a positive point of view the importance of educators' awareness of context in relation to young children's learning, the 'people involved in it, and the values and beliefs which are embedded in it' (DES, 1990a, para. 67), and while they suggest that the principles upon which an under-fives curriculum should be based complement those underpinning a curriculum for older children, they urged the use of a 'framework' rather than a 'National Curriculum' for three- and four-year-old children. Further, the committee argued that the aims of education for this age-group are basically the same as those for any other phase, as the House of Commons Select Committee stated in their earlier report (House of Commons, 1989).

The Rumbold Committee (DES, 1990a) considered alternative ways of defining the curriculum and came to the conclusion that the best approach would be a framework based on areas of experience and learning; additionally, they stressed that the process of learning — *how* children are enabled to learn — was just as important as *what* they learn. This *how* is usually expressed by early childhood educators as 'through play', and this view has been supported by official documents (e.g. DES, 1985b; DES, 1989a), by research (*see* Moyles, 1989), and by bodies such as the House of Commons Select Committee, as a result of their wide-ranging investigations (House of Commons, 1989).

WHAT DOES OUR CHOICE OF CURRICULUM TELL US ABOUT OUR BELIEFS ABOUT CHILDREN AND CHILDHOOD?

Robin Alexander (1988) identified seven different types of primary school curriculum. Preference for one of these, or even a particular mixture, will be derived from one's knowledge and beliefs about children and society. Alexander's seven curricula are as follows: classical humanist (initiating the child into 'the best of cultural heritage'); behavioural/mechanistic (hierarchies of observable and testable learning outcomes); elementary (preparation for being a worker); social imperatives (1) — adaptive (enables children to adapt to meet society's economic, technological and labour needs); social imperatives (2) — reformist, or egalitarian (enables children to fulfil potential and contribute to the progress of society); progressive (an open and negotiable curriculum enabling children to achieve individual potential); developmental (underpinned by knowledge about children's psychological and physiological development and learning).

Drummond *et al.* (1989) offer ways of exploring one's own view of an appropriate curriculum framework for our youngest children by critically examining examples of curricula based on the following models: High/Scope; Rudolf Steiner; Maria Montessori; structured, pre-planned lessons, as in Peabody, Distar and 'Teach them to speak'; Portage; and HMI guidelines *Curriculum Matters 2* (DES, 1985a). The last is in fact the framework adopted by the Rumbold Committee (DES, 1990a).

Children under five are the most vulnerable and powerless group in our society. The way they are treated, their access to high-quality life experiences, whether at home or outside the home, is dependent upon those with more power than themselves, and in turn, their parents are often at the mercy of those more powerful than they are. For this reason it is important that those of us involved in working in, or promoting, early childhood care and education facilities should really examine questions about the curriculum that every individual child takes home. There is no such thing as a curriculum for young children 'set in tablets of stone' — it will be developed and modified according to what the people in a society believe it is appropriate for children to learn, and this will depend upon their view of early childhood, the position of children in that society, and the kind of people that society wants children to be and to become. In the early 1980s, Dowling and Dauncey (1984) suggested that an 'aims and objectives' model of curriculum may not be appropriate for children in this age-group, and that a set of principles, with ideas about their translation into practice, might be much more helpful to teachers of this age-group. In fact, this is the type of approach to curriculum which those who have worked with and focused on the very young have often adopted.

YOUNG CHILDREN AS LEARNERS – CONTEXT AND PROCESS

It is often said that we should begin with the children and their needs. Do we believe this, and if so, how is this made manifest in our practices? Are the adults involved able to 'see through each child's eyes', because these adults have the ability to de-centre and have observed each child's learning patterns, or schemas (*see* Bruce, 1991; *see also* Chapters 5 and 9 in this book)? Do we believe in valuing what each of the children 'brings with them', as a result of earlier experiences, and if so, do we demonstrate this in ways that children and their families recognize? Is there a chosen body, or content, of 'worthwhile' learning activities, which we feel it is important for children in this age-group to have access to, and if so, what is it, and why do we consider it to be important? Are children given opportunities to control their own learning, through choice of activities and the availability of resources to enable the next steps in that self-chosen experimentation and discovery? What kinds of learning styles do we want the adults involved to encourage, who should these adults be, should they be specially trained, and if so, how? What level of adult–child ratios do we consider 'right'? What kinds of language, ways of talking to and with children, do we expect the adults to adopt, or to encourage among the children themselves? What kind of environment do we consider an appropriate setting for young children, what kind of hidden messages does each individual group setting convey?

All these items are part of the curriculum – factors from which children learn. Some are overt – they are factors from which it is intended children should learn – while others may be hidden. For example, many of us, over the years, have derived great benefit for ourselves and our children from playgroups which, because nowhere else was available, were sited in dusty church or community halls, with splintery floors, no outdoor play areas, and adult-sized, distant toilet facilities. I now ask myself whether this is a good enough way for a society to treat its youngest children and the dedicated women (for they are usually women) who work with enthusiasm, for 'peanuts'. What group of company directors would hold even one meeting in such a setting, let alone session after session? What messages are children picking up from such aspects of their provision?

Sally Lubeck's (1986) study of two early years groups in the United States showed how children from different socio-economic and racial backgrounds were learning different ways of interacting with each other and with adults, and learning different ways of 'being and becoming'. Children from an affluent, 'white' area were learning to be individualistic, competitive and independent. In the same city, children from a poor, 'black' area were learning to support each other, to co-operate, to be dependent, in the sense that they complied with adult demands. As Lubeck points out, there may be times in our lives when we should be capable of operating in each of these ways. We need to be aware of limiting children through the curricular context, or through failing to encourage the learning process.

The Early Years Curriculum Group suggested that the learning context for young children should provide 'a broad and stimulating environment which reflects the cultural backgrounds and interests of the children':

> Each child starts school with a unique set of experiences gained at home and in his or her community. A learning environment should respond to each child's need for something familiar, something new and challenging, and something which enables him or her to pursue a current interest. An environment and daily programme which offer maximum choice to individual children in terms of access to equipment and space, use of time, and opportunities for collaboration with others is most appropriate.
>
> (EYCG, 1989, p. 2)

Although some of the points mentioned above, such as space, or range of equipment, are aspects of the curriculum which may sometimes be out of our control, we need to be aware of their influence. We can, however, be particularly rigorous about those aspects for which we are responsible, so we need to be able to probe, individually and with other educators, parents, and the children themselves, what we really think our provision is helping children achieve and learn. This evaluative activity then helps us move on towards forms of provision which everyone involved considers high quality.

WHY SHOULD AN EARLY YEARS CURRICULUM BE BASED ON PLAY?

Even before the start of the twentieth century, pioneers, such as Robert Owen, Froebel, Montessori and Pestalozzi, had rejected, in both theory and practice, formal teaching for young children. Their espousal of play as appropriate activity for the young was reiterated by Margaret McMillan, and later, Susan Isaacs and the early members of the Nursery Schools Association (now BAECE).

They believed, and concluded from their observations, that small children needed time to play, with a variety of equipment, with opportunities to play alone, or with other children or adults, in order to learn. Furthermore, the kinds of activities children were afforded by their environment (Piaget, 1951), together with social interactions were an important part of the learning process. At around the same time, Vygotsky (1978), in Russia, was formulating his theory of the child 'as apprentice', suggesting that adults should take into account the affective aspects of learning (the emotions becoming overpowering when too much new learning is being presented), and act as facilitators helping children move on in manageable steps from what they already know and can achieve, to a new, self-chosen level of proficiency.

Although there continue to be those who challenge this view of early learning, expecting children during this phase of their development to be capable of long periods of adult-directed, formal or passive learning, for example from workbooks, the news from research carried out in the USA and the UK is that what is called 'the pressure-cooker approach' or 'the academic pre-school' does not work (e.g. Osborn and Milbank, 1987; Katz, 1987; Zigler, 1987). During play, children are free to make choices and to follow interests, are self-motivated, engage in play about what is relevant to themselves and their lives, dare to take risks, learn from mistakes without any feeling of failure, and negotiate and set their own goals or challenges.

Perhaps as a reaction to those who have tried to restrict children to a narrow, inappropriate, formal curriculum, some early years practitioners, for example in Germany and Denmark, find it anathema to discuss the idea of 'play-based programmes' or 'a curriculum based on play'. They believe that this implies too much monitoring, interference and pressure on the part of the adults, and that young children should be 'allowed their childhood'. An example of this monitoring, interference and pressure, according to Danish colleagues, is the way in which many early years practitioners in the UK foster children's early literacy development. On a recent visit to Danish pre-schools, we were discussing children's early awareness of print, and I asked whether Danish pre-school staff would help children set up a hairdresser's shop, together with appointment books, invoices, etc. I was told that children in the UK only ask for these items because our whole society pressurizes them into the acceptance that literacy is of over-arching importance. While we have convinced ourselves that we are empowering young children who demonstrate interest in learning about print, and that we are not committing the 'crime' of applying too much adult coercion, our Danish colleagues 'see' the implicit messages to which we may be blind – or is it that they are missing out, failing to spot an interest in, and thus failing to provide for, learning activities which children incorporate into their play, in relevant and meaningful ways?

ARE ALL PLAY ACTIVITIES EQUALLY VALUABLE?

Perhaps the previous paragraph will raise enough questions about why we think it important for children to engage in certain learning activities for us to recognize that we may value some experiences more than others. We have evidence from research (Bloom, 1964) that children's learning styles laid down at three years of age persist at age six. Children who display curiosity about their environment and who are able to explore, experiment, discover, then represent, interpret and evaluate their findings in the early years will be likely to continue to engage in these learning processes throughout life. Children who are afraid to go through such processes in early childhood may become the unquestioning adults of the future. Activities lumped together and labelled 'play' have been thought to offer opportunities for all those processes. However, in the last twenty years psychologists in particular have begun to observe children at home and in group settings, with a view to finding out what we mean by 'play' and if it does indeed afford children the valuable learning opportunities practitioners allege.

If we decide that we trust children themselves to be self-motivating, to decide when they need certain experiences, we make the assumption that they also know what is possible, or that they can imagine many things they have never seen.

Shane and Dawn, just three, and from highly disadvantaged families, began nursery school. While staff were busy with other children these two noticed some small sorting equipment and, never having seen anything like it before, but without spending time looking closely at the tiny replicas, began to have fun tossing the small, brightly coloured animals into the air above their heads, so that they fell like rain on to themselves and the surrounding floor. If play is a valuable learning activity, what did they learn from this episode? Some adults might think that the appropriate intervention would be authoritative, encouraging the two to pick up every piece and to examine them with a view to future sorting activities. What would such an intervention have helped them learn? At the other end of the scale might be the adult who decides to ignore the children's behaviour, it was self-chosen and fun, so let them get on with it. In between is an approach which recognizes the children's lack of experience, lack of close observation skills, but which acknowledges that this may not be the moment in Dawn and Shane's development to build on these. Intervention may entail the provision of a special space and a large sheet of paper on which to continue the activity without the risk of losing expensive small equipment, and with the excitement of a new way of clearing up the pieces from the floor, funnelling the piece of paper into the appropriate container.

Corinne Hutt (1979) built upon Jean Piaget's ideas about play and learning by suggesting that in the early years there are two equally important phases in children's play activities. She concluded from her observations that when something – a toy or material, clay for example – is new to a child, he or she will *explore* it, with serious and purposeful intent, as if asking the question 'what does this do?' Corinne Hutt labelled this the 'epistemic' phase – the child's search for new learning. In the next phase the child will engage in 'ludic', or true play, activity, when, according to Corinne Hutt, the child gains no more new knowledge about the toy or material, but becomes competent at using that gained during the epistemic phase. This means having fun, laughing with one's collaborators, sometimes using funny voices – as if asking the question 'what can I do with this?'

Work by Chris Athey (1990) and Tina Bruce (1991) has given even further insights into the ways children learn through play. Like Corinne Hutt, Bruce (1991) separates out children's need to explore, manipulate, discover, practise and represent, which she refers to as first-hand experience, as different from play. Bruce and Athey's approach demands not only careful observation of children during 'free-flow play' bouts, but close and positive collaboration between workers and families, since they suggest it has become clear that children have individualized patterns of learning interests to which they return in their play, and, given the opportunities, will engage in them in as many different forms as possible.

These patterns are called 'schemas'. By knowing children's interests intimately, staff and parents are able to provide for, intervene in and extend children's learning according to individual needs and wishes, and not according to the adults' hierarchical, content-based idea of what should be learned next.

From the work of Piaget, Hutt, Athey and Bruce, then, it would appear that children need a balance between those activities offering challenge through first-hand experience following the introduction of an unthreatening yet unfamiliar 'starting point' (a new piece of equipment, material, outing, etc.), and those activities allowing for children's 'free-flow play'.

There have been numerous studies (e.g. Sylva *et al.*, 1980; Smith, 1986; Meadows and Cashdan, 1988) demonstrating which types of play provided challenging learning activities, and the role of the adult seems to be crucial in determining whether this occurs, for as Parry and Archer (1974, p. 5) wrote concerning the distinction they made between two types of 'play': 'It is possible to detect the differences between occupational and developmental play experiences.' One merely keeps children occupied; the other contributes to their educational development.

Furthermore it is important to add, as Janet Moyles states (1989, p. 24), 'children can and do learn in other ways than through play, and often enjoy doing so.' Helping an adult bake, lay the table, wrap a present or feed the rabbit are simple examples of such non-play, enjoyable learning possibilities.

BREADTH, BALANCE AND DIFFERENTIATION

Discussions about appropriate curricula usually include questions concerning the steps which need to be taken to ensure 'breadth, balance, differentiation and progression'.

Breadth and balance

Breadth and balance means that providers should ensure that each child has access to a wide variety of experiences, in order to develop a range of skills and concepts, positive attitudes towards, and knowledge derived from different disciplines, and that no one area of experience predominates. The guidelines given in the Rumbold Report (DES, 1990a) provide useful information for planning ensuring breadth and balance in the early years curriculum, in all the areas of experience (aesthetic and creative; human and social; language and literacy; mathematics; physical; science; technology; spiritual; and moral).

For example, young children who attend a group where the adults are unable to provide any 'plastic' materials, such as clay, dough, sand, water, etc., may be missing out on science as an area of experience.

By observing the range of activities in which individual children engage, one can not only become aware of children's particular needs concerning breadth and balance, but also evaluate the strengths and weaknesses of the group's provision for particular areas of experience. Staff at one centre were worried because Yussuf spent most of his time with the Lego. They began to ask themselves why. Were they failing him because of their lack of his mother tongue? Was he intimidated by an unrecognized undercurrent of institutional racism? What should they do, and how could he be encouraged to branch out, so gaining a broader and more balanced curriculum?

Differentiation

Differentiation means ensuring that the needs of individual children are met. When Emma began nursery at three-and-a-half, she was painfully shy and adult-dependent in the melée of large-group life, having spent the first years of her life as the focus of parental and grand-parental gentle adoration. It would have been easy in a formal classroom situation for a child like Emma to become one of 'the invisible children' (usually quiet and well-behaved little girls) who, although often unsure and nervous about what is expected of them, get on with what they have been ordered to do. In a nursery where children were expected to make choices and engage in first-hand experience and play, Emma seemed lost at first. As Woodhead (1976) and Hutt *et al.* (1989) pointed out, a nursery or playgroup in which everything is implicit, unplanned and not discussed makes overwhelming demands on the children to understand and take advantage of what is offered. In Emma's case, her teacher and nursery nurse discussed their observations and listened to the family's ideas. At home, Emma talked of her wish to play with other children, but could not find a 'way in', could not find 'a voice'. Her teacher decided to provide the children with a starting point which might mean some would make puppets, and she made sure materials for this were available. Emma was one of the children who made her own glove-puppet, and she then used the puppet as her intermediary, holding it in front of her face, speaking for it. The puppet gave Emma the confidence to begin communicating with other children. If a rejection occurred, it was the puppet, not Emma, who was being rejected – but fortunately, that did not happen.

Studies (e.g. Bennett *et al.*, 1984) in infant classrooms have shown that early years teachers are generally good at diagnosing, or assessing, individual children's needs, but find it difficult to address those needs. The problem is that in the situations observed in these studies, the children's activities were adult-directed. In contrast, other research (for example, Sylva *et al.*, 1980; Meadows and Cashdan, 1988) suggests that in guided play situations, where the children take the lead in making decisions about their own learning activities, there is a much closer 'match' of challenge and child. This is the result of the 'competent adult's' (Faulkner *et al.*, 1991) ability to 'scaffold' the child's learning through appropriately gauged discussion, questions and provision of materials. This point about scaffolding brings us on to 'progression' – each child should have opportunities to move on, developing greater competence and learning. In order for progression to occur, there is also a need for continuity, since children will not be able to 'make sense' of irrelevant activities which do not build on their earlier experiences.

CONTINUITY AND PROGRESSION
Children moving from one context to another

When children move from home to a group setting, or from one type of group to another, they can experience damaging discontinuities. Later changes can be equally traumatic, and for this reason the strategies which promote positive experiences for babies can be adapted for children in the three to five age-range, moving from group to group, or group to school, and even later – why are we not sensitive to the stress that change of school, home, work-place, team, etc. induces right through life?

In particular, however, I want to suggest that educators need to recognize children's entitlement to continuity in curriculum, irrespective of the setting. In order to achieve this, in the light of the Children Act 1989 and the Rumbold Report (DES, 1990a), there will need to be greater development of co-operation, co-ordination and collaboration between services; sharing and valuing of expertise and resources; greater investment in both initial and in-service training of early years educators. One of the most valuable contributions in all this, however, will come from the individual children's parents, who must be recognized as the first educators and the 'link people' between settings.

Children in primary school — the relationship to the National Curriculum for five- to sixteen-year-olds

The House of Commons Education, Science and Arts Select Committee reported that

> early education should be seen not as something separate and apart, but rather as the first step on the path into a relevant, coherent and integrated curriculum.... 'The purpose of nursery education is the learning and development of skills, attitudes and understanding in order that children will have full and satisfying lives and become confident, useful, active members of a diverse, constantly changing society'.
>
> (House of Commons, 1989, paras. 2.5, 2.6)

I have referred to Audrey Curtis's (1986) delineation of the early years curriculum as distinct from curricula for older pupils, and Margaret McMillan certainly believed this early years curriculum should be available for children up to age seven. Thus we have a recognition not only that children in this age-group should be entitled to appropriate, high-quality educational experiences which complement home experiences, as entitlement and enrichment for *now* (that is, not *pre-* anything), but also that the curriculum offered in the statutory school years will build upon that early years curriculum: 'education is a seamless robe' (House of Commons, 1989, para. 2.5).

Vicky Hurst writes of the concern engendered by the requirements of the National Curriculum for five- to sixteen-year-olds and suggests that the subject-based learning in these documents

> adds to the impression that play is seen as separate from the high-quality learning that is aimed for. Yet it is possible that without the learning opportunities offered by play, the aims of the National Curriculum will not be achieved, since it is through play that learning becomes meaningful to children.
>
> (Hurst, 1991, p. 49)

By analysing the National Curriculum within the context of the early years principles and curricular framework (*see* Sylva and David, 1990), it is possible for educators to feel confident that they are providing children with a meaningful education, and at the same time helping them develop firm foundations on which later learning can be based.

ADULT ROLES AND RELATIONSHIPS

The roles and training of educators is discussed in the later chapters of this book and it is not my intention to debate this at any length here.

However, it is important to reiterate the point made earlier about scaffolding, namely the ways in which educators facilitate learning. One vital aspect of this is, of course, language. The Rumbold Report (DES, 1990a) drew attention to the abundance of research evidence demonstrating the importance of talk. Children need access to adults who will behave in ways which stimulate and encourage dialogue, often about shared experiences (Wood *et al.*, 1980). As Gordon Wells (1985, p. 73) put it, 'teaching thus seen is not a didactic transmission of pre-formulated knowledge, but an attempt to negotiate shared meanings and understandings.' In other words, the learning process is dynamic, and not additive, and children themselves shape the sequencing and pattern of that education process through these negotiations. The further implications of such a view of children's learning are that they need a setting and equipment which will promote opportunities to engage with other children. Further, for children whose mother tongue is not English, equal opportunities for access to the curriculum on offer will be provided by the involvement of bilingual educators.

Providing a high-quality curriculum for young children is a complex and demanding task (Lally, 1991; McLean, 1991). Children begin learning from the moment they are born, perhaps even before, and we know that the first five years of life present an optimal learning period; further, that if the desire to learn is suffocated, or the variety of learning opportunities limited, children may come to later educational provision with neither the will, nor the ability, to benefit from that education. The level of education and training of the educators is therefore crucial, as research has shown (e.g. Clark, 1988; Whitebook *et al.*, 1990).

CONCLUSION

The early years curriculum, while distinct, must be one which offers all our young children high-quality experiences which make sense to them because they are based on the curriculum already experienced at their earlier stage. And since children learn in individual ways, at individual rates, it is essential that the principles relating to early childhood provision are adopted and continued into the infant school, for older children but especially when there are four-year-olds in infant classes (Barrett, 1986; Brown and Cleave, 1991). These principles include: attention to the whole child; integrated (not compartmentalized) learning; starting from children's own concerns, abilities and interests; first-hand experience and play; the ensuring of time, i.e. self-regulated activity bouts; and access to adults and children with whom they can interact, and who show respect for all children as valued human beings with a right to equality of opportunity. The curriculum each child takes away should have been relevant, challenging — and fun.

5

OBSERVING AND ASSESSING YOUNG CHILDREN

Mary Jane Drummond and Cathy Nutbrown

INTRODUCTION

In this chapter we will identify some of the questions that educators face as they engage in the process of assessment; we will discuss each question in turn, looking at its implications for practice; and conclude by offering a set of principles that educators might reflect on in developing practices for themselves that answer the questions we raise. We believe that this will be more worth while than attempting to give an account of observing and assessing young children that would tell educators everything they wanted to know. A step-by-step guide to observation and assessment in a few thousand words is not a realistic undertaking, and, perhaps, not a very useful one. Following other people's instructions is rarely the first step towards learning to think for oneself. We believe it will be more helpful for us to raise questions about assessment, rather than try to sketch in the full range of possible answers. Asking questions can stimulate thinking, while listing answers may forestall discussion and debate.

WHY ASSESS AND OBSERVE YOUNG CHILDREN?

When we ask ourselves 'why?' questions about aspects of our work with young children, we are looking for explanations and justifications of two different kinds. Sometimes we are trying to establish reasons for what we do by drawing on our own past experience. We interrogate the understanding of young children's learning and development that we have, as a body of educators in different disciplines, built up over the past. Sometimes this accumulated experience does not offer substantial or sufficient reasons for our practices. Historical precedent is not always a convincing justification for some of the things we do, or do not do, although it may help us to understand how practice develops over time. For example, the lack of multi-disciplinary training opportunities in the past is no justification for their not being available now. We also try to establish, through 'why?' questions, the purposes and outcomes of our work: these questions are focused on the future, rather than on the past, on what will come of our work, rather than on what has shaped it into its present form.

Asking 'why assess?' and 'why observe?' will, in the same way, lead us to different kinds of answers, different kinds of reasons and justifications.

One powerful reason for observing young children's development, and assessing what we see, is simple. Children's learning is so complex, rich, fascinating, varied and variable, surprising, enthusiastic and stimulating, that to see it taking place, every day of the week, before one's very eyes, is one of the great rewards of the early years educator. The very process of observing and assessing is, in a sense, its own justification. It can open our eyes to the astonishing capacity of young children to learn, and to the crucial importance of these first few years of our children's lives. But the process can do more than make us marvel at our children's powers – it can also help us understand what we see. Our own observations can help us learn from others who observed before us, and from whom we have learned in our own professional training. So, for example, the work of Piaget, Donaldson, Wells and Athey can be vividly illustrated for us by our own observations of children's activities: their drawings, their questions and their games with rules. Our own first-hand experiences of individual children's learning can help us to see more clearly the general principles that other researchers and educators have established as characteristic of that learning. Indeed some of the pioneers of early childhood provision worked in just such a way themselves, moving from the specific to the general, from single observations to generalized conclusions. Susan Isaacs, for example, ran an experimental school, The Malting House, in Cambridge from 1924 to 1927, and her gripping accounts of the day-to-day doings of the children in the school show clearly how her analysis of children's intellectual development is the product of a mass of detailed anecdotal insights. For example, she describes the development of the basic concepts of biology, change, growth, life and death, illustrating this process with a wealth of evidence:

18.6.25: The children let the rabbit out to run about the garden for the first time, to their great delight. They followed him about, stroked him and talked about his fur, his shape and his ways.

13.7.25: Some of the children called out that the rabbit was dying. They found it in the summerhouse, hardly able to move. They were very sorry and talked much about it. They shut it up in the hutch and gave it warm milk.

14.7.25: The rabbit had died in the night. Dan found it and said: 'It's dead — its tummy does not move up and down now.' Paul said, 'My daddy says that if we put it into water, it will get alive again.' Mrs I. said, 'Shall we do so and see?' They put it into a bath of water. Some of them said, 'It is alive.' Duncan said, 'If it floats, it's dead, and if it sinks, it's alive.' It floated on the surface. One of them said, 'It's alive, because it's moving.' This was a circular movement, due to the currents in the water. Mrs I. therefore put in a small stick which also moved round and round, and they agreed that the stick was not alive. They then suggested that they should bury the rabbit, and all helped to dig a hole and bury it.

15.7.25: Frank and Duncan talked of digging the rabbit up — but Frank said, 'It's not there — it's gone up to the sky.' They began to dig, but tired of it and ran off to something else. Later they came back and dug again. Duncan, however, said, 'Don't bother — it's gone — it's up in the sky,' and gave up digging. Mrs I. therefore said, 'Shall we see if it's there?' and also dug. They found the rabbit, and were very interested to see it still there.

(Isaacs, 1930, pp. 182–3)

The diary entries made by Isaacs and her colleagues were more than entertaining anecdotes: they formed the basis for her analysis of children's scientific thinking. Isaacs was able to learn about learning by intently studying her own detailed observations.

The importance of close observation is also illustrated by Goldschmied's work with babies under two (1987). Observations of babies playing with the Treasure Basket can give the watching adult valuable insights into the children's learning and into their interactions with one another.

Other reasons for observing and assessing concern the adults' part in providing care and education. Young children's awesome capacity for learning imposes a massive responsibility on early years educators to support, enrich and extend that learning. Everything we know about children's learning imposes on us an obligation to do whatever we can to foster and develop it: the extent to which we achieve quality in day care and education services is a measure of the extent to which we succeed in providing appropriate environments for young children's learning and development.

The statements of criteria for quality in provision for young children, which have recently proliferated in response to the requirements of the Children Act, are attempts to identify and specify the necessary conditions for this learning and development. The processes of observation and assessment have a crucial part to play in achieving quality: they have important work to do in shaping the present, the daily experiences of young children in all forms of early years provision. The evaluative purpose of assessment is central for early years educators. We cannot know if the environments we provide and the support we give are doing what they should for our children, unless we carefully monitor the learning and development that take place within them.

Our observations can work for us by providing the starting point for reviewing the effectiveness of our provision: we can use our assessments of children's learning as a way of identifying the strengths, weaknesses, gaps and inconsistencies in the curriculum we provide for all children. Further, we can use the assessment process to plan and review the provision we make for individuals. We can identify significant moments in each child's learning, and we can build on what we see to shape a curriculum that matches each child's pressing cognitive and affective concerns.

Observation and assessment can also illuminate the future for us, as well as help us improve the quality of the present. This forward-looking dimension of assessment is the means by which we can explore the possible outcomes of our provision, curriculum, interactions and relationships. In this country, when pupils are sixteen, formal assessments are used to determine the type of education they will receive in the years sixteen to nineteen. We are not suggesting here that assessment at the age of two, three or four should be used to determine the type or quality of a child's statutory education, but it *is* important to be able to use the process of assessment to identify, for each individual, the learning that is just about to take place, in the immediate future.

This is the area of development that Vygotsky labelled 'the zone of proximal development', and he used this concept to argue passionately that assessment does not end with a description of a pupil's present state of mental development; in his own words, 'I do not terminate my study at this point, but only begin it' (Vygotsky, 1978, p. 85). Effective assessment is dynamic, not static, and can identify for the educator what the learner's next steps might be; assessment reveals learning potential as well as learning already completed. Vygotsky's arguments show how 'learning which is orientated toward developmental levels that have already been reached is ineffective from the viewpoint of a child's overall development. It does not aim for a new stage of the developmental process but rather lags behind this process' (Vygotsky, 1978, p. 89). Observation and assessment are the processes by which we can both establish the progress that has already been made, and explore the future, the learning that is yet to come.

WHO IS TO BE ASSESSED?

Other authors in this book (Moss and Pugh, for example) argue the case for a co-ordinated approach to services for young children, and demonstrate the need for equality of opportunity in terms of access and provision. The principles of co-ordination and equal opportunities also apply to the practices of assessment. If observation of children can increase educator's understanding, enrich curricular provision, and improve the match between individual children's development and the provision made for them, then observation and assessment must be part of the provision in every group setting for young children outside the home. If we take the Rumbold Report's conception of 'educator' seriously, it is no longer possible to categorize some forms of provision as more educational than others (DES, 1990a). Every child in every form of early years provision is a learner with a right to equality of learning opportunity. Every child's educators, therefore, have the responsibility of observing, assessing, understanding, and so extending that learning.

Through the process of assessment we have opportunities to enhance the individuality and the self-worth of each learner. The great educationalists, on whose work we draw in designing a curriculum for young children (*see* Chapter 4), have shown us some of the common characteristics of all young children's learning. However, the task of the educator includes the identification of differences, as well as similarities, between individuals. Through assessment we can distinguish what is unique and particular about a particular child: this distinction will make it possible for us to support each child's individual growth, as a learner and as a person. We can go further: by involving children in the process of assessment (*see below*, page 101), we can not only share our perceptions with them, but also help them to articulate their own perceptions; and so we can support them in the gradual process of synthesizing this self-knowledge, as they grow more truly independent, individual and autonomous in their learning.

Prosser (1991) studied her class of eight- to nine-year-old children in a primary school and found that just less than half the class (ten out of twenty-two) were prepared to state that they were aware of their teacher's assessment of them as learners. Seven children stated that they did not know, and five children did not know whether they knew or not! In follow-up interviews with individual children, Prosser investigated the complex thinking that surrounded the children's original statements, and revealed some surprising inconsistencies. For example, the interview with Chris (aged eight) contained this passage:

T.   Chris, aren't you really sure what I think about your work?

Chris I know you think I'm good at maths. I am good at maths but I should be. My Dad's a maths teacher. But I don't really know about the rest of everything.

T.   Yes, you are very good at maths.

Chris But I'm useless at reading.

T.   Chris, what a ridiculous thing to say. You're super at reading.

Chris (Very animated and interrupting me.) My Mum says I'm useless. I know you say I'm good at it but my Mum says I'm useless.

(Prosser, 1991, pp. 9–10)

Prosser's study, though small in scale, usefully alerts us to ways in which we may lose out on possibilities for fostering the growth of individual self-esteem. She shows how we need not only to make individual assessment an explicit, sensitively framed reality, but also to help children understand their own growing individuality as, in some ways, distinct from other people's perceptions of it. After further discussion, she encouraged her class to develop a self-assessment schedule, to which they gave the title 'What makes me, ME'. As they worked on completing the schedule, she was horrified by the children's anxiety as to whether they had fulfilled the task 'correctly', asking her several times if what they had written was 'right' or 'true'. Assessment practices that deny children individuality and autonomy as learners cannot be truly effective. Prosser's study suggests that some classroom practice in assessment may indeed have such an unintended outcome, and that teachers would do well to ensure that, from an early age, children start to contribute to the assessment process.

While all young children can benefit from the processes of observation and assessment, the focus of any specific act of assessment is always an individual child, whose uniqueness is revealed and reinforced in the process. Yet this account is not the whole story. Taken for granted at the heart of any statement about a child's individuality is a whole set of unquestioned assumptions about the concept 'child'. And taken for granted at the heart of many of our assessment practices are the very same assumptions. The ways in which we assess children's learning, and the purposes for which we do so, are based on an implicit value system, built up of beliefs about children, about what kinds of beings they are, what kinds of ways they behave, and what kinds of feelings they have, or are expected to have. A description of the normal child, or, indeed, the ideal child, is rarely made explicit in the process of assessment. Nevertheless, as we set about observing, assessing and evaluating young children's learning, we do have, deep in our mind's eye, some dearly held beliefs about what we are looking for. These beliefs are likely to be different for different groups of educators in different settings and different cultures; the exploration of such differences can be both challenging and rewarding (Tobin, 1989).

WHAT DO WE OBSERVE AND ASSESS?

The short answer to this question is — children, and everything they do: exploring, discovering, puzzling, dreaming, struggling with the world, taking their place in it, and making their mark on it. The statutory requirements for the assessment of seven-year-olds, laid down in the Education Reform Act 1988, represent only a part of the whole process of assessment. There is much more to know about young children than their levels of attainment in Maths, English and Science at the end of Key Stage 1. The need for a broader view of assessment was explicitly recognized in the Rumbold Report (DES, 1990a), which warned that educators should 'guard against pressures which might lead them to over-concentration on... the attainment of a specific set of targets' (para. 66). Assessment of six- and seven-year-olds for National Curriculum purposes is one small part of a more comprehensive process, in which educators assemble detailed and meaningful pictures of every child with whom they work.

What features of learning and development do these pictures contain? Bruce (1987) draws on the work of the pioneers of early childhood education to establish key principles for practice, one of which is directly relevant to the practice of assessment. 'What children can do, rather than what they cannot do, is the starting point in the child's education' (p. 25) — and so, by implication, it is the starting point of assessment too. Educators will observe and try to understand everything that children do, in their talk and in their play. Watching children at their work of interacting with their environment will tell their educators some of what they need to know about children's needs and development.

From their first days of life, babies are observed by their parents, not with a checklist and pen but with concern, interest, curiosity and love. They reflect on what they see and draw meaning from their observations: 'She's sucking her fist — is she hungry?' 'He turns his head when he hears me speak — can he recognize the sound of my voice?'

Such human, open and implicit observations are the cornerstones of meaningful assessment. As children grow older, the adults who observe them attend to everything they reveal about themselves. It is sometimes appropriate to observe a child with a very specific question in mind; for example, 'How do these three children co-operate when working in a group?' Or 'What objects does this six-month-old baby choose to explore in the Treasure Basket?' 'What does Rashid really do in the playground?'

However, it is still important to keep a wider view as well, and ensure that our assessments of children are balanced, reflecting all that we can possibly know about their thinking, their knowledge and their understanding. This is a daunting task. Happily, early years educators can turn to the work of other educationalists who have shown us how the observer can learn to map the growing world of a child's understanding. The work of Athey (1990) is of particular importance in this undertaking, not least because she also teaches us how our observations and assessments can enrich the curriculum we provide.

Athey builds on the work of Piaget, whose extensive and detailed observations of his own young children gave us a wealth of understanding of children's developing cognitive structures. Athey focuses on particular patterns of behaviour and thought – the 'schemas' of two- to five-year-old children. In Athey's use of the term, any particular 'schema' is at the core of the child's developing mind, and is thus a central element of intellectual growth. The vital corollary for the child's educators is that curriculum experiences can be provided to match this core, this growing point, this centre of the child's thinking and doing.

Three illustrations from a study of nursery children's schemas (Nutbrown, 1987) will show how the concept of 'schemas' can enrich both a short observation, and even more vividly, a series of short observations made over a period of hours or days.

Adam (3:2) used stones and a thin strip of tree bark collected in the nursery garden to construct two pillars with the tree bark balanced between. He spent time testing which things could go under and which had to go over or across because they would not fit underneath. He said, 'this is a bridge, some can go over it and the little bits go under'.

What understanding of Adam's thinking can we achieve through reflecting on this observation of a child's play? If we consider the processes and not just the end-product, we see Adam describing, explaining, organizing, constructing, selecting materials, forming hypotheses, testing and categorizing. Adam used the natural materials he could find in the garden to develop his own forms of thought. It would seem that at the present, the schema that absorbs him is related to things that 'go over and under', simple spatial concepts, which will develop further in time. His surroundings enabled him to explore his schema, and the observant and listening adult could identify and support his actions and thinking. Much more is learned by reflecting in this way than by simply looking at the content of his work;

so much would have been lost here, were the observation simply to record 'Adam made a bridge of stones and tree bark'.

Kate (4:1) was partially sighted. She was familiar with the environment of the nursery and used it to extend her own 'enveloping' schema. The following observations of her took place over two days on four separate occasions.

(1) Kate was dressing up and wrapped first a sari and then a large shawl around her.
(2) She went into the home corner and pulled the ironing board across the gap, 'I'm here now – it's private.'
(3) She took a wicker basket and went around the nursery collecting objects such as shells, nails, screws, small boxes and paper bags. She felt each object, apparently exploring texture and shape. On reflection, the adult who made this observation realized that each object that Kate selected was either a form of container or, in the case of nails and screws, 'went into' something else.
(4) Kate was talking on the telephone, the line went dead. 'It's the inside that's broken I think,' she said.

These notes show a consistent thread of thinking over the two days, a thread running through four separate activities. Kate was exploring 'enveloping and containing' with all the experiences available to her. In the process she was collecting according to clear criteria and categorizing objects, using her senses. She was defining space, hypothesizing and using language to express her thinking.

Adam and Kate make it clear to us that children have their own agendas for learning, which can flourish in rich learning environments, where adults tune into children's forms of thought, meet their needs and extend and challenge their interests.

In order to build up a complete picture of every child's learning, assessments of cognitive developments, like those above, will be complemented with assessments of other aspects of development. The concern of the educator is with children in their wholeness.

Josie (4:5) was absorbed with 'connecting'. She chose activities which enabled her to explore this schema. She built 'a street with people going in and out of the shops' using large bricks. She put gates in her drawings. She liked making jewellery using beads and pieces of foil, threading them together to make them 'connect'. She made elaborate structures of tubes, funnels and valves in the water play which represented 'a factory making sweets'. Josie developed and extended her connecting schema with competence. There was an interesting development when Alan (3:2) wanted to use the construction bricks which fastened together. His manipulative skills were not such that he could fully master the materials he was using. Josie noticed his problem, and (possibly spotting the opportunity for more connection) offered to help:

> Josie: 'Give it here to me − I'll fasten them.' Alan seemed reluctant and held on to his bricks. Josie tried again: 'You tell me where and I'll click them on.' Alan pointed to one brick and held up another to be fastened to it. Josie: 'You want this on there − see it clicks on − give me another − where shall we put this one?'

Josie worked with Alan to make the structure. She talked with him − skilfully matching her words to the actions she was performing, probably modelling this on experiences she had had with adults reflecting her own actions back to her through talk. When both were satisfied with the process Josie took Alan to the teacher: 'Alan made this − he said what to do and I helped a bit − he tried hard.' She then turned to Alan and said, 'When your Dad comes you can show him.'

Josie shows us the way in which children can support each other, when the experiences they assimilate are appropriate to their thinking. The social interaction displayed here and the emotional support given by Josie to Alan is of a quality to be marvelled at. When adults attentively watch the children with whom they work, they can learn to provide a model for affective as well as cognitive development, thus giving children, like Josie, the opportunities to co-operate and support their peers.

HOW DO WE SET ABOUT OBSERVING AND ASSESSING YOUNG CHILDREN?

For many practitioners, this is the sixty-four thousand dollar question. Questions of why, whom and what to assess have a certain abstract and intellectual appeal, but the question of how it is to be done is remorselessly practical. All early years educators are familiar with the cry: 'So *how* do you expect me to do all this *and work with children*?'

The most important task for educators considering how best to build observation and assessment into their practice is not to learn a handful of new techniques but to become more aware of their own, already existing powers: their power to think for themselves, to look for themselves, and to act for themselves. Early years educators can, we believe, develop a pattern of working which is not wholly dependent on instruction from outside. We can, through our own efforts, and through building on our existing skills, learn about our practice, and about our children's learning and development.

We will not discuss specific techniques of observation here as there are other sources for this purpose (for example, Walker, 1985; Hopkins, 1985; Sylva *et al.*, 1990). Although these are all concerned with observation in schools and classrooms, the insights of these authors can be applied in other settings where care and education are provided.

All early childhood educators already use observation as an integral part of their daily work. The implicit, covert skills of these acts of observing can be developed, and made more explicit; the fruits of observation can be stated more confidently as we learn to record, examine, reflect and act upon the knowledge we gain through observation and assessment. What do educators need in order to develop in this way?

Firstly, they need to know for certain that their assessments are worthwhile, important, valued and put to use by colleagues, parents, children and other professionals. Secondly, they need access to training whereby they can develop their already existing skills; this training should be available for all early years educators, with opportunities for cross-professional training whenever possible (Sheffield LEA, 1991a; Drummond and Rouse, in preparation). Thirdly, although the activity of observation is inseparable from the other daily activities of working with children, and should not be confined to a particular time of day or week, educators need time to reflect on the meaning of their observations, time to select and record information. They need time to talk about their observations with colleagues and parents, and time to put their insights to work in building a richer and more fulfilling curriculum for young children.

WHAT NEXT? HOW IS ASSESSMENT TO BE USED?

All the preceding sections of this chapter have included some reference to the purposes of observation and assessment. We have noted a number of different ways in which observation and assessment are used: as a way of appreciating and understanding learning; as a way of recognizing achievement; as a way of distinguishing between individuals, identifying significant differences in their development; as a way of shaping and enriching our curriculum, our interactions, our provision as a whole; and as a way of identifying what children are going to learn next, so that we can support and extend that learning.

Under the Education Reform Act 1988, the assessment of children in primary schools and classes has become a statutory process, combining continuous teacher assessment with the results of a number of Standard Assessment Tasks (SATs) in Maths, English and Science. This process, specified in considerable detail by the Schools Examination and Assessment Council (SEAC), is intended to raise and monitor standards, nationally and locally, and to ensure the early identification of learning difficulties. In the years to come, as teachers of young children in primary schools learn to comply with the requirements of the Act, it will be important for early years educators to continue to carry out their own informal and non-statutory assessments for all the purposes we have described. In particular, the growing number of four-year-olds in school will not be well-served if assessments of their learning are confined to establishing numerical Levels of Attainment in Maths, English and Science. The educators of young children in schools can confidently assert the value of the whole range of their continuous and purposeful assessments; they will not be prepared to narrow their practice, or to restrict their attention to one small part of children's learning.

Two further important purposes of assessment remain to be discussed here: those of continuity and accountability.

Observation, assessment and continuity

The dictionary definition of continuity (*Chambers*, 1972 edition) includes the words: 'uninterrupted connection'. This succinct phrase contains two elements: the idea of interruption and the idea of connection. When we talk of continuity within any form of pre-school provision, or continuity between one provision and another, we are bound to accept that some interruptions are inevitable. Children's pre-school experiences are interrupted by illness, removals, weekends, snowstorms, holidays, changes of staff, family upheavals, and reaching the age of statutory schooling. We cannot do much to prevent these interruptions, but we can focus on connections, and thereby explore how it might be possible to establish 'uninterrupted connections', in other words, continuity. How can observation and assessment help us to do this?

First, at the level of the individual child, we can see how regular observation and assessment can be used to establish and maintain connections within and between forms of pre-school provision, in a variety of different ways. Daily observations in one setting have an important part to play in ensuring that each child's experience is stable and secure; daily efforts to watch, to reflect and to understand children's development can help us build on one day's events in planning the next, establishing fruitful connections between each day of a young child's experience.

Between settings, too, connections can be made. An understanding and appreciation of children's growing bilingualism, for example, will form part of a vital connection between different periods of their pre-school experience. Parents who pass on knowledge of their children's current schema will enable the educator in a new setting to shape a curriculum that will continue to match their cognitive concerns. A set of detailed observations of children's fantasy play, showing how they are exploring a range of powerful emotions, will help other educators, reading a summary of those observations, to appreciate children's struggles and challenges, and to recognize and encourage the advances they have made and are making. Assessments of children's developing sociability, as they learn to interact in groups of different sizes, will ensure that young children moving to a large playgroup or classroom are not overwhelmed by a sudden change in what is expected of them. Records of children's developing physical skills will prevent children from being expected to start all over again, with equipment they have already outgrown, when they move from one setting to another. Babies who can feed themselves, or climb unaided on to a changing mat, will not appreciate being interrupted in their development by having these achievements ignored; connections between different rooms, or different settings, informed by records and assessments, can sustain the babies' continuous development. As part of its developing co-ordination of services for under fives, Sheffield LEA has produced a variety of record formats which can be used by educators in all domestic and group settings (Sheffield LEA, 1991b). The use of such records can make a valuable contribution to the continuity of a child's early experiences.

Observation and assessment not only benefit individual children and their educators: the process may also have a part to play in achieving the continuity of some practices that affect the whole group of children who are in transition, from year to year or from place to place. Observations and assessments, made over a period of time, and summarized at the point of transition, will also be a record of the values and belief systems of those who made them and wrote them down. Assessments always say something about what the assessors believe children *should* do, say, feel and understand, as well as recording what they *actually* do. These assessments, when carefully read, could form an important connection between the values and practices of one form of provision and the next. They could become the first step towards a greater awareness of a set of beliefs that diverges from one's own, or a further step towards a greater shared understanding of what it means to care for and educate young children.

Some of the practices of assessment are themselves part of this value system, which may, and probably will, differ from setting to setting. The involvement of parents in the assessment process is an important example. Some educators, who involve both parents and children in the assessment process, would trace this practice to a core principle of partnership, underlying many different aspects of their general practice. For these educators, making connections between their practice and other people's will entail making connections between principle too. The principle of parental involvement cannot be seen, by them, as something that can be casually interrupted: they will be prepared to work hard, through discussion and debate, establishing practical connections, maybe small and apparently insignificant at first, until a continuity of principle, across a variety of practices, is achieved.

Observation, assessment and accountability

All early years workers are accountable for their work, to one or more of a variety of audiences: the management committee, the board of governors, the funding body, the community forum, the staff group, parents, employers, children and so on. An effective working relationship between educators and any one of these groups depends on the quality of the communication between them. When educators set about explaining and justifying their work, they will draw on their principled understanding of young children's learning, but they will also speak convincingly of their daily experiences in their own setting. By rooting their beliefs in real-life events they can explain how and why they care and educate as they do. By drawing on their assessments and observations of learning they can demonstrate clearly how principles are transformed into practice.

WHO IS TO BE INVOLVED?

A further step in ensuring the usefulness of their assessment will be for educators to give some thought to the people who might be involved in the process. Who can most helpfully contribute to monitoring the developmental needs and growth of young children? Which people are best placed to do this? And who owns the process of assessment?

In schools and classrooms, it has traditionally been left to teachers to carry out assessment. Teachers made the assessments, wrote the records, held the records, and made decisions about how to communicate what was in them and to whom. In recent years this monopoly has been broken. The trail-blazing ILEA Primary Language Record was designed as a collaborative exercise in recording achievement. The development of the child's language – or languages – in the home is seen as quite as important as progress in school, and so the contribution of parents is an essential part of the recording process (Barrs *et al.*, 1988).

In early years settings away from schools, there has been great interest in the developmental record *All About Me* (Wolfendale, 1990), an anecdotal format for parents and other educators, who work together to build up a vivid personal picture of many aspects of a child's development.

As parents, educators and teachers come closer together, discussing and sharing their insights, the benefits for all concerned become clear. Nursery teachers in Sheffield have worked on a joint approach to assessment, sharing records with parents and giving them the opportunity to comment (Sheffield LEA, 1986). They report an opening-up of the whole process of recognizing and reporting development. Parents made comments such as the following:

> I never thought she was as clever as that — it's good — to say that she's only three!

> It just shows how much they learn, even when you think they're playing, and to see it written down.

> Some of this he does at home, drawing and things, it was nice to have the chance to write a bit myself on his record sheet.

Over the past few years, the development of records of achievement, which started in the secondary sector, has stimulated the development of similar approaches in primary schools. These records are based on the continuous involvement of pupils in their own assessment. This initiative, now endorsed by SEAC (1990) for all primary schools, has the effect of giving assessment a much wider ownership: parents, pupils and teachers are all active partners in the process. Even very young children can talk about their learning and development, and so make positive contributions towards their own assessment profile: 'I *can* write' or 'My book is about a dog, I like reading it', are comments which four-year-olds might make about their developing literacy. Young children can be encouraged to comment on themselves in this way, playing an active part in recording their development, and laying the foundation for further, more evaluative contributions later (Nutbrown, 1991).

Another initiative, the Sheffield Early Literacy Development Project (Hannon *et al.*, 1991), suggests that when educators work with parents to share the children's experiences at home, their understanding of young children's literacy development is enriched and extended. Parents were invited to watch and to comment (often in some detail) on their children's early literacy activities. The comments from parents make clear their perspective on the value of such involvement:

I noticed his writing more by going to the meetings than I think I would
have.... One time when he was drawing it was all lines. Then after a few weeks
he changed and started doing circles.

(ibid. p. 15)

I didn't make a point of reading with him before — then I did. He looks at
books a lot more now.

(ibid. p. 18)

The project team considered ways in which parents might reflect on
and record their children's development. They devised a way of providing
pointers to different aspects of writing development which could be combined with a method of recording a child's progress. Parents were offered
a record format resembling a jigsaw, with each piece representing one
small element of literacy development. They found this a valuable
exercise, and one parent commented:

I got a surprise when filling in the jigsaw bit. It surprised me how much he
could do. There was only one blank.

(Weinberger *et al.*, 1990, p. 16)

These initiatives show how observation, assessment and recording
can be more widely shared, more openly discussed and so become
more reflective and evaluative. We can learn from these examples how
the purposefulness of the educator's assessments can be enhanced by the
contributions of others.

CONCLUSION

In this chapter, we have tried to indicate some of the questions that face
early years educators engaged in assessing young children's learning,
without suggesting that there is only one possible set of answers to these
questions. However, the answers that educators arrive at, in the process
of reviewing and developing their practice, will not add up to effective
assessment unless they are based on a coherent set of principles, which
can provide justification and explanation for particular practices. By way
of conclusion, we will take a more personal note, and outline four fundamental principles that we believe should underly the practice of assessment
in the early years.

The most important of our principles is that of *respect*. We believe that
assessment must be carried out with a proper respect for the children
themselves, for their parents and other carers, and for their educators.
This respect will be expressed in actions, in words and deeds, in our daily
interactions and in our attitudes. So that, for example, in respecting

ourselves as educators, we will acknowledge both our expertise and our fallibility; we will respect our judgements enough to build on them in practice, but without elevating them into infallible dogma. We will respect our determination to work hard for our children but also the physical limits of our energy and endurance. We will respect each other's judgements, even when differences arise, and we will respect our own professional ability to have our judgements challenged and questioned. Our skills in observing and assessing children will be used by others with respect for their accuracy and validity; we will be able to build confidently on our own work.

Our second principle that we see as central to the practice of assessment is that the *care* and *education* of young children are not two separate, discrete activities. In our work as educators, we both care and educate. Quality care is educational, and quality education is caring. Children's enhanced learning and development are the outcomes of our work in whatever setting. Our assessment practices will recognize the close relationships between these concepts; and we will struggle to develop a pedagogy that recognizes learning and development in all their human manifestations, as processes in which all the child's faculties and powers are employed. In our assessment practice, we will recognize children learning to love one another, as well as children learning to count.

Our third principle concerns the awesome *power* of the early years educator. We believe that it is important, first, to acknowledge that power, and second, to use it lovingly. The psychotherapist David Smail (1984) writes of 'the loving use of power', in his discussion of relationships within families. We believe that the 'loving use of power' in the assessment of young children is an absolutely central principle.

Our fourth principle is that the *interests* of children are paramount. Assessment is a process that must enhance their lives, their learning and development. The educators' needs are secondary to those of the children they work with. Assessment must work for children. Their minds and their futures are entrusted to our hands for the brief years of childhood. We must do all in our power to serve them well.

6

WHY UNDERSTANDING CULTURAL DIFFERENCES IS NOT ENOUGH

Iram Siraj-Blatchford

The States Parties to the present Convention shall respect and ensure the rights set forth in this Convention to each child within their jurisdiction without discrimination of any kind, irrespective of the child's or his or her parent's or legal guardian's race, colour, sex, language, religion, political or other opinion, national, ethnic or social origin, property, disability, birth or other status.
(Article 2, Part 1, The Draft Convention on the Rights of the Child, Unicef, 1989)

The United Nations recognized that it is the right of every child and his/ her guardian to be free from oppression and discrimination, and that every state has a duty to ensure this. While the state may articulate policies and shape provision, it is of course the service providers and those in daily contact with children on whom the ultimate reality of providing a discrimination-free environment depends. It is beyond the scope of this chapter to attempt an analysis and to provide practical strategies for early years educators to overcome all discriminations. (Note: the term 'educators' is used to refer to all those who care for and educate young children; c.f. Rumbold Report, DES, 1990a.) What I will attempt, however, is to deal with one area, racial discrimination, as a case study. Readers may well find parallels with other forms of discrimination under the sub-headings that follow, and indeed would be encouraged to transfer concepts.

RACIAL DISCRIMINATION: WHY WE VALUE SOME RACIAL GROUPS MORE THAN OTHERS

It will not surprise most early years educators to learn that Britain's relationships over the last four hundred years with Africa, the Caribbean, South East Asia and other countries nearer home such as Cyprus were grounded on the subjugation of the people of these areas and that vast human and material resources were exploited. The wealth created by black slavery and colonialism was, and still is, to a large extent, enjoyed by British society. Britain is no longer the imperialist power it once was but the beliefs and institutional and cultural practices which were normalized in past centuries still exist and manifest themselves in discriminatory beliefs and practices today.

As a country we have recognized the existence of the more crude and apparent effects of racism in the Race Relations Act 1976 and more recently the Children Act 1989. This legislation acknowledges and offers practical measures for removing racially discriminatory practice and procedures in early child care/education provision (Lane, 1990). What may surprise early years educators is how well we continue to absorb both subliminal and overt racism in our lives today. We shall look more closely at the effects of this on young children's lives later. It is true that we no longer celebrate Empire Day in our schools (a common practice till the 1940s), and that it is unlawful to discriminate against people on the grounds of 'race' in care, housing, employment and education. So how is racial discrimination still normalized? Why do many British people still continue to hold negative beliefs and attitudes about South Asian and Afro-Caribbean people? It is worth considering some of those ideas we take for granted, accept without questioning and do not notice in our omissions or transmissions about black and white people. (Note: the term 'black' is used to refer to all those groups which share the common experience of racism, in particular Afro-Caribbean and South Asian people.)

Our environment is a hothouse for propagating notions that present black people as a problem and inferior. It will be useful to consider a few examples of this:

(1) *The press.* The press largely sensationalizes and focuses on black people only when writing about items of violence, famine, political unrest and sport.

(2) *Television.* Viewers are continuously presented with negative images on the news. Old Hollywood movies are shown where black people

act as servants or martyrs to white people. Repeats of many popular comedy programmes from the 1960s and 1970s also contribute.

(3) *Books*. Our literature is read uncritically, e.g. in *Robinson Crusoe* the labour relationship between 'Man Friday' (a name given to him) and Crusoe is absorbed by generations of children as normal. School biology, history and geography texts in particular have been shown to convey racist messages.

(4) *Grafitti*. There are rarely positive images of black people in large advertising displays in our environment, but almost everyone has seen racist grafitti. It is significant that very few individuals take active steps to get it removed, because it is accepted as an everyday occurrence.

(5) *Jokes*. Racist jokes about black people, Irish people and Travellers are commonly heard and usually accepted as innocent fun. The fact that they degrade, hurt and humiliate certain groups is often ignored. Racist jokes are only funny if you share the underlying stereotypes and assumptions.

(6) *Language*. Our culture accepts that 'black' is generally negative (blackleg, blackmail, black mood, etc.) and that words such as 'nigger' should be part of our stock of dictionary words. In the English language there are dozens of disparaging words to describe people who are not white and English (e.g. Taffy, Paki, Kraut, Yid and Wog). Name-calling is a 'normal' part of our children's experience.

(7) *Traditional British tolerance*. Employers and landlords/ladies are often tolerant of intolerance, accepting without question the assumed or expressed xenophobic desires of their employees and tenants. Such cynical and fatalistic attitudes by those with the power to effect change yet seeking a 'quiet life' may be the greatest barrier to equality.

Through these dynamic and continued happenings racism is perpetuated and absorbed by all around. The continued overt and subliminal messages to children and adults alike is that there are groups of people in our society who are inferior from birth because of their racial background. Simultaneously the message of assumed white superiority is constantly promoted. This kind of stereotyping leads to gross inequality at an institutional level. Where white people wield power over other people (e.g. educators over children and parents, teachers over children, employers over employees, policy-makers over practitioners and housing and social workers over the public) the consequences can be devastating for the lives of black individuals and families.

We carry with us our baggage of experience and part of that experience is growing up in a racist society. Racism affects our attitudes and beliefs. However, the real damage occurs when more covert institutional practices result in the conversion of people's personal beliefs into action. Early years educators are not exempt from these influences. We need to understand what our own past experiences have been and how and why we feel the way we do about tackling racial equality issues. Unfortunately our experiences feed into each other and this may not be such an easy task. The model in Figure 6.1 may be useful and can be added to further.

We must understand that if our home language is English then that gives us more than a national identity, there is also a global significance. I shall try to unpack some of the assumptions upon which the foregoing is based before going on to the next section.

YOUNG CHILDREN'S IDENTITY AND ATTITUDES

'Research shows that racism damages the emotional, intellectual and social development of black and white children' (Brown, 1990, p. 9). Many early years educators believe that racial equality is exclusively about black and other ethnic minority children, but racial equality is as much an issue for the ethnic majority. The dehumanizing effects of racism on white British ethnic majority children is an issue which must be raised and addressed. If educators remain unconvinced about this and fail to analyse the facts, racial equality cannot, and will not, be achieved in the early years. This is a serious responsibility which *all* of us have.

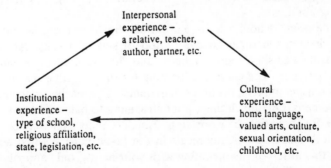

Figure 6.1

Very few educators would dispute that young children learn from their environment. If we are to believe that the early years are the most formative in a person's life, a time for learning through associations in the environment and through observation (Sylva and Lunt, 1982), then we should accept that children inevitably absorb racist values too. The work of some social psychologists shows that children demonstrate a clear awareness of 'race'. Three- to five-year-olds learn to attach value to skin colour (Milner, 1983). They are aware of a pecking order which places white at the top of the hierarchy and black at the bottom. The inevitable impact on some children's self-image can be very damaging.

Apart from white being the norm, children also witness and learn to accept the position of black people in our society. Ian Menter cites an example from a nursery school where

> A four-year-old child was showing a painting, which she had just completed, to her teacher and some other children. She had painted a wide brown border all around the large piece of kitchen paper. Inside this frame was a large yellow sun, a human figure and some yellow 'ground'. She explained that this was a picture of Africa. The frame, she said, was because she had seen Africa on the television, in a programme about hungry people.
>
> (Menter, 1989, p. 95)

Menter goes on to analyse how this image may consolidate into a stereotype of Africa and black people.

In the absence of any positive black role models, either in the early years care/education setting or in the immediate community, a young white child may have no choice other than to absorb negative views about black people. These will be further reified by the media at home and in school as the child grows older. The cognitive development of black children may be seriously damaged if they encounter adults with stereotypical and racist views about their culture, language, skin colour or learning abilities.

In one infant school a four-year-old continued to struggle with a knife and fork at lunch times over a period of several weeks. At home his parents ate Pakistani food, chapattis and rice were eaten by hand, as is normal practice. The child was learning for the first time that food could be eaten using implements other than hands. The teachers encouraged his development. One lunch time, after struggling to balance baked beans on his fork for some time he resorted to using his hands. The school secretary (who collected payment for meals in the lunch hall) shouted across the hall to this little boy, 'Stop eating with your hands, only animals eat with their hands!' The look on the four-year-old's face was one of bewilderment, hurt and embarrassment. He and all his black and white peers were interpreting the secretary's words to make meaning of them. She had indicated not only that his behaviour was deviant and animal-like but by implication so was his parents' and that of his community. Anti-racist work must include all those working with young children, for they are all in a sense 'educators'.

The cumulative effects of discrimination and stereotyping can leave some black children feeling isolated, angry or rejected. It can leave some white children with false notions of superiority and encourage the perpetuation of racism through bullying and name-calling. Fundamental concepts of justice, fairness, equality, co-operation and sharing are distorted. Children are denied the opportunity to learn, appreciate and value the aspirations and achievements of others. All those involved are in effect being dehumanized and disadvantaged. If we accept that *all* our children have an equal right to achieve their full human potential then we need to move on to look at what specific changes are needed in early years education.

POLICY AND RACE EQUALITY ACROSS EARLY YEARS PROVISION

There is little doubt that most power in our society is held by white, middle-class males (Epstein and Sealey, 1990). Our policy-makers at national and local authority level are not therefore generally drawn from any of the oppressed groups in our society and have little experience of discrimination. In fact, their experience has been, and continues to be, one of positive discrimination towards their own group. If we do not believe that women, ethnic minorities, working class and disabled people are inherently inferior, and I suggest that very few people would actually argue this, then policies aimed at sharing power and a wider experience of life must be a prime democratic objective.

Of course, power is a relative concept. At a micro level we need to focus attention on the power of educators. Educators are not generally powerful in economic or policy terms; indeed, given that most are women, they may often feel completely powerless. However, educators *are* powerful in terms of the power they have over the children in their care. If educators are to exert any influence over economic and policy decisions they need to apply their understandings of government policy and legislative effects at both a national and local level within whatever voluntary and private sector groups they have access to (e.g. National Childminding Association, Pre-School Playgroups Association, National Nursery Examination Board, etc.). Policy statements are gradually beginning to incorporate 'race' equality issues as part of the agenda. The policies do, however, vary in terms of commitment and extent, and the practicalities of implementation need to be explored.

Government legislation

There are three major Acts of Parliament which can effect change for racial equality in early years care/education.

Race Relations Act 1976

This legislation outlaws racial discrimination which is defined in four ways: 'direct' and 'indirect discrimination', 'segregation' and 'victimization'. This has clear implications for exclusions from and admissions to the care and education of young children and for the training and recruitment of staff. It is widely acknowledged that black people are under-represented in the field of early years care and education and that provision and service practices can be racist (Lane, 1990). The Commission for Racial Equality (CRE) booklet, *From Cradle to School* (1991), which is a practical guide to 'race' equality and child care, provides a clear framework for analysing the role of local authorities and highlights the research evidence, indicating widespread discrimination in local policies.

Children Act 1989

This Act appears to be an exciting move towards equality as it is the first piece of legislation on the care of children which refers specifically to catering for children's racial, religious, cultural and linguistic backgrounds. The Guidance, Volume 2, *Family Support, Day Care and Educational Provision for Young Children* (DH, 1991), is a particularly valuable document for local authorities (LAs). Ethnic monitoring is now required by law and services will be evaluated according to the extent that they are non-discriminatory. LAs will need to set up monitoring and evaluation procedures and guidelines.

LAs will also need to develop a framework with clear guidelines and criteria for the registration and cancellation of day care provision if it does not meet the 'race' equality criteria of the Children Act. A 'fit person' to look after children should, for example, have 'knowledge of and attitude to multi-cultural issues and people of different racial origins' (para. 7.32, p. 54). LAs have been given the power to cancel registration if 'the care being offered to an individual child is considered by the local authority to be seriously inadequate having regard to his needs including his religious persuasion, racial origin and cultural and linguistic background' (section 7,4(1)(b) and (2)(b), p. 60, para. 7.51). Many examples are cited to illustrate the need not only to rethink provision and services but also to reconsider training and the kind of knowledge needed to be able to offer services free from racial discrimination.

LAs will need to review their training schemes and the expertise required of day care advisers, childminders and others. Those in positions of power as directors of social, health and education services will need to re-evaluate their own commitment to 'race' equality. 'Race' equality should now be the responsibility of someone with 'status and commitment'. The experience and perspectives of black staff are crucial and recruitment practices that lead to increased participation are considered essential to progressive change.

Education Reform Act 1988 (ERA)

Under the ERA schools are required to cover multi-cultural issues across the curriculum and section 1(2)(a) of the ERA requires that a broad and balanced curriculum should be provided which 'promotes the spiritual, moral, cultural, mental and physical development of pupils at the school and of society'. This legislation applies to all five- to sixteen-year-old children in our schools but the ERA is vague regarding the practicalities of such provision and there is some evidence to suggest that schools are too worried about the assessed elements of the National Curriculum to bother very much about multi-cultural/anti-racist education which is often perceived as a 'bolt-on' inconvenience.

Policy initiatives

For children under five the Department of Education and Science (DES) has published the following statement:

> Good social relationships are often fostered by planning a curriculum that provides opportunities for the children to learn more about the lives and work of the people in school and the wider community. The children's awareness of diversity in custom and culture and their respect for and understanding of cultural differences are effectively developed through planned activities and the use of carefully selected stories and picture books, artifacts and materials.
>
> (HMI, 1989, p. 12)

We will focus our attention more closely on such specific planning and practice later in the chapter. Education and care practices and policies that may contravene the Race Relations Act are monitored and continuously acted upon by the Commission for Racial Equality (CRE).

Government Acts lay down edicts and these can be used to increase accountability and promote change.

Many of the changes that have taken place are the product of grass-roots action, where educators with a firm belief in, and commitment to, achieving racial equality have recognized inequalities and have been determined to effect change in their organizations and institutions. In the past five years a number of early years organizations have asserted their commitment to achieving racial equality. The National Childminding Association (NCMA), for example, has produced a bold statement of commitment and local regions such as Warwickshire have provided training for their childminders on race equality. So far such activities have been voluntary, but the Children Act may change this. The NCMA subcommittee on equal opportunities is working towards an implementation policy:

> NCMA is committed to a childminding service which views children as different but equal and which strives to meet the needs of the whole child, physical, emotional, intellectual and cultural.
>
> To this end, it is the responsibility of all childminders to acknowledge that racism exists, and that it harms all children in their care.
>
> Good quality child care involves valuing each child equally and affirming the positive value of different skin colours, cultural and family backgrounds. It involves giving children a realistic picture of the world they live in and correcting the distortions and prejudices about that world.
>
> Good child care is anti-racist child care.
>
> (The Anti-Racism Subcommittee of NCMA)

The National Nursery Examination Board (NNEB) is also facing this issue well and has reviewed its recruitment and selection processes with the help of the CRE. NNEB has an equal opportunity statement and is presently working on integrating this statement throughout its practice. An active equal opportunities working party is monitoring and advising on racial equality as well as on other equal opportunities issues.

> The Board's policy is:
> (a) that it is committed to promoting equal opportunity throughout its activities;
> (b) that no applicant for a course of study leading to one of its awards should be disadvantaged compared with another by virtue of class, ethnic origin, gender, marital status, race or religion;
> (c) that no student undertaking a course of study leading to one of its awards should receive less favourable treatment than another by virtue of class, ethnic origin, gender, marital status, race or religion;
> (d) that in the examination of students, both internally and externally, teaching institutions and the Board should ensure that no student receives less favourable consideration or treatment than another by virtue of class, ethnic origin, gender, marital status, race or religion; and
> (e) that the curriculum for all its schemes should reflect a commitment to

promoting equality in all the aforementioned aspects and so help to establish a concept of equal opportunity amongst all sections of the multiracial society to be found within the United Kingdom.

(NNEB, 1990, p. 16)

Similarly, the Pre-school Playgroups Association (PPA) has for some time had progressive regional activity (e.g. in Camden) and a national working party has been looking at racial equality in their practice. The PPA has sought advice from the CRE and has now integrated some of its deliberations into its guidelines for practice (PPA, 1990). Although there are several sound attempts to promote racial equality through statements appearing in pink and green at the end of most sections of the guidelines, e.g. on management, staffing, play activities, etc., these provisions do suffer from such presentation which suggests that they may have been added as an afterthought. It is hoped that future editions will provide an integrated and proactive approach to equal opportunities central to the text. That said, the PPA guidelines do cover a broad range of issues related to equal opportunities and are still well worth reading.

The National Children's Bureau (NCB) Early Childhood Unit has developed a clear policy and commitment through its working group on anti-racism, and this is now monitored by its advisory group and by the Bureau's Equal Opportunities Committee. It is interesting to note that the NCB as an organization now has a Bureau-wide policy. The Bureau's policy statement highlights its positive approach: the Bureau recognized that passive policies will not in themselves provide equality of opportunity and that specific positive programmes of action are needed. More recent publications with a sound, integrated equal opportunities perspective include the training pack, *Ensuring Standards in the Care of Young Children* (National Children's Bureau, 1991) on the registering and development of quality day care and *Young Children in Group Day Care* (Cowley, 1991) which offers guidelines for good practice.

The European Childcare Network has one funded project looking at racial equality and child care in Europe, and this project is being led by Britain. There is a need, while continuing to work towards racial equality in Britain, to raise the standards of early years racial equality throughout the European Community.

It is clear then that an increasing number of early years educators and policy-makers have felt this issue to be of utmost importance and approximately 80 per cent of local education authorities now have a policy on multi-cultural or anti-racist education. Unfortunately, many schools have still failed to respond and there is a growing fear that with ERA, as the power of LEAs is being eroded and combined with the effects of local management of schools (LMS), which is leading to increasing competition between schools, the gains in recent years may be lost and it is difficult now for LEAs to implement any policies. Many of those working towards greater equality of opportunity are working in isolation. Wider support and training is thus needed at a regional and national level, and such support should be provided by all organizations which work with educators.

PRACTICAL IDEAS FOR RACIAL EQUALITY

Policy initiatives are useful exercises and do convey commitment, but policies can be seen as mere paper exercises without any impact on the daily practices of practitioners (Cole, 1989). If parents and children are to benefit, a well-intentioned belief in racial equality is not enough, action is necessary. It is the responsibility of every organization that deals with early years education and care to provide training for this area and for every educator to seek training.

A curriculum and environment free from racial discrimination has to pay attention to the ethos and ambience within which children grow up and learn. It is not enough to offer a narrow multi-cultural curriculum which focuses on the diversity and difference of 'exotic' cultures. Such a tokenist form of curriculum promotes what has been referred to as the 'zoo' effect or the 'tourist' curriculum. Derman-Sparks is critical of educators who depend upon information gleaned from celebrating festivals, school visits and exchanges and holidays:

> Children 'visit' non-white cultures and then 'go home' to the daily classroom, which reflects only the dominant culture. The focus on holidays, although it provides drama and delight for both children and adults, gives the impression that that is all 'other' people — usually people of colour — do. What it fails to communicate is real understanding.
>
> (Derman-Sparks, 1989, p. 7)

The multi-cultural curriculum is problematic when it focuses on information about Indians or Chinese rather than on British-Indians or British-Chinese, for such an approach focuses on differences more than upon similarities. One of the most worrying aspects of a multi-cultural curriculum is that educators often assume that it is only relevant to multiracial settings. When it is applied to white children, multi-culturalism assumes that there is a set content of knowledge to be transmitted to children about 'other' groups. The fact that 'other' groups may be as diverse as 'we' are is ignored. While few educators would attempt to explain Christianity in all its forms in a twenty-minute discussion, drama or story, this is precisely what is attempted with major world religions in many schools.

There are many areas to review when developing a racial equality approach, whatever the situation (childminder's home, playgroup, classroom or hospital). This chapter can provide little more than an overview of some of the issues and references for further study. I have argued that every adult working with young children holds power and acts as a role model. If the adult stereotypes, omits or provides inaccurate information about our multiracial society, children will learn what is important to their educator and emulate those behaviours and attitudes. If we are to avoid this we need to consider how an early childhood setting can promote racial equality in practice.

The visual environment

While young children are still struggling with language, the impact of images is all pervasive. Images provide the means by which they absorb symbolic understanding of who 'belongs' in our society. There should be images, in our posters, books, jigsaws and other resources, that demonstrate and celebrate our racially diverse society. The images should be positive ones of children and families involved in normal, daily activity, e.g. meal times, in the park, visiting the dentist. Images which are negative, e.g. poor hungry children from areas of Africa or South America, should be counterbalanced — children receive enough of these images from the media. Children will, of course, at times want to talk about famine, water shortages or war and adults must respond to these issues in a well-informed and honest manner appropriate to the child's age. The visual environment should not be tokenist with only one or two black faces — there should be a numerical balance of different racial groups. In fact, Derman-Sparks (1989) recommends that more than half, although not all, of the images and other materials should reflect black people to counter the predominance in society generally of images of white people.

Language

Children should have the opportunity to hear and see various languages, and alternative scripts including Braille and sign. Children will only develop an awareness of the literary achievements of other cultures if we present the product to them. Language is the single most important factor in shaping a child's self-identity, esteem, culture, social, emotional and cognitive development. It is essential that educators value the whole linguistic resource that a bi/multilingual child brings with her/him. It is not enough to value only the English part of it; any such neglect of the home language will impart negative messages to the child about a part of them that is also a part of their whole identity and community. The educator does not require fluency to show they value their pupil's language. Monolingual educators can support bilingual/multilingual children in a variety of ways (Siraj-Blatchford, 1990). They can use bilingual story tapes, learn a few everyday words in the predominant minority language in their setting and encourage activities which allow children to use their home language. Monolingual children's awareness of other languages should be encouraged through bilingual labelling. Alphabet and number posters, dual language books, songs, rhymes and finger games are all things that all our children can join in, enjoy and ask questions about.

Educators require knowledge of the languages in use in our communities. They need to understand what it means to be bilingual/multilingual. That means understanding that words carry culturally specific concepts; for example, the word 'saucepan' may mean 'something to cook food in' to most English children and while it may have the same meaning (although involving different food) for a South Asian child it will also be the receptacle that tea (Chai, a special spiced, sweet tea) can be boiled up in. An incident in a nursery setting illustrates the need to understand this sort of thing well. A nursery nurse observed a Pakistani child 'making tea' in a saucepan in the home corner and demanded that the child use the kettle! One cannot suggest that *all* culturally specific meanings should be equally understood by everyone — that is neither possible nor perhaps desirable — but we can avoid making value-laden assumptions. The nursery nurse could have asked the child *why* she was using the saucepan or *how* she was going to make the tea. Through this process she would have learned the child's culturally specific understanding of 'saucepan'.

It has been noted by a number of nursery workers that where extra visual, auditory (puppets, sound effects) and bilingual resources are used, it helps *all* the children in their language development and not just the bilingual children. This is an interesting issue for us to reflect on. We need to recognize that bilingual and race equality education *is* simply good practice.

Books are a mixture of language and images and they reflect social values and attitudes. Since books and reading activities make up such a significant part of young children's lives in school and care, texts should be selected and used very carefully. The Council for Interracial Books for

Children (1980) provides a clear set of criteria for selecting and evaluating books on the basis of racism and sexism.

Toys and activity materials

The issue of toys is not as simple as buying black dolls or getting rid of the golliwog. As Bob Dixon (1989) suggests, the toy industry is strong and thrives on exploiting sexist and racist 'norms' in our society. Toys are a very strong socializing force in children's lives.

Dolls should be reasonably authentic in their shades of colour when representing black and brown skin tones. Unfortunately, some manufacturers believe that there is little demand for black dolls and therefore little profit is to be made. In the present circumstances, if we want black dolls we need to urge our local department stores to stock them. We also need to explain the kind of authentic looking dolls we wish to have in our education and care settings. It is clearly unacceptable to buy dolls with black faces which have the same European features as white dolls or dolls which have black/brown hands and faces but a pink body. Such dolls exist and suggest to children that black people are pink under their clothes! Dolls and puppets should represent a balance of the major groups in Britain, e.g. Caribbean, South Asian, Chinese, as well as white.

Dressing-up clothes should represent everyday clothes from a range of cultures rather than 'national' costumes. We would be shocked if the only English clothes in an Indian nursery were those of Morris dancers. Similarly, black people are often surprised to find what they consider rare dressing-up clothes from their own cultures being promoted as 'normal'. It is also worth considering why children dress up and what it means to them. Being a 'Red Indian' involves playing out a stereotype, offensive to Native Americans. What sort of knowledge could a young child possibly have of 'Red Indians' other than from the many aggressive and racist wild west films? Similarly, any early years topic based on 'Red Indians' is misconceived at best and discriminatory at worst. The children could only be misinformed. Dressing-up clothes should be chosen carefully and, if at all possible, with the consultation of local minority groups.

Arts materials should always reflect the home background of children and a wider community. For collage work such materials as mustard seeds, a range of legumes, rice, paints (brown, tan and black) and crayons can be provided. Mirrors should be on offer so that children can learn about, and articulate, their physical features and how best to describe them. The educator has much to offer here in helping to develop a child's self-identity.

All toys should be checked against clear guidelines to promote anti-sexist and anti-racist practice. The Working Group Against Racism in Children's Resources has produced an excellent set of Guidelines (1990) for the evaluation and selection of toys and other resources for children.

Food and festivals

As a society our attitudes about food have changed considerably in the last twenty years. A diversity of restaurants is commonplace in most towns and cities and most supermarkets stock an international range of foods. Nevertheless, there is still a lot of prejudice against certain foods and against the people who eat them regularly. Children at a very early age should be introduced to a range of foods within and across cultures. Children can learn that all groups have staples in their diet such as potatoes, rice and breads. A good time to introduce a commonality of experience is at Harvest time. Many early years settings display a range of breads – these could include chapatties, wholemeal bread, French stick, pitta, etc.

British society is particularly concerned about smells and children should be encouraged to cook with a range of herbs and spices. Young children enjoy cooking as a real activity in which they participate in a process from start to finish. Engaging in baking and smelling pizzas, sweet rice with saffron or fresh chapatties is not only a delightful learning experience but one in which language can be developed and the senses (both smell and taste!) enhanced.

Children are often asked about their favourite food and many children from non-English cultures may feel they can only give the answers which the educator (if white) will understand. Therefore the way we phrase questions is important. We could ask children what they have to eat or drink every day, or what foods they can eat with their hands, e.g. fruit, samosa, sandwich, pizza, chapatti (roti) and curry (salan), etc.

Festivals are strongly associated with food and celebration as well as religious ritual. Many early years settings only celebrate a few festivals, e.g. Chinese New Year, Eid ul Fïtr, Diwali and Christmas. Educators need to question what children learn from these experiences. Is it merely promoting a 'tourist' curriculum? Children need to understand why they are celebrating. Stories and the educational part of a festival need to be seen as much more important than simply an excuse for celebration in itself. Many infant schools start Christmas celebrations several weeks before Christmas Day, with the children making cards and decorations, writing letters to Santa, talking about presents, rehearsing their plays, holding discos and so forth — by the time the nativity play/story comes round they are all too 'high' and excited to learn anything! Similarly for Eid and Diwali, a one-day celebration with dancing and spicy food is hardly an educational experience for any child.

Early years settings need to set clear guidelines on the purpose of festival celebrations, on the use of foods and on cooking policy. We need to question who cooks with the children. Must it *always* be the Bangladeshi mother who cooks Bengali food with the children? The children would have a more balanced world view if the English teacher cooked a curry with them and the Bangladeshi mother made fairy cakes. Role models are important.

Interactions which promote race equality and deal with racist behaviour

If our early years learning environments reflect the black presence in our society, we are working towards 'race' equality. It is not enough to leave things at that. Children are naturally curious and have absorbed values from outside. Educators will want to read stories and have discussions with children which raise the issues of racism and sexism and allow children to express their feelings, views and experiences in this area. These issues will inevitably arise in the children's minds. When they are expressed they learn about their educator's views on the matter. They learn whether she/he thinks racism acceptable or very unacceptable. It is vital for *all* children to know that they are safe, secure and loved by their educator.

Children's indoor and outdoor play should be monitored carefully and their interactions listened to. Adults often assume stereotypes about boisterous Afro-Caribbean boys who do not concentrate or quiet Asian girls who never speak. The adults' interaction with children should also be monitored. All children should be offered a great deal of encouragement to engage in the full range of activities.

Many educators fear dealing with incidents of racial abuse, name-calling or ridicule. This is often because they do not have enough knowledge to deal with the issue with clear explanations or are ignorant of the damage this form of behaviour causes. Racist behaviour and name-calling is a form of mental violence on the victim. If a child is called 'Paki' or told 'you can't come to my party because my mummy doesn't like blackies', how can the victim react? The hurt, humiliation and damage is done. The message is that the child's colour/racial background is by its very nature unacceptable and inferior, and by implication that white/English is superior. Educators must *learn* to handle these situations. Victims must be supported with love and care and shown that we recognize the gravity of the crime committed. The perpetrator should witness this support and be talked with. Punishment is not enough, the reason *why* what the perpetrator said was wrong and unacceptable should be *clearly* and *gently* explained by the educator.

All these issues are equally applicable to parents. Parents should be involved in developing and understanding the educators' policy, and the reasons why racist behaviour is damaging, wrong, unacceptable and against the law!

A PROCESS FOR CHANGE: FIVE STEPS FORWARD

(1) *Staff/personal commitment*: develop children's learning through racial (and gender, class and disability) equality and develop a learning programme with all your colleagues. This approach ensures the ownership and commitment of all those involved − it will be your own ideas you are all working towards. A typical group might convene ten meetings over one year by which time a policy could be written and put into practice.

(2) *Looking at resources*: look at existing materials using anti-racist evaluation sheets. It would be helpful to identify the gaps and the existing good practice in the curriculum, and check thoroughly what messages the hidden part of the curriculum conveys (e.g. childminders may become alerted to the value of keeping some dual-language books), including resources used to assess children.

Educators will want to try out anti-racist materials and resources and discuss and research the potential of new resources. Human resources should also be considered. Local authority multi-cultural/anti-racist education support services may well be able to contribute.

(3) *Learning from others*: it is always worth inviting speakers to give their experiences and knowledge of working in an anti-racist context or speakers who will clarify one area of concern, e.g. how to support bilingual pupils, or working in an all-white area.

Try to develop a library collection with useful books, journals, any union literature on racial equality, newspaper cuttings and specific guidelines and addresses. The local authority may also offer specialist help. If it cannot, you are in a position to recommend it should.

(4) *Role models*: who is employed in your organization? What does this convey to young children? Schools often find that the only black person in their school is a cleaner or a helper; all other people who have real authority are white. Similarly, you should look at your local playgroup organization, childminders' association, private nursery staff, etc., and ask yourself how this affects our children's lives.

Once we recognize that role models are important and that inequality has resulted in the exclusion of black people from our work-places, then we have to do something about it. Policies which discourage black applicants should be discarded in favour of those which encourage, and we can campaign both locally and nationally for fairer recruitment procedures.

(5) *Monitor and evaluate*: policies and practices need constant evaluation so that practice is improved. We need to identify what to monitor, e.g. schools may want to look at teaching styles or language use while day care advisers may prioritize looking at value-laden child-rearing practices. From this process a new set of steps should emerge for staff development. There are no simple solutions to eliminating racial inequality but accepting the need to take the first step is the most important.

7

MEETING SPECIAL NEEDS IN THE EARLY YEARS

Sheila Wolfendale and Janine Wooster

IDEOLOGICAL PERSPECTIVES

It is a mixed blessing that, in a book devoted to a diverse range of perspectives on the early years, there should be a chapter on special needs. The dilemma for early years/special needs workers is encapsulated by the presence of such a chapter, integral to the book but with a title that potentially marginalizes 'special needs' into being an adjunct to mainstream day care and early education.

Aware of the paradox, we feel that readers might wish to know our stance at the outset. We plan to acknowledge if not celebrate achievements in recent years in special needs/early years becoming much higher profile, commensurate with early years issues becoming higher on the care/education agenda. So we shall chronicle a number of notable developments. At the same time we want to demonstrate a broad responsibility on the part of all early years practitioners towards the distinctive learning and developmental needs of all children, in creating opportunities for them to flourish. One way of achieving this is to describe the contemporary framework that provides hopefully a conducive context for realizing these aspirations. We therefore attempt at the end of the chapter to synthesize a number of legislative and policy matters which have a bearing on future provision for special needs in the early years.

Rights and opportunities

It is only a recent phenomenon that special needs and disability areas have been perceived to come within the orbit of equal opportunities, belatedly joining 'race, sex and class' as the major educational and social issues over which positive action was seen to be needed (Roaf and Bines, 1989). The language of Warnock, the Education Act 1981 and its accompanying Circular 1/83 were not couched in these terms, but that report and the ensuing legislation have in part paved the way for the perspective propagated within the Education Reform Act 1988 that pupils with special educational needs have a fundamental, inalienable entitlement to the National Curriculum. These rights of access to all available curriculum and educational opportunities are becoming a bedrock principle that is permeating educational thinking (National Curriculum Council, 1989) and which is informing the thinking and writing of educationalists (Rieser and Mason, 1990) including those working in pre-school and multi-disciplinary settings (Cameron and Sturge-Moore, 1990).

The broadest universal context for these developments is the moral imperative provided in the Convention of the Rights of the Child (Unicef-UK). This Convention adopted by the United Nations General Assembly in 1989 is being signed by an increasing number of countries. It is a set of international standards and measures that 'recognizes the particular vulnerability of children and brings together in one comprehensive code the benefits and protection for children scattered in scores of other agreements and adds new rights never before recognized' (from Unicef-UK leaflet). Once it has been signed and ratified by twenty countries (and this has been attained, including recent ratification by the UK) the Convention will have the force of international law.

This will and should have implications at every level of policy, decision-making, provision and practice for children from birth, if the fundamental premise is to protect and guarantee children's rights. A number of Articles within the Convention are explicitly geared towards special needs and disability.

Definitions and terminology

The debate on the meaning, purpose and adequacy of the terms 'special needs', 'special educational needs' and disability shows no sign of diminishing. There have been a number of recent critical and reflective appraisals of these terms, from philosophical and educational viewpoints (Rieser and Mason, 1990; Cameron and Sturge-Moore, 1990; Norwich, 1990). A term that started out, pre-Warnock in fact, as intended to be benign and advantaging towards children perceived to be vulnerable and educationally at risk, has become contentious. At its worst, 'special needs' has been perceived as being a separate area, with its own panoply of procedure and personnel, and in education, 'SEN' is too often used as a shorthand label that does indeed encapsulate this view.

With the advent of the Children Act 1989, and its own definitions of 'need', relating particularly to the early years, these controversies are not abated, indeed are probably exacerbated, as different practitioners from different disciplines, employed by diverse agencies, operate within their own frameworks. Woodhead, in a microscopic analysis of the concept of 'need' (1991), starts his critique with a portrayal of how 'need' is defined in a number of key documents and reports emanating from different disciplines and spanning twenty years. He challenges a number of 'givens' and unelaborated hypotheses that have informed policy-making in the early years and beyond, not the least being an unspoken contention that all children's needs are universal whereas in fact 'while in certain very general respects "need" statements may have universal validity, detailed prescriptions about children's needs are normative and depend on a judgement about processes of cultural adaptation and social adjustment' (Woodhead, 1991, p. 48).

A *sequitur* from Woodhead's thesis is that it behoves early years workers to 'recognize the plurality of pathways to maturity within that perspective' (*ibid*. p. 50).

Such cultural imperatives need to inform our practice as a backcloth to the need to provide for a range of 'conditions' listed by Cameron and Sturge-Moore (1990) in their definition of 'special needs' and their justification for using the term within early years contexts (*see* their Introduction).

This is our justification, too, in this chapter; whilst acknowledging flaws in the concept and unease at employing such shorthand, nevertheless we proceed to define our territory, thence to consider recent and current developments in provision and thinking about special needs in the early years.

For the purposes of the chapter, our 'early years' go up to school entry at five years but not beyond. We are aiming to integrate a number of key influences and interests, ranging from some evidence from research to practice innovations, with policy implications, within legislative contexts. Thus, in the case study, we shall illustrate from current practice in one London borough known best to both of us and in which one of us (JW) works as Co-ordinator of the Pre-school Home Visiting team. We shall do this, not only because such a case-study format illuminates the issues, but also because issues of process 'on the ground' can highlight and inform the discussion at other levels.

THE PLACING OF SPECIAL NEEDS IN THE EARLY YEARS ON THE AGENDA

The public agenda

The Warnock Report (DES, 1978) gave under fives and special needs a higher profile than that area had hitherto had by recommending it as a priority area in terms of teacher training and increased provision (Wolfendale, 1987a). Emphasis was give to the proven effectiveness of Head Start programmes (and *see* Woodhead, 1987 and Nielsen, 1989), including Portage, partly to justify this call for increased investment in the early years as both a preventive and 'remedial' measure. Equally, the Court Report (Committee on Child Health Services, 1976) had focused attention on health and development in the early years and had recommended implementation of local early screening and surveillance systems to detect developmental delay and early-appearing disability.

Other government reports on early years include the Select Committee on Educational Provision for the Under Fives (House of Commons, 1989) and the Rumbold Report (DES, 1990a), which includes brief mention of special needs.

The Warnock Report paved the way for the legislation that amended existing law on special education, namely the Education Act 1981 (implemented from 1 April 1983). This conferred new duties on local education and health authorities in respect of identifying and assessing young children with possible special needs. The accompanying circular to the Education Act 1981, updated in 1989 (Circular 22/89) to take account of the Education Reform Act 1988 as well as recent developments, has a whole section on under fives with special needs, doubtless influenced by the House of Commons Select Committee (1987) criticisms into this phase of education and provision.

The Education Reform Act 1988, whilst not statutorily covering pre-school of course, nevertheless has implications for the early years in terms of those four-year-olds who are receiving infant school education (NFER/SCDC, 1987) and, too, in terms of the 'knock on' effect of the National Curriculum (NCC Curriculum Guidance 2, 1989).

Finally, mention is made of the Children Act 1989, in which this area looms large, and to which we return later.

The practitioners' and professionals' agenda

The fact that, without exception, these reports and Acts recommend close inter-agency and multi-disciplinary links is, as we know, no guarantee of this coming about, especially where there are resource implications.

So, for practitioners and providers themselves have official pronouncements had an impact upon their work? If anything the reverse has operated, namely that recent practice has been impressive enough to be quoted in government reports (reference to Portage in the Warnock Report was cited above and *see* Cameron, 1989) which after all are intended to reflect and synthesize current and emerging good practice.

There is now plenty of evidence to show that at every level of practice, management and policy-making, special needs in the early years is in receipt of more attention, resources and provision than at any other time.

Despite this agenda, however, and the fact that there is some kind of consensus over the importance of the early years, the known variation in provision (Pugh, 1988) reflects the lack of co-ordination and commitment to explicit policies at government levels, and the anomalous status of non-statutory pre-school provision (except for under fives with a statement of special educational needs which must be met and provided for by the LEA).

The parents' agenda

Each of the aforementioned reports emphasizes the importance of parent-professional dialogue, and the various Acts have enshrined, and therefore strengthened, a number of parental rights. Many parents themselves have translated rhetoric and principles into a number of realities, which include:

(1) finding a collective voice: a number of local and regional parents' groups have emerged, within, now, a national umbrella (Wolfendale, 1989a);
(2) empowerment, via the emergence of parent advocacy, representation, self-help and parent-professional coalitions (Hornby, 1988; Russell, 1990);
(3) participating in assessment processes (Wolfendale, 1988; Russell and Gatiss, 1991);
(4) parents as educators, as in Portage and other home-based early learning schemes (Cameron, 1989; Wells, 1989; Russell, 1990).

As the 1987 Select Committee noted, however, there is a long way to go in terms of inclusion of parents into more levels of decision-making, let alone partnership.

SOURCES OF INFLUENCE UPON PRACTICE AND PROVISION FOR YOUNG CHILDREN WITH SPECIAL NEEDS

At any one time the factors and forces governing special needs decision-making are intricate, complex and pervasive. There is no unitary source of influence in the early years field as we have already noted. A number of influences cohere at the point of practice and provision, their origins lying in:

(1) *ideology and principles*, such that commitment to provision based on concepts of entitlement and meeting needs informs decision-making processes;

(2) *pragmatism and needs analysis*, where pressures resulting from identifying needs determines expedient responses;

(3) *findings from research*: this particular source of influence will be explored in more detail than (1) and (2) because research is often invoked to justify local action and confer legitimacy and respectability on to decision-making. Each of the major reports cited above refer to seminal research, though the most frequently invoked areas, those of the alleged longer-term effectiveness of early childhood education and accelerated programmes, remain the most inconclusive and the hardest to 'prove' definitively (Woodhead, 1987; Howe, 1990).

In the anomalous area of pre-school, reliance upon research is perhaps the greater, for provision is optional, variable and unequal and the case has to be made with whatever ammunition there is to hand. These points are emphasized by Clark who, whilst acknowledging the influence of the National Curriculum, nevertheless cautions that 'it would be unfortunate if the current move "Back to Basics" ignores the insights we are already gathering from research into ways of encouraging and supporting the learning of young children' (Clark, 1989, p. 114). Clark identifies five main types of research − laboratory-based, questionnaire surveys, descriptive case studies, observational studies, and practical work by students in training. Collectively these embrace qualitative and quantitative methodologies.

Table 7.1 lists some contemporary research in the early years that

Table 7.1 Examples of research into early years

Topic/area	Authors/source
(1) *Survey/questionnaire*	
• Community Child Health Services	Elfer and Gatiss (1990)
• Inter-disciplinary support for young children with special needs	DES (1991a)
• Survey of thirteen Portage projects	DES (1990b)
(2) *Observation, recording, interaction* in situ	
• Children with speech and language difficulties in an integrated nursery	Robson (1989)
• Completion by teachers in sixteen nursery classes of behavioural questionnaire on 778 children	Davis and Brember (1991)
• Examining teaching styles in nursery education	Meadows and Cashdan (1988)
(3) *Measuring or reviewing effects of intervention* (epitomized by evaluation of Head Start programmes)	
• Critical appraisal of early language intervention programmes	Harris (1984)
• Reviewing USA and UK early education	Woodhead (1989)
• Review of evidence on parental role in the education of children with severe learning difficulties	Wells (1989)
(4) *Development, evaluation, applications of assessment instruments*	
• Parent-held child health records	Saffin and MacFarlane (1988)
• Parent-completed developmental profile	Wolfendale (1987, 1990)
• Schedule of growing skills	Bellman and Cash (1987)
(5) *Experimental and hypothesis-testing studies*	
• Cognitive foundations and social functions of imitation	Meltzoff and Moore (1991)
• Early parent-child interaction	Trevarthen (1990)
• Perceptual and cognitive development	Psychology Dept., University of Bangor, North Wales

ranges across topic areas, different ages, and groups of children. A small selective number of examples are given within each type of research.

We have not distinguished between research directed at young children with special needs and that directed at *all* children. In selecting this broad range of examples we want to emphasize that the appraisal and formulation of the most appropriate pre-school learning opportunities for special needs should take place within the all-encompassing perspective of entitlement and access outlined at the outset of this chapter. Indeed, current early years special needs provision is located and embedded or linked with mainstream settings (*see* Wolfendale, 1989b, for a continuum of such provision and discussion on the characteristics of specific curriculum approaches for young children with designated special needs; *see also* Robson, 1989).

We do have a sufficient range of evaluation approaches as well as research findings which ought to be used routinely to appraise the effectiveness of intervention programmes and early curriculum opportunities. Whilst this applies to all young children, such close scrutiny is especially important for those children whose next educational setting needs a careful match and prior planning based on a comprehensive assessment.

CASE STUDY

This case study describes current practice and provision in one locality. It typifies the range and organization of services and inter-agency collaboration that increasingly can be found in many areas, and, too, reflects the mix of policy and pragmatism that has been the hallmark of developing services for under fives and special needs. In the London Borough of Newham there has been much commitment, discussion and planning which have brought about present levels of staffing and resourcing. Readers will judge which aspects of practice seem to represent 'good' emerging practice and which areas are in need of further development.

One prime purpose in presenting an 'on the ground' picture is that services are rooted in the realities of restricted funds, with provision that is targeted at early years special needs being potentially vulnerable. This portrait of the current scene in Newham focuses upon:

(1) early identification and assessment processes and multi-disciplinary co-operation;
(2) staffing and services – description of the Learning Support Team with reference to pre-school;
(3) integration, via two illustrative case accounts.

The early identification and assessment process in the London Borough of Newham

Children start with a medically based assessment when initial diagnoses are made. For many children this initial stage will take place in hospital although it is likely to come later for those with difficulties or conditions which are less obvious or easily detectable. Those children diagnosed as having a condition such as Down's syndrome usually enter immediately into a pre-designed and tested package of 'follow-up'. In Newham these children will be referred to the Child Development Centre (CDC) on leaving hospital and they will soon receive a home visit from one of the senior medical officers who will examine the baby and outline the programme for follow-up with the various options involved. There will be a great deal of information given on this visit but parents will be advised that it will all be repeated at a later stage. Some parents may wish to take up some of the options immediately and most will be referred to physiotherapy at this stage. Assessment has begun and so far only one or two people have seen the child; probably these will have a medical background — hospital staff, health visitor, GP and medical officer.

The next stage will involve a visit to the CDC itself and yet another assessment which will usually take place at between three and six months. Any number of the other professionals could be introduced now (*see* flow diagram, Figure 7.1). A broad based multi-disciplinary team will now

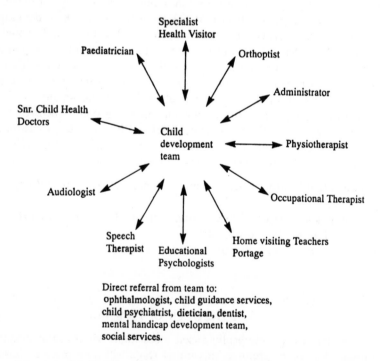

Figure 7.1   A multi-disciplinary approach to special needs.

look at the child and assess her/his development right up to the time she/he is five. Obviously children with different conditions will enter this system at different times between the ages of one or two months right the way up until school entry at five. This multi-disciplinary method of assessment via a team approach does mean that the children are receiving a wide range of input from various professionals and it also means that we as professionals can use the knowledge of those around us to give ourselves more scope for using the best possible methods for each individual child. When a child attends for review a plan is made to detail what is to happen over the next three or six months before the parents and child return to the centre. This plan may advise the parents of other appointments that need to be kept, e.g. audiology clinic or hospital appointments for medical tests; it may equally advise the parents of what they should expect from the professionals involved, e.g. regular visits from the occupational therapist or a more detailed assessment by the speech therapist. The parents will take away with them a copy of this plan and a further copy will be kept in the child's file at the CDC for reference. Everyone is in this way made clear of what is to happen and any assessments that have been made formally or informally are used to form the basis of a plan rather than simply being filed away.

If a child is referred at a later date, often by the school, the options may not be as clear-cut or as helpful. At later stages the whole area of communication seems to cause far more problems as there is no one forum from which to operate as there is in the CDC. There is, however, in Newham a Learning Support Team (*see* Figure 7.2).

Staffing and services

The London Borough of Newham LEA was one of the first in the country to produce a policy statement about the integration of children with special needs into mainstream schools. There was an immediate commitment to support the integration programme with a Learning Support Team in one base, on the ground floor of an old, no longer used, primary school. It is right on the edge of the borough and transport systems are non-existent but nevertheless it provides a base for co-ordination and communication. At first there was a pre-school team and a couple of primary teachers. This has now grown dramatically to a service with a headteacher and incorporating three distinct teams – pre-school, primary and secondary, with some staff obviously working across all three phases (*see* Figure 7.2).

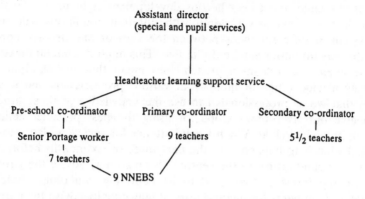

Plus two teachers working on 'whole school policy on assessment'.
Plus welfare assistants at present based in school and supporting
children over seven or those with particular difficulties.

School age pupils: Roll 199   Pre-school pupils: Roll 154
                    Waiting list 8   Waiting list 15

Figure 7.2   London Borough of Newham Learning Support Team (correct as at
April 1991)

In addition to the teaching members of the team there is a team of
welfare assistants providing support to older children and/or those with
specific physical difficulties. The nursery nurses share the caseload of
home visits and provide long-term support to children in nursery and
infant provision, whereas for the majority of children of school age they
will operate in a purely advisory role monitoring progress and liaising
with staff. Each child receives a visit from a teacher at least once a week,
while they may have a welfare assistant or nursery nurse with them for up
to four sessions. However, it is rare for a child to receive full-time
support and this would only be agreed in very special circumstances. All
support is provided subject to review (this may be an annual statement
review or a special review called specifically to evaluate the support that
is being offered).

The pre-school team contributes fully to the Learning Support Team's
programmes of training and support activities, such as advice on individual
children, information on assessment and curriculum. The whole team is
currently compiling a Skills Directory. Training is also directed to non-
teaching personnel such as governors, welfare assistants and parents, and
the head of the team also produces a termly bulletin entitled 'Support for
Learning'.

Present and future plans

With current staffing ratios and a waiting list of referred children it is essential that we work together to streamline our methods of keeping and storing information about children. This is even more necessary with the pressures of the National Curriculum and the generation of even more paperwork. In the pre-school department we are currently working on developing a profile to be completed on an initial visit to a child, giving us in the minimum of time with the minimum of questions to the family all the information we need to provide a picture of the child. We are also trying to develop a format for passing on information to colleagues when children move from us to the primary team.

We need to ensure that we keep a check on the current rapidly changing situation *vis-à-vis* the National Curriculum, the Standard Assessment Tasks (SATs) and methods of profiling children in order that we can be of the most help to colleagues in mainstream education in providing information and in correlating and keeping tabs on the required paperwork rather than in adding to it unnecessarily.

One essential task of the Learning Support Team as a whole is to liaise with all services provided in the borough and to spend time on communication. We need to look closely at the service we offer and at how effectively we are able to work with other adults (Lally, 1991).

Integration

We now examine the process of integrating young children with assessed and identified special learning needs. This is effected via two case accounts, that of 'C' which to date has proved more straightforward and that of 'N', whose complex needs are such that one change of provision has already taken place and on behalf of whom intensive monitoring of his next placement is a fundamental requirement and basis for making the most appropriate longer-term decision. In both cases team work is paramount.

Example 1: 'C'

'C' was referred to the pre-school home visiting team by the Child Development Centre when she was two years and four months old. The physiotherapist was seeing her regularly and it had just been suggested that 'C' attend a local children's centre funded partly by the social services department and partly by Barnado's. Speech therapy had also received a referral but as yet had only seen 'C' when she visited the CDC for a review. It had also been suggested that she be placed on the waiting list for occupational therapy. There was some question of her attending hospital for further tests under anaesthetic but her family were undecided about this.

'C' was the younger of two children and her family had not been unduly concerned about her but the health visitor had begun to worry when she attended the clinic as she seemed to be reaching her motor milestones very late. She was therefore referred to the CDC at twelve months and waited three weeks before she was sent an appointment.

The team that had seen her on that initial visit were clear that she had some motor problems but they felt that they would like more time to visit and get to know her before making any other decisions.

Visits from the speech therapist and the teacher commenced and she continued to be seen by the physiotherapist, until she was fairly steady on her feet. After this time the occupational therapist was introduced to work on her finer movements. Tests were carried out at the hospital but little new information was revealed. 'C' settled well into the routine of the nursery and enjoyed her time there. The work that was being done with her was clearly helping her and improvements were seen in all areas.

This pattern continued with minor variations, the only other milestone being that we began to use Makaton signs and symbols with 'C' and her parents agreed to the formal assessment procedure beginning when she was three-and-a-half. At four the question of school became a priority and her parents began to look closely at local schools. The two which were nearest to home were unfortunately ruled out as they were old buildings on three levels which it was felt would prove very difficult for her. The next school considered was small and under the threat of closure, so we looked slightly further afield and settled on a newer building that seemed to meet all her needs. An interview with the head-teacher was positive. The education authority agreed with the parents' decision and said that they would provide transport to and from school. All went according to plan and 'C' entered the school at five and joined a reception class. Now as a top infant she is still receiving one session of support a week from a support teacher and two from a nursery nurse. There have, of course, been minor set-backs but generally things have gone well.

Example 2: 'N'

'N' is a little boy who has autistic-like difficulties. He has a few words which are sometimes used in context and he flaps either an object or his hands in front of his face. He has many difficulties resulting from obsessive behaviours and his parents find him very difficult to handle. He was referred to the CDC at almost three when the speech therapist saw him and realized that his difficulties were much more complex than purely speech. He attended the initial appointment and immediately the wheels were set in motion for other members of the team to see him. Domiciliary speech therapy was agreed and he was referred as an urgent case to the home visiting team. An initial visit was arranged to the home by a teacher and an educational psychologist and the behaviour problems and sleep problems combined with feeding difficulties were discussed.

The speech therapist was finding it very difficult to work and after discussion it was decided to make the teacher the key visitor at least for a time in order to try and assess the possibilities for intervention and to work out a draft plan of action. 'N' was already attending the local playgroup and they were finding him very difficult so a session was arranged to discuss the possibilities of activities for staff to undertake. A programme was built up and seemed to be taking effect so it was decided to look into a nursery placement at the local nursery. A place was set up for just one morning a week to be supported by the teacher. At first this seemed to be going well and he was settling well into school. However, at about this time he developed an obsession for cereal boxes. The nursery had a large stock of these boxes for junk modelling – he refused to do anything else in the nursery and determined to find these boxes; it did not seem to matter how well they were hidden he would search until he found them.

He was still very happy and would try and enter the school when passing with his mother but at home his behaviour began to deteriorate and previously organized patterns of behaviour were lost. After much discussion it was agreed to terminate the nursery visits at this time. He seemed to be in a state of panic and consequently he received some holding therapy. The Educational Psychologist saw him again and agreed to begin the assessment at the parents' request. All the reports were sent in and it has been decided to send him to another nursery school where a special class has been set up with the school, to offer support to children with severe communication difficulties. This has yet to occur but we hope this will be a means of offering a more consistent input to 'N' and his family.

CONCLUSION

In conclusion, we summarize the special needs in the early years agenda and identify key issues for the short and longer term.

Each of the other chapters in this book has a pertinent bearing on special needs issues and to that extent each of these major topic areas has profound implications for meeting the distinctive needs of young children who have a developmental delay, a disability, and who, unless such acknowledgement is made for them, remain vulnerable and at risk.

The challenge for carers and educators is to ensure that the general aspirations for guaranteeing quality provision genuinely embrace *all* children. Translation of this beyond paying lip-service to entitlement and

Table 7.2 Suggestions for specific action for special needs in key areas

Topic	Comments	Key references (some already cited)
• Policy and local provision	(1) Tie up between Education Acts 1981 and 1988 and Children Act 1989 *vis-à-vis* definition and action	DH (1991)
	(2) Co-operation between statutory and voluntary agencies and work towards service integration	Pugh (1988)
• Equal opportunities and special needs	(1) Anti-racist statements and procedures in all day care	Celestin (1986) CRE (1991)
	(2) Equality of access and translation facilities	
• Integrated pre-school	Continue to integrate children along 'inclusive' lines	Stephenson (1990) Robson (1989)
• Curriculum	(1) Pursue 'educare' concepts	David (1990) Rouse (1991a)
	(2) Differentiate learning experiences	Hurst (1991) Anning (1991)
• Assessment	(1) Use of array of differentiated assessment and record-keeping	Drummond and Rouse (in preparation)
	(2) Use fine-grained, child-focused, context-relevant measures	Fox (1990)
• Partnership	(1) Ensure participation and representation at all levels	Pugh (1989)
	(2) Maximize 'parents as educators'	Russell (1990)
• Training	(1) Towards competency-based training including special needs awareness	Curtis and Hevey (Chapter 11 of this book)
	(2) Training for teamwork	Lally (1991) Whalley (Chapter 9 of this book)

equal opportunities principles involves specific action in the key areas covered in some of the other chapters. Some suggestions, following other chapter topics, are given in Table 7.2 in the form of comments with key references where appropriate.

Collective responsibility

What this means in practice as far as special needs in the early years is concerned has been explored elsewhere (Wolfendale, 1987a). Since then the advent of the Children Act 1989, implemented from October 1991, represents a significant landmark *en route* to the sharing of responsibility. It not only provides very obviously the larger frame of reference, within a legislative context, but is also a catalyst for action in the early years and shapes and unifies perceptions over:

(1) concepts of needs;
(2) duty to make provision for identified need and disability;
(3) involving parents in decision-making and acknowledging parents' needs.

The Guidance on these parts of the Act (DH, 1991) is explicit on core principles and clear about the necessity of having local policies and achieving co-ordination, collaboration and co-operation.

We concur with the philosophy outlined in Part III of the Act which is that children with disabilities are treated first as children and then as persons with a disability.

8

QUALITY FOR THE UNDER THREES

Dorothy Rouse and Sue Griffin

INTRODUCTION

This chapter explores two contemporary issues relating to the care and education of children under the age of three, and their families. These issues apply to a range of play and learning environments, in a variety of communities:

(1) children's needs for relationships with significant responsive adults;
(2) children's needs for developmentally appropriate learning experiences.

There are many criteria for defining quality, and because values and beliefs vary in a pluralistic society, so will ideas for giving a priority to any issue; even so we have settled on these two issues as they are of contemporary concern to a broad range of providers as well as to parents.

This chapter considers issues relating to children under three because of the distinctive development and learning needs of this age group, and because of a number of current developments. These include:

- a need to consider the continuity of learning from birth onwards. There has been very little discussion about this in Britain as there has been so little day care here. Now that there are more combined nursery centres and childminders, and a growth in the commercial sector to meet the needs and wishes of working parents, the inter-relatedness of education and care should be priority for discussion.

- a new duty (section 19 of the Children Act 1989) requiring local social services and education authorities to work collaboratively to ensure quality standards when reviewing all childminding and day care for young children (*see* Elfer and Wedge, Chapter 3 in this book).

- the links which are beginning to be made with colleagues in Europe and internationally (for example, Melhuish and Moss, 1990; Moss, Chapter 2 in this book). We have much to learn from international exchange and networks which will challenge, enrich or inform traditional practice in Britain.

- the demands of integrating children with special learning needs into all early childhood settings. This reinforces the need for all educators to have detailed knowledge of the characteristics of learning and development of *all* children. Skilled observers will use this understanding of the continuum of development from birth onwards to inform curriculum planning for children whatever age they may be.

Definition and clarification is required of two key terms used in this chapter. 'Educators' is used to apply to people who care for and educate children in a variety of settings. These people may be parents, grandparents, childminders, workers in day nurseries or family centres, teachers, playgroup or parent/toddler group workers, nannies, home visitors – and so on. All these adults affect children's development and learning, and so we use the term 'educator' to refer to them all (Rumbold Report, DES, 1990a). Education and care are inextricably linked. It is not possible to educate a young child without being concerned with her well-being and aspects of her daily care.

Children learn and develop as a result of a set of experiences which are provided consciously or unconsciously. We shall use the term 'curriculum' to include:

(1) all the activities and experiences provided for babies and toddlers by educators:
(2) all the activities children devise for themselves;
(3) the gestures, vocalizations and language that educators use to communicate with children and all the language they use with each other;
(4) all that children see and touch and hear and taste and smell in the environment around them.

It is from this curriculum, however planned or unplanned, consistent or inconsistent, explicitly based on particular theories of how children learn or derived from observations or respected responsive colleagues, that children learn and are educated (Drummond, Lally and Pugh, 1989).

We begin from the premise that children have a right to good quality care and education in whatever setting their parents choose. Children in group day care, children with childminders or in the family home all have the right to experience responsive education and care which has been sensitively arranged to meet their distinctive developmental needs from birth onwards.

The Children Act 1989 has a fundamental principle that the welfare of the child is paramount. In the context of day care, this is elaborated in the Guidance and Regulations (DH, 1991). We examine children's development and learning in the context of their rights to 'individuality, respect, dignity' and to equal opportunities in their play and learning experiences.

The purpose of this chapter is to identify imaginative practices for improved quality care and education. It is not enough to provide 'adequate care' or a 'fit person' to work with children (Children Act 1989). Children deserve the best we can offer them.

QUALITY RELATIONSHIPS BETWEEN CHILDREN AND ADULTS

It is recommended that staff use a primary (or key) worker system during the nursery day. Thus each staff member will have responsibility for an identified group of children, and will be able to form a stronger attachment with them...and babies should spend the majority of their nursery day in the care of the same adult.

(Cowley, 1991, p. 42)

These National Children's Bureau day-care guidelines clearly describe policy and practice for working with young children and emphasize the accepted ideology in the UK that the provision of responsive and sensitive educators allows children the opportunity of familiarity with, and *attachment* to, their significant adults.

More than a generation ago, Bowlby (1953) cautioned mothers about the negative aspects of institutional group care and the dire consequences of maternal separation. More recently, Belsky (1988) offered further evidence that full-time day care of more than twenty hours a week before twelve months of age may have detrimental effects. On the other hand, Andersson (1990) points to the benefits of early educare, particularly where educarers have more and better quality education and training themselves. These conflicting views can be confusing, on the one hand deeply worrying and on the other constructively hopeful. Melhuish (1991) and Calder (in Rouse, 1991a) summarize the research debate.

Earlier research (Ainsworth *et al.*, 1990; Bowlby, 1953; Schaffer and Emerson, 1964) supports the view that a close emotional tie between young children and their day-to-day carers is the solid base, a secure safety net, a protection against strange and overwhelming experiences, and a comfort in coping with new sensations and relationships. This concept of attachment underpins all good practice. Secure attachments to educators are thought to increase the chances of developing successful relationships in later life. The films of James and Joyce Robertson in the 1950s will haunt all educators who witnessed the distress of children like 'John' who was seventeen-months-old when he was separated from his mother for nine days, in a situation where no individual or continuous care could be provided. John was not able to feel *attached* and safe in the arms of a particular trusted adult. The conclusion of these studies of early separation is that separation in infancy can have long-term effects which may disable children in forming successful, warm, responsive relationships later in life. This frightening warning still lingers and means that we place heavy emphasis on the importance of secure attachments. Later studies, however, show clearly how flexible children can be. Experience has shown us that little children are able to form attachments with a number of care-givers including childminders, and fathers as well as mothers (Schaffer and Emerson, 1964).

We believe that children need trusting, dependent relationships in order to be able to learn to love, and to venture out and learn from the curriculum available to them. However, we recognize that not all cultures develop the quality of their provision for babies and toddlers from this premise and we welcome the opportunity to examine these long-held views.

Le Vine (1989) shows that societies in which 'insecure' and 'avoidant' attachments are more typical than 'secure' attachments are not marked by greater incidence of psychopathology than are countries where 'secure' attachments are typical. Indeed, Japanese child development experts, in a discussion on spoiling children, describe the attachment-like behaviour of mothers as narcissistic, over-involved maternal investment in children. This occurs when mothers are isolated and emotionally needy and so look after their children to provide gratification otherwise lacking in their lives. In China, group day care is regarded as a benefit because children can get away from the dangers of spoiling (over-attachment?) in a single-child family, and so be liberated from smothering maternal attention and love (Tobin *et al.*, 1989). In Italy, key relationships with a significant adult are not seen as necessary to children's successful development in group day care. Group settings may be seen as attempts to counterbalance the clinging, suffocating closeness of mother and child. An Italian colleague explained her alternative ethos to the key worker system. She stresses the *system* of reference rather than the *person* of reference with interchanges of relationships emphasized within a group (Rinaldí, in Rouse, 1991b).

Children are encouraged to respond to the environment and the team of educators and to their peer group, rather than to a 'significant adult'.

These alternative philosophies challenge our own ideology and we would welcome further formative research to investigate attachment in different forms of high-quality education and care.

When parents share their parenting role they need the complementary support of educators. It is not enough for educators to tide things over until the parent returns, unless the arrangement is only as an occasional 'babysitter'. A day educator must also develop a strong and complementary attachment with the infants and toddlers in their care. They will not be a replacement or substitute for mothers or fathers or grannies, but they must be able to form special relationship which nourish, protect, and are available on a regular and predictable basis during the day. The quality of these complementary attachments depends on a number of features including:

(1) responsive and loving attention by a significant adult;
(2) opportunities for children to develop a positive self-concept, personal identity and autonomy.

Responsive and loving attention by a significant adult

Appropriate gestures, words, deeds and attitudes enable infants to develop hopeful, trusting and essentially joyful interactions with adults. For example, a person who sensitively changes her voice and the arch of her eyebrows to match the slow-motion finger patterns and the arching of a new born's back is giving loving attention and developing trust.

On a recent visit to a nursery school for children from birth to six-years-old in Bologna, Italy, it was found that the educators in the baby and toddler unit had found a number of ways to give loving, physical attention to a baby who was causing some concern. The baby, from a family of Chinese immigrants, cried pitifully and clung to her mother during the initial transition process from home to school. The arrangements to meet the needs of the baby and her family included:

• the educators learning to carry the child in the same way as established by the family, the baby's legs astride and seated on the adult's hip with her arms clasped around the adult's body. Every effort was being made to let the child lead while the adults responded to and supported the child's body. There was an opportunity to value the significance of parents' preferences and to learn about their child-rearing style.

- the educator noting that the Italian intonational pattern of her voice was distressing for the Chinese baby. So she babbled and made up song and rhymes for this baby by imitating the intonational rhythms of the Chinese language. The baby found this comforting and was reassured by the educator's voice.

- tapes being made of the father singing lullabies in Chinese. These were played to help the baby feel tranquil at siesta time but also for all the other children too.

As children develop language it is also important that adults should be verbally stimulating and responsive. There was a time when we were told that we should bathe the child in language and surround them with books and stories. If this were sufficient, it would be enough to settle a two-year-old in front of the television or with his own sackful of taped stories. However, quality experiences which support children's language development need to be reciprocal exchanges; responses should follow the pattern, tone and nature of the children's communication.

Language and communication are closely interrelated with all other aspects of development, especially emotional well-being, social competence and the child's sense of distinct, capable self. Therefore it is important that educators take time for individual turn-taking games, songs and activities with even the youngest babies. The example of the relationship with the Chinese baby and her Italian educator demonstrates the baby's ability to initiate, participate and regulate her interactions with her care-givers. Children need adults who can attribute meaning to their utterances and gestures, who are sensitive and responsive in their physical movements, and in the intonations, rhythms and pace of their interactions. Educators must develop the ability to follow the initiatives of needy, vigorous infants, to meet their needs for security and conversational exchanges of gestures and movements.

Holding on and letting go

Physical care and loving attention will be required in different ways as a toddler becomes mobile. The child will still come close to the educator — approaching, following, reaching out, cuddling in — but exploratory behaviour will also take the child away as she crawls, walks and inspects the world about her. The educator is required not only to protect the child through closeness, but also to let go to encourage the growing independence.

The toddler can explore from a safe base, returning for solace if stressed, in danger or feeling apprehensive, before moving off again

(Lieberman, 1991). If her foray into separation brings her up against too unfamiliar or unexpected circumstances, she may cling and be cuddled; as she grows in self-reliance, she may need only to check that her special adult is still close by if needed. Where babies and toddlers experience the opportunities and challenges of groups in the company of their educators (parent and toddler groups, childminder drop-ins), thoughtful arrangement of adult furniture, carpeted areas and play equipment and materials can enable the child to have control over holding on and letting go. The educator should remain alert, watchful and ready for action, but the child must not feel constrained or under constant observation (Ruddick, 1989).

Educators should never lose sight of the prime role of the parents in the child's life. They need to think about the nature of the beginning and ending of the day: the 'letting go' to return the child to her parents. The childminder who accompanies the child and the parents along the garden path each day to the car, making almost a ritual of parting and farewell, is marking the boundaries of her complementary but not usurping role. The child, the parent and the educator are all clear about the extent of that role and of the sustained central role of the parent.

Educators are required to make a commitment of attachment to children they nurture, to be open to intimacy, not only with the children, but also with other members of families. They are also required to relinquish the care of the children to their parents each day, and eventually to subsequent educators. People selected to be educators should therefore be adults capable of attachment to children without clinging, suffocating closeness. They must not be seeking to compensate for their own unresolved early experiences of separation and instability (Bain and Barnett, 1980).

Opportunities for children to develop a positive self-concept, personal identity and autonomy

The significant key adult has a many faceted role in supporting children's identity, autonomy and positive self-concept. Through the interactions and physical closeness described above, the young child learns the boundaries of her own identity, her separateness, and her competence to influence and affect the people attached to her through touch and inter- actions. As children learn to do things for themselves and to become autonomous, they define their own sense of self. By trying out the boundaries of their skills, children are defining themselves. Adults need to support children to manage this on their own while also recognizing, describing and valuing each child's individual contribution.

Another important part of this relationship between children and adults and their evolving autonomy is the arrangement of space, furniture and play materials. These aspects of the child's surroundings have a profound influence on the opportunities and constraints for enabling children's exploration of their own capabilities. A number of nurseries in Emilia Romagna in northern Italy are carefully and imaginatively designed, built and arranged, as collaborative projects involving architects, teachers and parents. A number of features suggest ideas for developing quality practice in this country even if they are not all ones we would emulate directly.

The sleeping rooms in one nursery for the under threes, for example, are arranged to give even the youngest children a sense of control and autonomy. The cots are not cages on stilts which small children have to be hoisted in and out of by adults, but baskets with children's own entrances which mean babies can help themselves to sleep or comfort. In each sleep 'nest' are the child's personal bedding and comfort objects. These arrangements are evidence of the respect and support children receive to help them be autonomous and take initiative for their own needs as well as playing their part in group routines. In the nappy-changing and toileting areas, children able to climb are provided with little steps to the changing mats. The towels and nappies are stored in low cupboards. Children can help themselves, and adults are able to avoid unnecessary lifting and back strain.

The outside play area has scope for solitary exploration. One child was observed on a piece of equipment – a series of toddler-sized steps and ramps. She was about fourteen-months-old and was repeatedly practising the techniques needed for scaling the stairs, and then tackling the more challenging task of coming down again. She worked for twenty minutes at this task with perseverance and absorption, playing alone. No adult stood within approximately twenty metres. She had toddled through some chin-high meadow grass to reach this discovery. The adult's role was to plan and create the environment containing safe, stage-appropriate equipment, in an inviting setting. The adults were not waiting with outstretched hands to catch her fall, nor was it necessary to praise her for being a 'clever girl'. The adults remained behind the scene, observing unobtrusively, not directing. This child was given the space, the privacy, and the opportunity to learn a new skill. She enjoyed the satisfaction of testing her own capabilities and achieving her own goals. An adult's praise or protection would have been superfluous.

During conversations with educators in Italy they identified a primary educational feature as the development of identity. They explained that children's need to identify themselves as individuals, and their need to know and use their own bodies, was central to the curriculum. This philosophy was evident in the places visited. For babies and toddlers large wall mirrors from floor to waist height, and often two or three metres long, are fixed behind an arrangement of mattresses and cushions. A rail for grasping, for babies to pull themselves up to an upright position, is a common fixture in front of the big mirrors. Along another wall at skirting board level and on the baby's 'nests' are large head-and-shoulder photographs of the babies. These photos are covered with wipeable film and above was a mirror of the same size. One child of about eight months was observed exploring both the photos and the mirrors with his lips and tongue as well as an intense gaze. Mirrors and photographs are also a regular feature in the sleeping and changing areas so that children can see themselves and others.

Supporting the development of positive self-image

Educators play a crucial personal role in helping children develop a concept of self, a positive image incorporating realistic self-knowledge, and self-esteem rising out of the valuing of the child's own abilities, gender and own particular combination of skin colour, facial features or hair type (Maximé, 1991).

The damage done to children's perceptions about themselves and others by absorption of discriminatory and mistaken concepts and values about gender, racial origin and disability are well rehearsed in other places (CRE, 1990; Siraj-Blatchford in Chapter 6 of this book). In the context of this chapter, the significant consideration is how early the development of such concepts begins.

It would be more comfortable and less threatening to believe that the youngest children somehow have an innocence which means that 'they don't notice' differences amongst themselves and the adults around them. However, we know that this is not true. There is clear evidence that by the age of three, children not only distinguish between skin colours, but also give different values to them, with 20 per cent of two-year-olds and 50 per cent of three-year-olds making such distinctions (Milner, 1983). Whilst there is less striking evidence available about gender differentiation in such young children, there are indications of gender-stereotyped choice of toys as young as eighteen months (Caldera *et al.*, 1989).

Issues of combating discrimination and prejudice and ensuring equal opportunities for all are significant in the nurture of a child's self-image. The differences and shared characteristics of children and families should be recognized, described and valued. Careful selection of materials and activities for play and learning should reflect and celebrate the racial, cultural and linguistic mix in Britain. Images and models of all people of various racial origins and cultural backgrounds, gender and/or disabilities should demonstrate active, responsible, influential and caring roles. In particular, educators working with babies and toddlers must be knowledgeable about a range of child-rearing practices, and demonstrate that they respect and value each family's preference so that their own practice can follow the lead of the family and be in harmony with it.

Educators should look inside themselves at their basic assumptions, values and beliefs about children and childhood, and think about where these ideas come from. Perhaps professional training provides us with a theoretical framework for working with children, but personal experiences of childhood, and early experiences of playing, learning and loving, will also have had an effect on the way educators understand and interact with children. Attitudes, beliefs and values have been forming from our own childhood onwards. If we look after and work with other people's children, we have to be able to recognize and explore these values. When you see a child with a dummy, do you see a tranquil child being comforted, enjoying the erotic sucking on the teat, or do you see a child with an unhygienic object stuck in her mouth which will inhibit her language development. . .or something else? Do you see the physical features of Down's syndrome on the baby who holds out her arms to be picked up, or do you respond firstly to a child who is asking for a cuddle and then secondly do you notice the signs of a child with a disability? Do you see a black toddler, boisterous and undisciplined, or a toddler who is black, and enthusiastic to join in the game? When a child is pouring sand down the drains do you see one of the 'terrible twos' being naughty and unbiddable or a bright, curious infant investigating the properties of sand and water? Why do we label children 'just babies' and 'terrible twos'? (Drummond and Rouse, in preparation.)

The development of a child's positive self-image is affected by our perceptions, prejudices and attitudes to children. Educators need to explore and reflect on their personal assumptions or 'labels' so that we can ensure that every child is positively valued.

DEVELOPMENTALLY APPROPRIATE LEARNING EXPERIENCES

What does education for the under threes mean? Some people who work with the youngest children have traditionally been seen, and have seen themselves, only in a 'caring' role. Their congruent role as educators must be acknowledged – it is central to their job in offering and extending play and learning experiences. What do we know about the distinctive learning needs of children from birth to thirty-six months old?

Education, training and care are interrelated. Caring for very young children involves a number of activities like the rituals of nappy changing, bathing, dressing and soothing children to sleep. Other activities might seem to be more directly 'educational', like sharing a picture book with a child or explaining the habitat and habits of the bumble bee that the two-year-old tries to pull out of a foxglove. Training is about teaching children 'no' so that they don't put the poisonous digitalis leaves of the foxglove in their mouths, or so that they don't offend social conventions by their child-like inclinations to explore, to pick the flowers in hedgerows, public parks or other people's gardens. Training is establishing the rhythms and patterns of daily routines for health, hygiene, safety and for establishing codes of behaviour so that families can live together where each member's needs and rights are considered. For example, the rituals of bedtimes, naps and night-time sleep may be matters for training so that the whole family or day-care group can rest during siesta, or during the evening, or so that adults can alternate their other work with child education and care as a child sleeps in a nest basket, a crib, a back bundle supported by a wrapper, or a coach-built perambulator. Training is particular to the customs and conventions of each family.

So, if we take the definition of curriculum as identified in the introduction to this chapter, then in practice it becomes impossible to separate education, training and care. As an educator dresses a child they may discuss the woolly texture of her jersey (learning about the properties of different materials), or count the buttons on her shirt (numerical experiences contributing to basic mathematical concepts). While explaining about the bee's search for nectar to make honey (new knowledge for the child related to her previous experiences of eating honey for breakfast), the adult would also protect and care for the child by restraining her from clasping the bee for a closer inspection as well as training her not to pick or eat foxgloves.

Education, training and care are interrelated in:

- *All aspects of the child's development*, including emotional, cognitive, sexual, social, physical, moral, aesthetic, and the development of self-concept. All these aspects of the child's development demand nurturing, are complex and require 'maternal thinking' (Ruddick, 1989), or educators who are knowledgeable and reflective about the distinctive learning needs of the under threes.

- *All areas of learning and experience*. Children's knowledge and skills evolve from mathematical, moral, physical, scientific, spiritual, technological, aesthetic, creative, linguistic, literary, human and social early learning experiences (HMI, 1989).

(Watching the bumble bee in the foxglove was certainly an aesthetically rich experience. Watching the furry, round body bustle and delve into the cerise trumpet and listening to the intermittent buzzing of the tiny creature in the sunshine may well have been a formative sensory and aesthetic experience for the toddler. The child could also have had mathematical experiences and formed mathematical concepts as the bee's vertical movements are described by the adults. 'The bee is going up and down the stem to look in all the flowers.' These words could feed a child's emerging thinking about spatial awareness. The explanation of the bee's work could be classified as learning about the 'process of life'. Attainment Target 3, Level 1: 'Pupils should be able to label or name the external parts of the human body/plants, for example, arm, leg, flower, stem' (DES and Welsh Office, 1989). Obviously a formative scientific experience!)

- *All aspects of the child's play.* As children track the movements and reflective lights on a mobile, when they splash water, examine the tickle in their belly button, gaze at their own image in a mirror, manipulate play materials by sucking, banging, fitting, filling, emptying, piling, demolishing, poking, and pulling out all the contents of the kitchen drawer, their childminder's handbag or the 'Treasure Basket' in the day nursery which is overflowing with a range of household and natural objects (Goldschmied, 1987), so they learn. Each of these bits of play represents specific stages in the child's learning, and in their education.

A number of individuals and groups have identified distinctive curricula for the under fives, some with their own formats for assessing children's learning; for example, High/Scope Key Experiences (High/Scope, 1986); identifying patterns of play or 'schema' (Athey, 1990); others have identified 'subjects areas', 'topics', or 'processes'. For a summary, *see* Section 9 in *Making Assessment Work* (Drummond and Rouse, in preparation).

However, in this chapter we are concerned with the learning needs of children up to thirty-six months. Too many books and training materials bunch the needs of under fives together, but we must take care to perceive the needs of each child as unique, and to acknowledge that they have special learning needs at different stages in their development. Just as schools must ensure that the curriculum meets the needs of four-year-olds in reception classes, we must also take care to see that two-year-olds have particular materials and activities which support their stage of learning. Children's interests and abilities change rapidly during their first three years, and it is only through careful observation and with imaginative use of resources that it is possible to create the stimulating, inviting, purposeful activities that will offer children opportunities to concentrate, to discover and to achieve, and for us to celebrate their achievements.

Much has been written about the stages of 'normal development' or 'developmental milestones' and there are copious checklists to celebrate children's achievements, or in some cases to worry about the empty boxes with no ticks. However, all these lists are arbitrary, especially when applied to children's behaviour, play and development. Only the child's basic physical perceptions, functions and growth may be noted and checked out as universal conditions. All development must be observed in context. All milestones, normal development or 'ideal' behaviour are recognized in the context of the educator's values, beliefs, cultural and social expectations of particular families and social groups. There is nothing that children ought to do unless we decide it must be so. Why is it important that children learn to say 'thank you', or kiss their grandmother, or dress themselves, or eat with a spoon, or avert their gaze when an adult is talking? All these things are 'normal' or expected, or discouraged in some families. It is our duty to socialize children into our kinds of families and communities so that they may 'fit in'. But does it really matter if children learn to manage without nappies before they are three? Why must they learn to stack bricks or play pat-a-cake? What do we want our children to learn, to know, to be and to feel? The kind of education we envisage is rooted in our own childhoods and in our values and beliefs. Accepting this plurality will enrich our early childhood programmes as well as accord respect for the rights of individual children in particular families.

It will also be important to distinguish, theoretically at least, between the training of infants and the education of infants more clearly so that the latter can be examined in more detail.

Training is about fitting in with the family's customs, morals, manners and routines. It is learning to adopt the patterns of behaviour which promote 'peace in the home or group' and which is acceptable in supermarkets, restaurants, the mosque, grandma's garden and society in general. Until or unless society changes to become more tolerant of children and is able to revere and extol the state of childhood, then even very young children will have to learn some of these patterns of socialization. Of course, children should learn to be courteous and considerate, this learning is interrelated to education. The training and socialization of infants will continue to be the kernel of educators' discussions and a focus for their energies and imagination. There are many contradictions for an educator to ponder. When groups of practitioners talk about the children they 'train' there will be feelings of guilt, amusement, controversy, indignation, self-righteous superiority, crushing inadequacy, joy, despair, frustration and accomplishment. The debate is philosophical and personal. We must draw up a curriculum based on children's distinctive learning needs but we must constantly make decisions which involve moral dilemmas, which require knowledge about children's perceptions and cognitive learning structures, and which have no clear-cut answers.

We are at the beginning of a new era of exploration and understanding of how babies and toddlers learn, and more importantly how we can meet their learning needs. Most of the literature on early education has concentrated on three- to five-year-olds, but some new research and discussion is opening up new concepts of education for infants and is illuminating our understanding. At last, the focus of research is building on from earlier formal laboratory experiments (Bower, 1977; Papousek, 1969; Moore, 1975) and practice-based new 'research' in natural settings is beginning to identify the distinctive patterns of children's play and behaviour which will inform education practice. The work of Bower and others has long indicated that babies are cleverer than we might think. He concludes his fascinating and detailed scientific study of infant development by suggesting that this new knowledge can be used to 'judge what kind of inputs are appropriate or necessary' (Bower, 1977, p. 166).

It is the 'inputs' that we are interested in, not to raise a brighter baby, not because we think plenty of stimulation must be better, nor are we making the erroneous assumption that by identifying the distinctive learning needs of babies we shall be able to accelerate development. A faster rate of development does not necessarily guarantee a higher level of cognitive functioning in the long run as far as we know. Instead we want to indicate how imaginative provision of materials and developmentally focused and choreographed experiences can broaden and enrich development and facilitate newly emerging patterns of activity and thought in young children (Korner, 1989).

Chris Athey's *Extending Thought in Young Children* (1990) is a milestone in describing the continuum of education from birth to the primary school. This work describes the development of patterns or commonalities of action and thought in young children which she calls 'schemas'. Examples of continuity in education include: how the infant behaviours of looking and gazing can be the first steps to map-making in the nursery class; and how the spontaneous vertical and horizontal linear patterns made with bricks, beads or toy cars in a toddler's play are the 'connecting schema' (or thinking and playing by joining things together) which can lead in turn to tessellation, measuring and numerical concepts. The Athey ideology has indeed inspired many educators to develop their practice by 'spotting the schema' or patterns of play, behaviour and thinking in young children's activities. The adults then use their observations to make curricular plans, 'to feed the child's schema' with appropriate talk and play materials so that they may support and extend the child's play activity and thinking (*see* Chapters 5 and 9 in this book). This approach of observation and support for children's play has many possibilities for the curriculum of children under three.

Stroh and Robinson (1991), in their therapeutic work with children who show many signs of developmental delay, describe their educational approach of enabling children to 'learn-to-learn'. They do this in the context of a psychotherapeutic and child/family therapy process which does not lose sight of the child's emotional needs as well as attending to their learning needs. Their work is based on an optimistic belief in the creativity of individual children and on detailed observations of children's intrinsically motivated play which can be concentrated, intense, persistent and enjoyable. In a fascinating description of the case study of 'Jonathan', they demonstrate their theory of a 'Functional Learning approach within an integrated therapeutic programme':

> Out of a baby's unspecific body activity, patterns begin to emerge. These patterns of behaviour are what we call *learning tools* (placing, pairing, matching, sorting and so on). . . . There are no rules which dictate the development of these learning tools in sequential steps, rather, it is a development continuum.
> (Stroh and Robinson, 1991, p. 6)

They then go on to chart the development of learning tools from the fundamental tool of *placing* as exemplified by the nursing couple when the nipple is offered, *placed*, and accepted by the baby, to the continuous behaviours of pairing, matching, sorting, sequencing, piling and banging and scraping with a held object. The work of this team, based on the ideas of Dr Geoffry Waldon (to be published posthumously), offers insights into how young children learn-to-learn and may inform curricular decisions for many practitioners.

Indeed, the work of Elinor Goldschmied has built on this philosophy. In her work in creating early play and learning experiences for babies who are sitting up, but are not yet crawling or mobile, she has invented a 'Treasure Basket'. This is a sturdy basket overflowing with a range of household and natural objects. Goldschmied (1987) demonstrates with video material how babies explore, concentrate and use the materials for interaction with other children of the same age. The video has a riveting sequence of two babies having a turn-taking game, a 'conversational' type exchange, by handing objects from the basket to and fro to each other. This material clearly demonstrates the potential abilities of babies to be able to interact with their peers. Many parents, child care 'experts' and educators have underestimated the capabilities and possibilities for sophisticated social behaviour of infants when they have company, and when they are given stimulating, developmentally appropriate play materials. Goldschmied's work with sitting babies shows how children explore play objects of differing weights, textures, sizes, colours, tastes, temperatures and smells. They do this with their mouths, their eyes, and with the energy of their whole bodies from their groping, sucking lips to their toes curling with pleasure and concentration. Babies are shown to be using all their senses to learn about the properties of objects in the presence of their trusted adult.

When a child becomes mobile, but before language alters her pattern of thinking, a new challenge is presented to the educator. Goldschmeid in her paper on 'Heuristic Play' (in Rouse, 1991a) describes how children move on to think about what they can do with the play objects. They discover or reach an understanding of what they can do with things in their spontaneous play. In her practical paper she suggests the materials needed, and how and when to introduce them to children, as well as the role of the adult in an Heuristic Play session.

These ideas for curriculum development and those of other innovative educators must be the basis of further observation and research so that we can extend our knowledge of how the youngest children learn.

As the child develops language, her play alters. Instead of wanting to find out what she can do with an object, she will explore the object's function in the real world. She will want to join in with adults' activities, to assist and copy the real world. Next the children will imagine what their play objects will become, will begin to pretend and later to fantasize.

If we were to observe a child's play with an object, for example a chain, over the first thirty-six months, it is possible that a continuum of learning would emerge. At a few months old John will play with the chain by sucking it, shaking it, dropping it and banging it and so *discover what it is*. As a toddler John may fill up a cup with it, rattle it round in a tin, drop it down a cardboard tube, flap it on a tin tray, coil it into a match box or dangle it over the banisters *to see what he can do with it*. At a later stage, he will explore *what they really are for*. He will imitate the adults around him. He will pull the chain to unplug the bath and empty the water, he will fasten the gold chain round his neck like his mother and he will hang the dog's chain on the hook at the back of the kitchen door as Grandpa does. By the time John is two-years-old he will use his *imagination*. The chain may become a wriggly worm, a garden path for his Duplo people, or a pretend rope to moor his boats in the bath. Maybe the same chain will later become the links and ties he needs for his 'connecting schema'!

Such phases are not distinct or an invariant sequence of play behaviour. They overlap and are part of a continuum of learning. Some objects are used as real ones at the same time as other objects are used imaginatively to represent something else. Two-year-old Rosie sits on the bottom stair, a doll sitting on the stair behind, an old handbag beside her, a toy radio in front of her and a teething ring/rattle which happens to be round and have spokes clutched in her hands. She is driving to the shops with her little girl in the back seat. The bag is a real object being used in an imitative way, the radio and the doll are toys representing real things, but the rattle is a play object from earlier sensory/discovery learning phases which has now been transformed in the child's imagination to a steering wheel. Rosie's play is imitative and imaginative and reflects her own needs to understand events as well as to explore objects.

Each of these phases in play demands knowledgeable and understanding adults to sustain the children's explorations, their learning work, and their imagination. There is a whole new language evolving to help us to think about our observations and assessments of children's behaviour and play so that we can find new ways to develop a curriculum which meets the needs of children at each phase as they move rapidly through changing patterns of thinking and understanding. As educators plan for children's learning, whether they talk about 'learning tools', or Heuristic Play, or 'Sensory Motor Key Experiences' (High/Scope, 1986), or 'schemas', the important thing is to distinguish the learning phases and needs of babies and toddlers, and to continue to grapple, to find words to enable discussion (not to create barriers) and to talk and think together about the distinctive role of the early childhood educator.

CARING FOR THE EDUCATOR

Educators have the responsibility, the awesome power, and the challenging task of organizing learning opportunities for children. Each child is unique, and has individual needs as well as common developmental patterns of learning and development shared by all babies and toddlers.

The interactions between young children and educators are mutually enriching but are also demanding. Educators can support, extend and nourish children's development, or conversely thwart, stunt and damage children's beginnings; the beginning of their sense of self-worth, and the onset of their capabilities as confident learners. To minister to needy, vigorous, demanding infants is significant and worthwhile work. This work can be a pleasure, and may leave the adult satisfied and emotionally replete. Young children are sensuous creatures who drape and cuddle, who smile enchantingly and fit the contours of our ambitions to love and be of service to humanity! Conversely, young children are eternally demanding and can drain care-givers' physical strength, and can evaporate the best intentions of conscientious adults. The insistent and continuous greedy gobbling of infants into adult time, love and patience can empty an educator of energy and imagination.

Educators must also be responsible for their own psychological welfare. They are emotionally vulnerable, their work involves them in repeated cycles of relationships with and commitments to young children. The demands of children and of parents can drain the emotional and physical resources of the adults. If educators are to maintain the levels of communication and intimacy needed for effective practice, with both children and their families, then this commitment and involvement must be respected and cherished. The distinctive demands on educators of the under threes cannot be taken for granted if personnel are to sustain their health and well-being. The educators themselves have great needs for support in 'letting go'. They need time to reflect on their practice and to share concerns with colleagues. Such needs may be met through sensitive supervision and in-service training, or through mutual support meetings and networks. Working with young children is often isolated as well as demanding, and careful planning may be necessary to create times and spaces for refreshing and strengthening philosophy and practice (*see* Whalley, Chapter 9 of this book).

CONCLUSION

We must have the courage to insist on the best, not just an adequate quality of education and care with 'fit persons' for babies and toddlers. We need the vision to plan for whole human beings who have a clear and realistic personal identity whatever combination of cultural or religious background, racial origins, gender, ability or disability that may be. Children who know who they are will have the confidence to love and learn and communicate in a world of mathematical, scientific, aesthetic and technological experiences. Children who can collaborate and learn together in harmony with other people are likely to respect and value differences. Children who are able to have intimate responsive relationships with their significant adult will have better access to relevant early learning experiences. Children who play in inspirational, safe and challenging environments will take these values into adulthood and pass them on to future generations. An ethos of respect for and dignity in childhood may be set from the cradle.

9

WORKING AS A TEAM

Margy Whalley

The feeling of power and confidence achieved by powerless groups who challenge their ascribed position in society by acting collectively.

(Dominelli, 1990, p. 126)

INTRODUCTION

In this chapter I want to outline the belief system that underpins the way we have worked at Pen Green since it opened in 1983. I want to look at the structural and pedagogic implications of adopting a community development model. I want to show how we evaluate our work and ensure that what we are offering is a quality service that can respond to constantly changing community needs. I want to describe how we work with parents, volunteers and workers from other agencies and to look in some detail at our staff development programme and our in-service training. Above all I want to celebrate the many mistakes we made, mostly with good intentions, and to be clear that making mistakes has become a very important part of our learning process. Making mistakes implies that we have taken risks; taking risks assumes that staff have the self-confidence and the ability to make decisions and to take on personal responsibility. I want to encourage children, parents and under-fives workers to believe in themselves and to congratulate them on taking risks and taking charge of their own lives.

I am aware that being a strong, assertive, challenging child or parent, or under-fives worker, may not make for an easy life. The children who leave our community nursery have been described by one local teacher as having 'the Pen Green Syndrome'. This is an interesting psycho-social disorder which presents in four-year-olds going up to big school – children who are not interested in what their infant teacher has decided to put out for them, assertively or subversively (depending on your viewpoint), put it away and take out activities that they really want to do, maybe even something they had planned to do on the way to school. The Pen Green Syndrome manifests itself in parents who boycott or protest at governors meetings called at inconvenient times, or at parents' meetings that have no crèche facilities, or where they are asked to sit on little chairs. It manifests itself in staff who challenge the assumption that they can plan and develop quality work for children and families without the non-contact time that professional colleagues with older children assume.

THE BACKGROUND: A SEARCH FOR A CONCEPTUAL FRAMEWORK

The Pen Green Centre for Under Fives and Families was set up in 1983 in an empty comprehensive school on a 1930s estate. The Pen Green estate is made up of thirteen streets backing on to the now defunct steelworks. The houses were only separated from the blast furnaces by a railway and a sixty-foot strip of land.

The 'bad news' for those of us who set the Centre up in those early days, was that the closure of the local comprehensive school had been much resented by the local community. The proposed new 'pre-school centre' was viewed with a great deal of hostility by both local people and other professionals. The most active voluntary group locally was a Community Action Group which had strongly protested at the lack of consultation between local community and county council.

The two lead departments were social services and education and neither had a clear understanding of how the Centre would work in practice. The education department described it as an extended-day, year-round, nursery school with some parental involvement; social services saw it as a day nursery for referred children. Corby then and now has no local authority day nursery provision. The two departments had no shared conceptual framework or language and geographically Corby was very isolated from the administration in Northampton. The district health authority, which had contributed to the capital costs of the new centre, became immersed in a reorganization and was unable to contribute to running costs, but retained its policy and management role.

The 'good news' outweighed the bad and still does for those of us working in Corby. There was strong local political support for the new project and the steering group that had been set up had strong councillor support. The steering group was truly multi-disciplinary having representation from the LEA, social services, the health authority and voluntary groups in the community. This steering group visited a well-established combined centre in London, read the limited amount of research available on joint provision, and resolved to put all staff on the same conditions of service, since differentials in holidays and hours of work appeared to be a real block to a creative partnership.

Social services locally was organized on a patch basis and local social workers were working as community development workers in the local community association. They influenced the decision to make it a local community resource rather than a town-wide service. Since the closure of the steelworks, male unemployment in this patch was as high as 43 per cent and there was a good working relationship between agency workers and the local community group – a 'partnership in adversity'. Many of those parents involved in the action group against the centre had already been involved in local housing campaigns and were very ready to express their concerns about the nature of the proposed centre for under fives. They were clear that they did not want it to be a 'dumping ground for problem families'. This action group was critical to the development of the Pen Green Centre for Under Fives and Families. Several of its members became vociferous spokespeople *for* the new centre and used it on a daily basis.

Most significantly, some of these parents were involved in the initial recruitment of staff and these staff, as a consequence, felt directly accountable to them. All newly appointed staff then had between two and six months to work together while the alterations to the building were completed. Much of this time was spent walking the streets, getting to know local people and local resources and visiting other centres. Parents and staff remember that blissful period when everything was open to negotiation; when we had an empty nursery waiting to be filled. People were invited in and started using the centre whilst the concrete was still wet, and rooms undesignated. Staff who remember that period are thankful that time was spent in finding out what was needed rather than imposing a predetermined 'neat and tidy' plan. In the life of an establishment it is rare to get that kind of quality time.

RECRUITMENT AND STAFF DEVELOPMENT

What we started with in 1983 was a commitment to set up a community-based, multi-disciplinary centre. The brief included offering year-round nursery and day-care facilities with provision for an extended day, a service for supporting families and a health 'resource'. Contextually we were working in a socio-economically depressed community with an active and critical community group, and some very creative professional colleagues well accustomed to working co-operatively in adversity. Some of the structural obstacles to a creative team approach had been removed, such as differentials in conditions of service, but some still remained. Chief among these were the grossly differentiated pay-scales between care workers and teachers or field social workers; and the inappropriate pay-scales for key workers like secretaries, cooks and other support staff (mostly women).

Most of the research on combined provision emphasizes the difficulties experienced when integrating staff who have always focused on the needs of children in a care capacity and those who see themselves as educators. Our experience was very different. In the first place we were recruiting staff from many different sectors, not only from education and day care but also from social work, health and the voluntary sector. They had a vast range of different qualifications including CQSW, PPA Foundation course, PGCE, B.Ed, NNEB, SRN, etc., and they were accustomed to different styles of working and different models of supervision and support. The varied backgrounds of many of the staff (some qualified in more than one discipline, some with no formal qualifications but enormous amounts of experience in the private or voluntary sectors) meant that there was no simplistic polarization between education and care. All their different experiences informed our practice, and made it possible for us to set up an appropriately flexible management structure and support system for staff working in a challenging and innovative way. We tried to take the best from all the different models of supervision and support.

The critical difference between our centre and those that had been modified from already existing schools, day nurseries or children's centres, was that we could be clear at interview about what the job involved. Even our adverts were 'different' and usually required major debates and sanctions from whichever personnel department was handling them. One department found them so idiosyncratic that they refused to handle any of the process and left it entirely up to us.

Parents who have been involved in interviewing, over the years, have found it to be a fulfilling and challenging process. Some parents have even been motivated to make career decisions on the basis of interviewing others! Parents were not 'pre-selected' for interviewing so that applicants met many different members of the community: some shy, some assertive and some negative. Interviews were always informal and candidates were told that this would be the case. On some occasions interview panels were very unwieldy. My own interview was conducted by the two Chairmen of the Social Services and Education Committee and twelve other officers, employees and members of the community.

All posts are advertised as 'family worker' posts, a generic title which embraces those primarily working with children and those who are chiefly concerned with adults. Some posts are more senior than others but we do attempt to distribute the unpleasant and mundane jobs fairly evenly.

All family workers in the nursery have a responsibility for up to ten families and they are the link workers with those families, home visit them and keep developmental records on the children. With some families, family workers liaise with the statutory social worker, attend case conferences and attend court. No one undertakes this sort of work without support and/or training or feeling confident and competent to do it: the important point is that staff can choose to take on that level of responsibility where they are involved as the key worker. Family workers in the nursery are also given the opportunity to work directly with parents by offering one session a week as part of a group work programme, again with appropriate training and with a co-worker. Other family workers recruited to work primarily with parents are asked to spend time in the nursery, to home visit families and to play with the children at lunch time.

There was no assumption that a teaching or NNEB qualification implied any differentiation in the core family worker role. Teachers appointed to family worker posts needed to be prepared to take on additional responsibilities commensurate with their substantially higher salary and different training. The responsibility that an individual teacher was able to take on had to be negotiated on the basis of what skills and experience they brought with them. Clearly a probationary teacher, leaving a one-year PGCE course, would only have a very limited experience of curriculum planning and development; they might, however, have a strong specialism such as dance and music or some life experience that they wanted to offer.

All staff when appointed are given some time to get to know the different aspects of the centre's work. In the early years staff had an enormous amount of freedom to visit other centres all over England. Such visits are still encouraged and most staff, including ancillary and support staff and many parents, will have been to a variety of different types of centre within their first few years in the job. Most recently staff have visited early years provision in Italy.

It soon became apparent that since the majority of new staff came from a teaching or nursery nurse background, most had a vast range of experience with young children but felt less confident in working with adults. Having said this, all three senior staff in 1983 had either PGCE and CQSW or PGCE and extensive community work experience. Overall, staff tended not to come from either mainstream education or social services but rather from residential/special schools, child and family guidance, or community nurseries.

Table 9.1 Staff development programme

Timing	Content	Geared to
Stage 1 (during the first eighteen months)	Listening skills Counselling Family dynamics Home visiting Working with parents	Most relevant for NNEB, teaching staff and support staff volunteers
Stage 2	Assertiveness Group work Marital counselling Boundaries with co-workers	For all staff colleagues from other agencies working with adult groups
Annual programmes	Gender issues Race issues Violence First aid	All staff
Child focused (on-going)	Child psychology and child development Early years curriculum Working with troubled children Assessment Record keeping – an educational model Record keeping – a social work model Child abuse/child protection	As part of planned individual programmes/all nursery staff
Responding to new legislation (when it comes out)	NHS White Papers *Promoting Better Health, Working for Patients* National Curriculum Children Act	As appropriate
Training relating to co-operative working (on-going)	Working with other agencies Working with volunteers Management, team-building Supervision/appraisal	All staff

We quickly realized that no single qualification could provide all the skills and knowledge needed for working in this new way. We had an enormous skills bank to call on for our own in-service training but we also needed a comprehensive in-service rolling programme that staff could opt into on the basis of their level of confidence and competence. Some key areas of work had not been addressed in any initial training course and these were management and team-building skills and budgetary control. Some training needed to be on-going, some addressed current issues (such as the AIDS awareness programme in the mid-1980s). Table 9.1 gives a rough outline of our staff development programme.

We do not view staff development as an optional extra. It enables us to provide a quality service. As Professor Tomlinson said in an open lecture (1986), what we need are 'confident and secure professionals well trained in their own service who can co-operate and see the part to be played by other services'. I make no apologies for the inevitable reduction in the quality of services when staff are attending courses or taking time back for courses they have attended in their own time. In the long term, staff are enabled, through training, to feel confident in, and to challenge their own practice. They have no need to put up a front of so-called 'professionalism'. I also make no apologies for having spent so much of my time in the first five years setting up in-house training courses. Training was the carrot that kept us all motivated. When we felt out of our depth we could hold on to our sanity in the knowledge that we would attend a course or a study day and understand a little more. Training was also one concrete way of showing low-paid (women) workers and volunteers that they were valued and that they too had choices and career prospects. We rejected the traditional model of training whereby emotionally fraught teachers or burnt-out social workers were sent off on expensive secondments. We believe staff have the right to a properly structured staff development programme which involves training, supervision and support, the majority of which should take place in work time.

MANAGING SERVICES

What I have tried to do is give an impression of an environment where:

(1) decisions are made as a response to the expressed needs of the local community and not their assumed needs. When we have set up groups or activities because, as a staff group, we thought they were 'a good idea', they rarely took off. Our rather self-conscious health food pantry was a disaster.

(2) staff were given time to get to know the local neighbourhood and parents were invited in from the word go. Parents helped to make the decisions about room allocation, use of space and what equipment we needed to buy.

(3) parents were on the interview panels for all staff appointments – not only the parents who might have had the confidence to fight for a seat on the school governing body, but also parents who would not even attend parents evenings in mainstream school.

(4) staff needs are seen as central and staff working in a different way need a whole range of training courses and a lot of personal support. All staff are involved in team-building, and 'all staff' includes ancillary support staff whenever possible. They also needed to be given time in lieu of training.

(5) everyone is learning – children, staff and parents.

To enable all this to happen whilst maintaining an extended-day, year-round provision for up to 70 families in the community nursery and 300 plus families in the 'drop in', parents' groups and health facilities, involves a lot of organization and a healthy and committed staff who enjoy shared responsibility. When I was first appointed I misread the advert and thought when it stated all staff would be on the 'same conditions of service' it meant we would all have the same pay! My naïvety must be attributed to having worked overseas on multi-disciplinary pre-fives projects for over six years and having earned 'local wages'.

Clearly the pay structure at Pen Green implies some sort of hierarchy with teachers' salaries being the most advantageous. Whilst it is obvious that differentials in salary do affect how people perceive their role, it is even more important that people feel valued for what they are doing. It is fair to say that most of the staff had already experienced hierarchical work settings. They were attracted to posts at Pen Green because they wanted to take on more responsibility and wanted to see rigid inter-agency role definitions relaxed.

The management structure that we established involved a co-operative approach. In our first naïve attempts to work together we sometimes skirted uncomfortably around issues involving those who earned more and those who were willing to take on more; sometimes we confused democracy and accountability and team work seemed to imply no management at all. We also at times avoided dealing with the 80:20 factor that our management consultant highlighted for us, i.e. 20 per cent of the people in most organizations end up doing 80 per cent of the work! Once or twice we did recruit staff who, like many in the caring professions, hoped to 'find themselves' through helping others, who were ungrounded and demanded too much personal support; usually they did not stay long. Very occasionally we recruited staff who despite the extensive interview process really did not understand how hard (emotionally and physically) the work was and who found the job just did not give enough back. The majority of staff we recruited have managed to balance their personal and professional lives. Perhaps in the early days when we were struggling to empower traditionally passive low-paid under-fives workers and families who felt deskilled, we underestimated the need for senior staff to have time together to reflect on how they were working, set targets, and review progress on a regular basis.

Instead of a hierarchy we established a 'side-archy' (Whittacker) which allows staff to focus on their strengths. Even in the early days we saw conflict as healthy, and felt that anger and resentment were better expressed than stored. Staff who work with young children and families almost always see themselves (and are defined by others) as 'nurturers', but that does not mean they have to be 'nice' all the time. We have learned to recognize the fact that there is a manipulative and controlling part in all of us.

Staff meetings

In practice, then, we spent time in pairs or small groups visiting other centres and seeing how they worked, bringing back ideas and arguing over 'good practice'. Staff quickly realized that with the wide range of views and experience we had amassed, we needed to continue to carve out time for ourselves as a staff group even when the centre was fully operational. We had seen many different models in practice from hurried after-school staff meetings and lunch-time meetings in educational settings, to interminable and unfocused team meetings in social services establishments.

We decided that a mid-week break was the answer and this has been the pattern for eight years. Nursery education, day care and family work take place on Monday, Tuesday, Thursday and Friday, and Wednesday became a community morning. This meant we could offer a session to any family on the waiting list and to foster parents and childminders. Wednesday afternoon was set aside for staff development, team-building and sometimes training events. It was the one time in the week when staff could work together without interruption, with clear heads and lots of energy. Professional colleagues from the LEA and other local authority day nurseries looked on it with some suspicion. Some felt we were 'neglecting' the children's needs. In fact, nursery children were getting far more time and continuity in the nursery sessions we did offer which gave them the opportunity for extended uninterrupted play. Children and parents accept the weekend break and just as easily learned to accept the Wednesday afternoon break and welcomed the choices and flexibility we could offer them at other times.

Having fought for it, how did we use the time? Our initial staff group of six permanent staff (plus four support staff) met in one group for the whole afternoon. When numbers increased to around sixteen, it became important to split the time available so that staff could work in small groups, meeting as a whole group for a relatively short period for an information exchange, diary dates, and general business session. Staff spend most of the time in two groups; those primarily concerned with the nursery children and those mainly working with adults. Senior staff try and move between groups but the head of nursery spends all her time with the 'nursery groups' since they are planning and exploring the nursery curriculum. This is a fairly crude division of staff since all have concerns for and are involved in working with both adults and children. Both groups use part of the session to focus on 'people' issues like problematic staff relationships, people's feelings about their work and sometimes personal issues. The rest of the session is task oriented, sometimes with an agenda that has come from personal support sessions or management meetings, sometimes coming from individuals within the group.

Meetings are informal with a rotating 'chair' and a minute taker. Minutes are essential both to remind us of what we committed ourselves to, and for sharing information between groups and for staff who are on leave or attending courses. Over the years chairing the meeting has been a real issue and the structure of the meeting has changed many times. Most recently staff decided to vote for five or six staff who could run the meetings most effectively and this worked well for a time. There is always a real tension between getting tasks completed and giving time to individual members of staff who need to share difficult work situations. Sometimes the balance is wrong and we go round in circles or become self-indulgent; when it is working well a great deal gets achieved. Whatever happens it is almost always the most demanding and stressful session of the week! Because we were often working with large numbers of staff (up to twenty-eight at one time, including our community service volunteers and social work students) and because it seemed important to increase our awareness of each other's different work-loads, we set up a tradition of 'Not the staff meeting staff meetings'. The main agenda of these meetings, which were planned by small groups of staff who did not usually get the chance to work together, was team-building and fun and the learning was kept light.

Feedback from colleagues and trainers who have taken part in staff meetings has been amazement at the energy and diversity of views, and the assertiveness of even fairly new staff when working in small groups. We realize that this is quality non-contact time and we do not see it as a privilege but as an essential part of our staff development plan. One vital lesson we learned within the first few months was that parents did resent the closure, for one afternoon a week, of their new play facility. They also welcomed the opportunity, when the space was handed over to them, and some staff support was offered, to set up their own playgroup one afternoon a week. Parents who used the service the rest of the week became service providers on Wednesdays; they went on courses and from 1985 set up two playgroups offering sessions in the next-door building, five days a week for about sixty children.

Staff meetings have been discussed in some detail because that is where most ideas are generated or debated, where policies are revised and where staff share knowledge and give each other support. Other aspects of the management structure are shown in Figure 9.1.

Parents' meetings

Parents in the first two years were encouraged to attend the part of the main staff meeting where general issues were discussed. Some did attend and brought a friend along. It seemed important, however, that staff should have their own time.

It also seemed important for parents to have a meeting, preferably chaired by a parent, where they could give critical feedback, exchange views about what was going on in the centre and share information with staff. Access to the group which runs in the evening was made easier by the centre covering the cost of babysitting fees and by staff offering transport on winter nights. The meetings were always informal with coffee and wine. One regular attender would always arrive half an hour late and the meeting would have to stop for a five minute summary of *EastEnders* before business could be resumed. Most recently an evening crèche is on offer, for in the current climate of anxiety over child abuse many parents are reluctant to leave young children with babysitters even when babysitters are available.

Both because of the change in employment patterns and because some parents said they would find it easier to bring criticisms and share

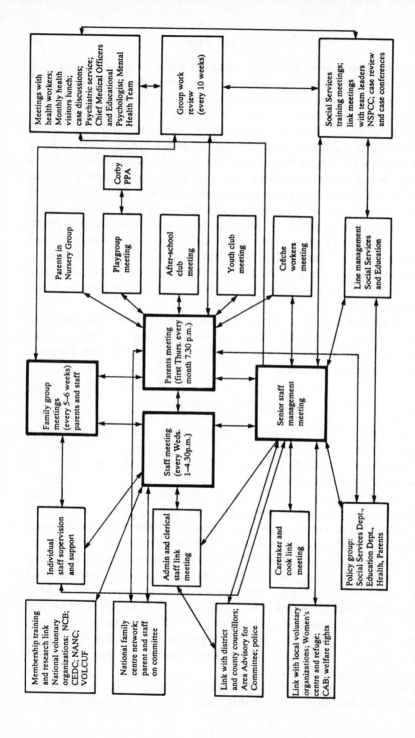

Figure 9.1 Towards communication, co-operation and collaboration: a management 'side-archy' and communication network (Pen Green 1991).

information in smaller family group meetings, these have now been set up during the day with a crèche. This gives parents an opportunity to discuss issues about their own child's education and care with other parents who share the same family worker. The family worker running the meeting is supported by a senior member of staff so that they can listen and get support during and afterwards, if the discussion has been difficult or painful. These meetings give parents a real opportunity both to understand how the centre works internally and how it is managed by the two lead departments and the policy group. Parents elect representatives to go from the family group meeting to the monthly parents' meeting. Two parents who attend this parents' meeting are then elected to represent all users on the policy group and in this way have a voice in the overall policy-making and management of the centre. The parents' meeting is primarily concerned with day-to-day events, staff appointments, training, social events, budgets, fund-raising and suggestions for the group work programme.

Sometimes it deals with more contentious issues. On two occasions the parents' meeting has formed itself into a community action group to protest at cuts in services and the possible closure of the adjacent building. On these occasions parents have become vociferous campaigners and have made many representations to the county council. Interestingly, parents who have been actively involved in the centre have moved on to become governors in the three local schools.

Staff support and supervision

At the same time as setting up staff groups and parents' groups to discuss central issues, we also looked around for the best possible model of supervision and support for individual members of staff. It would not have been possible for staff to remain open to criticism and to appraise their own work critically if they had not received consistent professional support. We set up a system where most staff receive supervision/support every three weeks from a senior member of staff. Senior staff then receive support from the Head of Centre who in turn has a monthly consultancy session with an external consultant (a lecturer in the University Social Work Department). This level of supervision is essential for staff working in centres for under fives and families which combine a social work and educative role. Clearly the LEA Inspectorate can offer curriculum advice, and senior officers from both lead departments fulfil the line management function, but what is needed additionally is a structure which addresses personal and professional issues. Problem areas such as leadership styles and personality clashes need to be discussed freely and confidentially. Time needs to be taken to give staff positive feedback, information on training, and careers advice. Supervision and support sessions need to be regular and uninterrupted. Ideas and problems that come up in supervision need to be appropriately fed back to management meetings and/or staff meetings. Staff have a right to this kind of support and it becomes a mechanism of quality control because it involves target-setting, goals and reviews. Staff may also need specialist support or outside consultants for particular pieces of work.

We have also adopted the social work model of taking time out for team-building and we spend two days each year away on a university campus with a trainer who has worked with us for four years. This is an important annual event and very hard work; the residental component was requested by staff so that they could combine self-development and team-building with a relaxing evening away from family and other pressures! Last year senior staff spent a weekend away on a management training weekend which proved to be very challenging and the management consultant was invited back to work with the staff team to great effect. Staff have made the request that this should also be an annual event roughly at the beginning of each school year and this has considerably enhanced our review process.

It may appear that staff spend most of their time being trained or in meetings. At Pen Green we have adopted a community development model of working with parents and children which involves planning, doing and reviewing at all stages and which aims at empowering not deskilling. To work in this way we need

> to be prepared to work with contradictions and confusions. It is not a field for people who like to be clear-cut, precise and polished...it is a field for compromise, negotiation, flexibility, sharing and a balance of conflicting interests.
>
> (Jordan, 1987, p. 36)

To achieve this we also need to work closely with other professional colleagues from other disciplines, so that we can develop a common philosophy and provide an effective service. To make this possible we share much of our in-house training with colleagues from health and social services, and with parent volunteers. (We pay for supply cover so that the playgroup staff can attend training sessions and meetings.) We try to avoid stereotyping and 'blaming' other agencies and we have gained an understanding of each other's management structures and the constraints that other agency workers experience through a programme of working lunches, reviews and seminars.

WHO BENEFITS?

Working as a team is a process not a technique. It is rooted in an ideology of empowerment, encouraging adults (whether parents or staff) to take control of their own lives and giving children permission to do the same.

Working as we do with parents and staff implies a different way of working with children and they are the beneficiaries both directly and indirectly. Instead of a fragmented service where children can be developmentally assessed twice in one day by different (well-meaning) professionals, where children's health, educational and social/welfare needs are kept separate, professionals and parents plan and work co-operatively. Instead of twenty different workers being 'involved' in the case of abused or neglected children and few making any impact, families can seek support from one or two people they self select and they can get it within their own community. In this way they are not pathologized. Instead of a perceived dichotomy between the needs of parents and the needs of children, where both end up fighting for recognition, there is an acceptance that they are equally important.

HOW DO WE KNOW WE HAVE ACHIEVED A QUALITY SERVICE?

I have outlined the forums we have set up for parents to express their views, and our own staff meetings and group work reviews give us a great deal of critical information on the service we provide. Parents evaluate all the groups they attend and staff who are well trained and properly supervised have learned how to take criticism and constantly review their own practice. Two examples are relevant here.

Example 1: Quality in the curriculum means parents and staff need to work together

Nursery staff spend many hours each week planning the nursery activities and assessing children's development. We believe it is critical that what we do is shared with parents and that parents have a great deal of the information that informs that process. Parents have always been encouraged to get involved in curriculum development, either through attendance at staff meetings, courses where parent volunteers and parent supply staff participate or through study groups. Several years ago staff were introduced to the concept of 'schema' (Athey, 1990 and Chapters 4 and 5 in this book) and have spent a great deal of their in-service training on increasing their understanding of the patterns in children's play. We had always based our curriculum on observations of children's interests and preoccupations but 'schema' gave us an intellectual framework and a helpful language to describe what we saw. Parents were involved in 'schema' training, and 'schema spotting' from the start, and were equally fascinated with the way we could all now reconcile bits of behaviour that had seemed random, or even counter-productive, with a cognitive structure. We were all equally impressed with how persistently children returned to *their* primary concerns (at home and at nursery) despite well-meaning staff trying to encourage them into more 'teacher-focused' activities. Staff and parents both gained from making videos and looking in some detail at their own children's behaviour, and then analysing it with the help of a very supportive early years consultant. Parents began to record observations on children at home and these observations were shared with staff and became the basis for planning for children in the nursery.

Now all new parents are encouraged to make observations after the initial home visit and are introduced to our ideas about curriculum development. The children's open files, which always contained records of work, home visits, and staff observations, have been transformed into rather splendid folders emblazoned with 'A record of my achievement'. These folders contain material from home and nursery. In our experience all parents, even where there has been child neglect or child abuse, care passionately about their children's development and are keen to collaborate.

This curriculum programme has moved a stage further with the advent of the National Curriculum and the important task of establishing nursery children's right to a curriculum that is not 'pre' anything but has intrinsic value. Nursery staff were reluctant to become familiar with unwieldy National Curriculum documents but when these were made more accessible, took pleasure in mastering the language of attainment targets and levels of achievement. Our new assessment 'pack' links National Curriculum objectives with our nursery objectives as simply as possible. Interestingly when this was shared with parents it was an after-school-club parent volunteer who expressed anxieties about the dangers of an over-rigid curriculum being imposed on young children. The same parent expressed concerns about other parents feeling the need to push children too hard. We concluded that for staff and parents simply having all the information in an accessible form was empowering. Perhaps most important for parents was the fact that staff recognized their enormous contribution to their own child's development and their key role in their children's learning.

Example 2: Information sharing between all those working with young children

Like most nurseries and day nurseries, more than half the children at Pen Green will have been referred because of emotional or social factors. Many of the referrals are linked to families living in poverty, or experiencing great stress, and some to actual child abuse. Whilst we strongly believe that all children whatever their socio-economic background have equal rights to a demanding and stimulating nursery curriculum, they also need an environment where emotional wounds can be licked and comfort given. As in the Italian nurseries which some of us were privileged to visit, we do not see our role as 'mother substitutes' and children are encouraged to help each other and get support from their peers. We do, however, feel that all children need someone who believes they are special and the family worker becomes very involved in the emotional and physical needs of the children in his or her family group.

Other workers and many of our support staff have been the 'special person' for children who perhaps find the warmth and comfort of the kitchen essential in their transition from home to nursery. Office staff and domestic staff have befriended children and to do that effectively have needed to have information shared with them. One example of this was when parents and some ancillary staff had real difficulties in accepting one small boy's need to dress up persistently in women's clothes. By this I do not mean occasionally appearing in the home corner in a hat or tutu but more a ritual change of clothes which was linked with lots of other bits of emotionally obsessive behaviour. Boys wearing 'girls' clothes has often been a problem for parents and we have worked hard on gender awareness issues in all possible forums. On this occasion *all* staff needed to know that the emotionally charged behaviour they were seeing was that of a child who was in and out of care. Clearly ancillary and support workers need to be bound by the same code of confidentiality that all staff work under. What is intolerable for them is trying to be caring and committed without understanding the context. We attribute much of the emotional GBH that children endure on school playgrounds to the fact that for most dinner supervisors it has to be the most unrewarding job in the world and they may not have any knowledge of where the children are 'coming from'.

Sometimes there is a simple explanation for children who display extremes of behaviour, but we just may not have the information. One parent who lived in a hostel had an only child, a three-year-old, who seemed very angry and wild and was demanding enormous amounts of staff attention. The family worker's visits were often the only ones the parent received and she welcomed the opportunity of working more closely with a member of staff. On one occasion she shared the information that a former boyfriend had offered to babysit her little boy while she worked. She made the discovery some months later that his idea of babysitting was to pick up her child from nursery and lock him in a cupboard under the stairs. She promptly dealt with the boyfriend and kicked him out. Her child's behaviour was then so much more understandable, and without the information our nursery response might well have been far from adequate.

WHAT ABOUT THE FUTURE?

We have survived cuts in services and enormous changes in legislation by constantly going back to the community users and asking what is most important to them; and by asking ourselves, 'is what we are doing "good enough"?'

We had a two-day closure and review of services this year when staff offered all-day crèche facilities so that as wide a representation as possible of our 300 plus users could come in at different times. The aim was to discuss what we could hold on to with a cut in staffing and what had to go. All the sessions were very well attended. We recorded all the passionate arguments that were made by parents, each fighting to maintain the corner of the service that was most relevant to them! Some were concerned with maintaining maximum flexibility in the nursery, others with retaining after-school provision for five- to eleven-year-olds or groups for parents. Symbolically, at the end of each session, parents and staff were given gas-filled balloons on which they wrote messages. Some gave the balloons to staff to keep, some sent them off with angry or poignant messages. This review marked an ending but was also a celebration of the future. It was also enormously helpful for our staff learning curve. The temptation for staff had been to try to be paternalistic and protect parents and children from the reality of the cuts and this was not helpful. Parents who use a service, value it and feel some ownership of it will probably want to fight for it when times are hard. With the kind of framework I have described it is possible for staff, parents and children to take risks and to take responsibility for services. This chapter started with a quotation from Lena Dominelli about powerless groups challenging their position in society. Parents (principally women) and children are, I believe, under-valued and often feel powerless. Working collectively there is nothing that they cannot achieve.

10

WORKING WITH PARENTS

Dorit Braun

This chapter will examine why working with parents should be an integral part of early years provision. Conventional wisdom in early years work suggests that parental involvement is 'a good thing' − this chapter will look at why this is, and at what it means in practice.

WHY INVOLVE PARENTS?

There is a wide body of literature which examines the thinking behind parental involvement. Tizard *et al.* (1981) explore the different debates surrounding parental involvement; Bastiani (1989) has written about why and how parents can be involved in schools; Edwards and Redfern (1988) outline the history and trace the evolution of involvement in the primary school; while Wolfendale (1983) provides a comprehensive guide to the rationale for involvement in a wide range of settings. Much of the literature traces the development of educational research, policy and legislation, and presents parental involvement as a concept to be developed by institutions. In thinking about why it matters to involve parents it is perhaps more helpful to step outside the confines of an institution and into the world of parents and families (e.g. Mayall, 1990; Atkin, Bastiani and Goode, 1988). It is an obvious truism that parents are the prime educators of their children. Of course, they are also their prime carers − and usually do not distinguish between these functions. Parents look after children from birth − some might say conception − and once they start nursery or school they continue to spend more time with their parents than with nursery staff. Yet for many who work with young children this truism is often seen as a problem. This is especially the case if parents differ in class or culture from nursery staff. Parents are sometimes seen by workers to inculcate their children with the 'wrong' attitudes, or are felt not to have prepared them adequately for nursery. Parents are seen to have failed to provide adequate stimulation, to have failed to promote language development, and generally to have a limited understanding of child development or of their child's needs. Thus, workers may feel that parents do not adequately care for or educate their children.

There is a failure to recognize just how much parents do in fact achieve for their children; and to recognize how much children do learn from everyday events and experiences without necessarily being provided with planned and structured learning activities. Tizard and Hughes (1984) have shown how this is the case for language development, while Mayall (1986) has shown how this is true in the case of health work.

This lack of recognition is not confined to workers. Parents of all social classes seem to share feelings of inadequacy in relation to the work they do on their children's behalf. Workers and parents often reinforce the sense of failure and inadequacy. From the workers' perspective, however, they are stuck with the influence of the parent on the child – whether they regard this influence as good, bad or indifferent, its existence cannot be denied, and it is the most powerful force in shaping a child in the early years.

To illustrate this powerful influence, think of a three-year-old child. Think of all the things she can do – talk, walk, use the toilet, eat unaided, run, express emotions – the list could go on and on. Think of all the things she knows – about time, about money, about people and places, about life. Most of these things have been learned in and around the home, with the love, support and instruction of her parents. Moreover, all these bits of learning, skills and experience cross the boundaries of education, health and care. Parents, along with other family members, are unpaid health workers, teachers and carers for their children. Mayall (1990) discusses an illustration of how this is true for health work, and shows how parents' perceptions differ sharply from those of health professionals.

Parents have the highest aspirations for their children although they may lack information and resources to ensure that these aspirations are met. Parents care very much about what happens to their children, and want to do their best for their children. How they interpret this will of course vary – to some extent these variations will reflect class, ethnic origin and culture — but there will be a lot of variety within any particular social grouping because of individual and family differences.

Thus, whatever a worker's opinion of the adequacy of a child's home life, many achievements have been made by the parents. Moreover, to the child, home is familiar, and in this sense, whatever its shortcomings, it is secure. For workers, it may be hard to acknowledge this security when working with children identified as 'at risk'. Within social work, the move away from day nurseries to family centres is an acknowledgement of the need to support parents in their child-rearing. Yet if workers do not believe in the work parents are doing with their children, how do they provide support? And if workers have the power to recommend that a child be taken into care, is it possible to develop a partnership of equals between parents and workers? This can only be achieved if workers do believe in parents, are willing to learn from them, and to offer them a wide range of support as suggested by parents themselves. This requires honesty between workers and parents and a recognition that even in cases of child abuse, parents will want the best outcome for their child. Such relationships are often developed in the voluntary sector, but are also possible in statutory services (*see*, for example, Braun, 1990, for a discussion of work at Hillfields Nursery Centre, Coventry).

When a child goes to nursery, or playgroup, or to a childminder, or crèche, she will feel more confident and secure if she feels that her parents are confident with the setting and if staff clearly respect her home and family. If these conditions are not met children may react in various ways, depending on their individual characteristics. They might cling to their parents, they might be defiant to their parents, they might be defiant and difficult with staff or other children, they might become withdrawn — they might simply accept it as how things are at nursery and separate home and nursery in their minds. None of these reactions are acceptable if we believe in doing our best by all children and in helping them all achieve their full potential. To do this we have to value and respect their home, and we have to help parents feel confident and comfortable with us and with our work. This is documented in research, for example by Woodhead (1985) who reviewed the implications of US early years programmes for Britain, and suggested that the involvement of parents improved children's performance, led to higher teacher expectations, increased children's motivation and increased parents' confidence and aspirations.

Thus, we have to work with parents in order to achieve our aims with children. But what does working with parents actually mean?

A number of possibilities can be found in the literature and in practice, but before we examine these it is important to clarify whom we mean by parents. Bearing in mind that the reasons for needing to work with parents lie in their role as prime carers and educators, it is perhaps not surprising that in much of the literature and of the practice, 'parents' is often synonymous with 'mothers'. In our society it is, after all, mothers who most frequently take the role of chief carer. But not always, and often not exclusively.

Partners may be involved, as may members of the extended family, or childminders, and others employed to care for small children. In terms of early years settings, it is important to think of parents in as wide a sense as possible, in order to maximize the opportunities to link home and nursery. If it is assumed parent means mother, this may exclude mothers in paid employment, grandparents, fathers and all the other people who may be closely involved with a child — and may in fact be the link person between home and the early years setting. Therefore, it may be more helpful to think about involving 'families' rather than 'parents'. In this chapter, both terms will be used.

WHAT DOES IT MEAN TO INVOLVE FAMILIES?

Families can be involved in a variety of ways in early years settings. For example:

(1) there might be space set aside, such as a parents' room where parents can meet or drop in for a chat to one another;
(2) parents or other family members might be used as helpers — in regular group activities, or less regularly, on trips;
(3) specific provision might be made, e.g. parent and toddler group or parenting groups aimed to support parents in their role;
(4) particular attention might be focused on communications at the beginning and end of a session, when families are leaving and then collecting their children;
(5) parents can be involved in the management of a service, through membership of its governing body or management committee.

These and other examples have been documented by Pugh *et al.* (1987) and Pugh and De'Ath (1989), while McConkey (1985) provides accessible and practical ideas about how to set up a range of work with parents.

Underlying each kind of provision will be staff values and attitudes about families and why they should be involved. Staff who feel that parents are ignorant about their children's needs, who feel that families and children with whom they work are 'socially disadvantaged', may set up provision in order to compensate for such 'disadvantages'. Such values can, however, be problematic. Do the parents feel 'disadvantaged'? In what senses? Using this compensatory notion as a starting point fails to build on the strengths that all families have, and may cause sharp conflicts of values between staff and parents — particularly as staff's expectations of how parents should be may be at odds with most of the parents' views, because of class and cultural differences.

Where parents feel they are being involved as a result of staff's desire to compensate, they are likely to feel devalued, and at times resentful. Parents may themselves have had difficult experiences of school, or may be unfamiliar with early years settings in Britain. So they may feel anxious and suspicious to start with. Any hint by the staff that they are not valued will be picked up very quickly.

A more helpful starting point is respect, where staff do not make assumptions about the neighbourhood or about individual parents, but base relationships with families on an explicit recognition that they share a concern — the welfare of the child — and that each person brings different skills and experiences to that task. This view is, of course, that on which the notion of partnership with parents is based. Recent literature has argued the case for partnership and has shown how hard it is to find in practice (Pugh and De'Ath, 1989; Bastiani, 1989). It is important to recognize that staff attitudes and values will influence whether parental involvement feels like a partnership to the parents. Thus, with any work undertaken to involve parents, staff will need to ask themselves how they view the parents and their potential gain from the involvement.

IS 'WORKING WITH PARENTS' THE SAME AS 'PARENTAL INVOLVEMENT'?

These terms have been used co-terminously and yet there are significant differences. 'Parental involvement' means that staff find and create opportunities for parents to be involved in various ways. 'Working with parents' is a much broader term, and implies an attitude to parents based on mutual respect. 'Working with' can include all manner of very informal links, taking advantage of opportunities as they arise (and not necessarily planning them), as well as joint planned activities between parents and staff.

In practice, involvement has often meant the physical presence of parents on site. Yet many parents find it difficult to get involved in activities provided by the nursery. They may have other family commitments, or paid employment, or be uncomfortable in the setting, or be ill-at-ease in English. Staff often confuse this lack of attendance with a lack of interest by parents, but all the evidence contradicts this (e.g. NCC, 1986). Parents are interested in what happens to their children, and if they are unable to be involved in activities provided by the nursery then the nursery needs to find ways of working on the informal links.

Working with parents encourages a more flexible approach, which can build on the opportunities that exist. Thus, the beginning and end of sessions will be very significant times; communications home will be crucial; providing a variety of ways and times parents can communicate with the nursery will be vital — and all these things will be seen to be part of the overall explicit policy of work with parents.

Where nurseries make the most of the informal opportunities to work with families they greatly increase the numbers of parents whose views are heard. This may not be very comfortable, because parents are not a homogeneous group, and will have different — and sometimes conflicting — views and ideas. This is where the notions of mutual respect and of a partnership of equals become crucial. Working with parents is not simply about parents learning about and supporting the values of the nursery. Nor is it about nurseries learning about and adopting parents' values — even if this were possible. It is about recognizing that the partnership is needed in order to benefit the child; that both partners bring equal but different skills to the task; and that both need to listen, learn, and change accordingly. Parents have a detailed and intimate knowledge of their child; staff know about children and their development. Both sets of skills and knowledge are vital for each child to achieve her full potential.

Unfortunately, in many settings, parents come to the partnership relatively powerless. This is most likely to be the case where the child has a place because of a referral, or because they meet a set of criteria which are about social disadvantage (e.g. single parent, low income, high-rise housing). But even where children have a place based on an entitlement to the service, parents may still feel they have little control over the situation. This means that for the partnership to work, staff need to make efforts to build relationships and to value what the parents bring and who they are.

The following section of this chapter describes some examples of how this has been done. Here, it is important to point out that work with parents is likely to have a cyclical as well as a developmental nature. When children first come to the nursery, staff need to focus on developing relationships; finding out what opportunities could be provided for involvement and learning about the parents and children – by listening to them. Then, opportunities can be provided, joint activities undertaken and new ideas for involvement will emerge as a result. When new children start, the cycle starts again – but several cycles may be operating at any one time with 'older' and 'newer' parents. In this sense working with parents is more about the process of working than about specific types of provision.

However, a word of caution may be important here. Working with parents sometimes assumes a life of its own, where all sorts of activities take place, and their links to the welfare of children become tenuous. This may not matter, if the nursery seeks to provide opportunities for adult and community education in addition to being a nursery. But if this is not its aim, then the question needs to be asked – how will this benefit the children? It has often been assumed that anything that you do with parents is good for children – that if you promote the well-being of parents, this automatically results in children who are better cared for. Most practitioners know that this cannot always be assumed. Sometimes, the well-being of a parent is in direct conflict with the needs of a child; for example, in some cases where parents are separating or divorcing. This is not to argue that all work with parents has to have an obvious link with their children's education or care, but it needs to be linked to their children, and to their aspirations for their children.

Some nurseries have staff whose specific role is to work with parents. It can be a huge advantage if someone has the time to build good relationships, and develop provision based on the needs that emerge. However, all staff should have a responsibility to work with parents – and particularly with those parents whose children are in their direct care.

In summary, then, working with parents in the early years is a process of getting to know, and learning from, parents and children in order to share effectively the responsibility for the child's development between parent and worker. There has, of course, been a considerable volume of legislation which demands that institutions work with parents as clients or consumers of services. Given that early years provision can occur in a wide variety of settings, workers are likely to be affected in some degree by all the major legislation relating to services – the Children Act, the Education Reform Act, and the changes in the health service.

The notion of parents as consumers of services for children is slightly misleading, since it can be argued that children are the consumers. However, working with parents is not a good thing because the legislation says so, but because it is good for children. The fact that legislation supports this is to be welcomed, but should not confuse the issue. Parents and workers need to work in partnership to ensure the welfare of children and to ensure that each child achieves her full potential.

It is clear, therefore, that nurseries need to develop explicit policies for their work with parents, so that the whole process can be effectively managed and supported. Such policies need to be shared with all staff and all parents. They need to state:

(1) why the nursery believes in working with parents;
(2) the formal and informal aspects of work with parents that the nursery intends to develop;
(3) the responsibility for work with parents (clearly it belongs to all staff, but someone may have a specific responsibility also);
(4) how the work with parents will be evaluated (which needs to include ways of getting feedback from parents and should include some indicators of success). Bastiani's (1989) work provides more detailed discussion of the development of whole-school policy, much of which is relevant to early years settings.

Having an explicit policy provides guidance for everyone and a way of containing and negotiating the work developed, so that provision is not a whim, but fits into the policy — and if it does not, then either the policy needs to be revised, or the provision may not be appropriate.

SOME EXAMPLES FROM PRACTICE

Much of the work described in the literature is about initiatives which meet the nursery's agenda of concerns they wish to raise with or share with parents. The work described below took a different starting point — to try to learn from parents about their concerns, and examine what those concerns meant for practice.

The first example is of a women's group, set up by a nursery class attached to a primary school. This group, the 'Spon Gate Mums' Group', arose out of a four-session course on the 'Highs and Lows of Parenthood' which was offered by the nursery as a way of supporting parents in their parenting, and learning from them about the issues and concerns they had. The work has been written up in a report (Braun, 1987) which analyses what happened in the group. One of the interesting by-products of this group was that the women identified that it had increased their confidence, and that this in turn had enabled them to become more involved in their children's schooling. From the nursery's point of view, it was a way of building relationships based on mutual respect and mutual support, and many group members became actively involved in aspects of the nursery as a result of being in the group. One of the difficulties, however, was to stop the group becoming a clique, which new parents found hard to join. This will be a familiar problem to most practitioners. It highlights the need for a paid worker to have the time available to support a group's development at various key stages, such as the beginning of the nursery year. This worker need not necessarily be from the staff of the nursery — it could be someone from another agency who sees this kind of support as an important part of their work. Health visitors and school nurses are both concerned with health promotion and often see parent groups as being one useful way to support their work with families. Some social work departments have community workers who may see this as being part of their role. Adult education services and adult basic education might be willing to take a role. In the case of the 'Spon Gate Mums' Group', some support was provided through the local community education project.

To make effective use of other available agencies requires time — to get to know who they are and what their objectives are, and to work out the ways of working together. However, time spent on this can mean a lot of time saved in the long run as agencies in a locality start to work together, pool resources and use their specialist skills effectively. Nurseries usually have very little available staff time, but can often create space, if someone else can provide the time.

In the example of the Spon Gate Mums' Group, the four-week course resulted in a demand to continue to meet once the course had ended. Members of the group took responsibility for running different sessions, planned them, researched them, structured learning activities, and provided opportunities for everyone to join in. There was a lot of support for individuals between sessions and many firm friendships developed. This meant, however, that people were often reluctant to allow new members to join the group. Since they had no responsibility for the group, or its relationship with the nursery, the school and the other parents, this was fair enough. Someone else needed to have this responsibility as part of their work, and to see it in the context of the overall policy for work with parents.

The second example is perhaps one which is easier to adapt and take on in other settings. It relates to a piece of work about children's perceptions of health and illness, which was undertaken in order to inform curriculum planning for health education (Combes and Braun, 1989). In recognition of the role that parents take as health carers and educators, this project invited parents of the children involved in the study to a short meeting at their school. The children were aged five to six and eight to nine. Meetings were held during the day and repeated in the evening where possible, to allow parents to come when it suited them. They were for two hours and some parents took time off work or rearranged work commitments to allow them to come. Men and women, parents and grandparents attended these meetings. Refreshments were provided, along with toys, and the invitations made it clear that babies and toddlers could come along. Invitations were translated into community languages. Parents were invited to look at their children's work, hear about the work that had been done with children and discuss their views on it. Parents were very interested in looking at what their children had done — the children's work was displayed around a room, and asking parents to walk around and look at the displays was a good ice-breaker.

Parents had a great deal to say about their own health work, and it was clear that they saw themselves as primarily responsible for the health of their children. At the same time they welcomed the support that school or nursery could provide.

The third example is similar, but relates to accident prevention work. Here, nursery children were involved in a project to look at their ideas of safety, and parents were invited to look at the children's work and talk about their concerns (Combes, 1991). Again, these were short meetings, with invitations in relevant languages. In this project, photographs were taken showing the children working, and in one case a video was made. Again, parents saw themselves as having prime responsibility for safety, but welcomed the support of nursery staff. They also welcomed the opportunity to talk to each other about some of the feelings they had when their children had accidents, and about the kind of support they wanted from the health professionals. As in the previous example, parents and grandparents of both sexes attended these sessions.

These last two examples could be adapted for use in various activities which many early years settings already organize, such as open days, or consultation sessions, or meetings about aspects of the curriculum. We particularly recommend having photographs showing the children at work, or even better, a video. This gives parents access to their child's experience of the nursery, and is very enjoyable. Video cameras can sometimes be borrowed from education development centres, or community projects. In some places parents themselves have attended courses to learn how to use a video camera and how to edit a film, and have taken videos to show to other parents — and sometimes to nursery and early years workers as part of their in-service training.

I want now to discuss less positive experiences. In the process of developing a pack of materials for use by and in parents' groups (Development Education Centre, 1991) we set up a number of occasions to consult with people who work with parents and run parents' groups. In these meetings it sometimes seemed to be the case that workers run groups not only for the schools' needs, but for their own needs – the need to be needed. Workers were sometimes very protective of what 'my parents could cope with'. This raises the very fundamental question of respect for parents, but it also raises the question of ownership. Workers frequently speak of 'my parents' or 'my children'. This is quite incorrect – people do not belong to anyone but themselves. Workers have no right to appropriate anyone who uses their service, nor do they have the right to patronize people by making everything simplistic. People live in the real world. They know that life is complex, difficult and confusing. It does them no favours to pretend that this is not the case. Indeed, the acknowledgement that life can be tough and some honesty about this can be very helpful for people who are experiencing stresses of some kind. In developing that piece of work we were reminded that far from 'empowering' parents, workers sometimes reinforce parents' sense of failure and lack of confidence in themselves as people and as parents. And because workers are relatively powerful in relation to parents, the effect they can have can be very destructive. The other side of this is that a relationship based on respect which does empower parents can have a very positive and long-lasting impact on parents and children, as Margy Whalley discusses in Chapter 9.

It is clear from the examples above that workers' attitudes to parents, and their values about child-rearing, are of critical importance. Yet workers have very few opportunities to reflect on their attitudes and values, to compare these with those of their colleagues, and to consider how these affect their relationships with parents and children. Moreover, workers have been trained to work with children, and have almost no training which might equip them to work with adults. This is not to say that training is a requirement for working with adults, but that practice and confidence are important, as are some specific skills. Some people relate very well to children but find adults more difficult. They will need support to feel comfortable and confident and will also need boundaries to what they are expected to do with parents, so that they do not feel overwhelmed by this aspect of their work.

OUTCOMES OF WORK WITH PARENTS
For parents

In all the examples outlined here, parents felt valued by the nursery or school. They felt their ideas and opinions were being sought, and this increased their confidence in relation to workers. In the groups run for parents, their increased support networks helped them gain support with the daily chores of parenting, and to do this in less isolated circumstances. In addition, they gained ideas and information about a range of topics related to child-rearing – and these ideas were relevant and practicable because they came from each other. Parents who were involved in the groups based in schools found it easier to get more involved in the school, and to contribute to it. In the shorter meetings, parents enjoyed the chance of having an insight into the life of their child at nursery, appreciated being asked for their ideas and opinions, and were better able to support their child's work in some specific aspects of the curriculum.

For children

It is, of course, very difficult to be as sure of the outcomes for young children because, quite rightly, they do not isolate specific pieces of work with parents as being of any special significance, especially in settings where this is the norm. However, one can surmise that parents who feel more confident generally, and who feel valued by the nursery, will be better placed to support their own children in the nursery. Children see the links between home and nursery, and see adults in both settings working together. As significantly, the work the children are involved in can reflect shared knowledge and understanding of home life and nursery life. It can build on what children already know and relate to the realities of their experiences in a way which is positive and affirming.

For workers

Working with parents provides essential insights and information about individual children. It provides insights into what they can do, and what they know, and how they think. This information is vital for planning the curriculum, and for forming caring relationships with children. Working with parents also provides workers with sources of help, of friendship and of support – but also of challenge and a constant need to review and rethink approaches. It ensures that no one and no place becomes static and complacent, but that things change to meet changing people, circumstances and needs.

THE BASIC PRINCIPLES

Some key threads run through the examples outlined here, which need to be drawn out. First, and most important, each of these pieces of work started by wanting to learn from parents, and set up a structure to ensure that parents felt welcome, relaxed and valued. In this context, it is important to remember that refreshments are crucial, as are adult-sized chairs, toys for small children, and a relaxed attitude by staff. Second, and probably of equal importance, was that staff were prepared to be people first and workers second. Thus, for example, in the mums' group the nursery teacher spoke very openly of the difficulties she was having with her own small child. These personal stories can be turning points in work with parents, because they stress the common ground between staff and parents, instead of emphasizing the power differences. A third thread is that staff were interested in hearing what parents thought, and in encouraging them to debate and discuss their ideas. These debates ensure that everyone recognizes the complexities, and that everyone can learn together by exchanging ideas and clarifying their own thinking. This process provides a basis for negotiation between parents, and between staff and parents.

This negotiation is, of course, of critical importance for partnership to become a reality. Parents' views are not all the same, and their values may conflict with those of the teacher or those of the school. Equal opportunities issues are the classic example of this. For example, Walkerdine and Lucey (1989) reviewed all the types of exchanges between mothers and daughters that had formed the basis of Tizard and Hughes' (1984) work, to show how mothers taught their daughters about gender, and about the role of women in a quite traditional sense. Yet most early years establishments have explicit equal opportunities policies that try to challenge traditional assumptions about gender; these may go against what parents actually do and perhaps also against what they want for their children. Similarly, some parents may hold views which are racist, or they may discriminate against people with disabilities. Workers need to discuss the nursery's policy with parents and to provide opportunities for them to reflect on their own values and how those fit or do not fit with those of the nursery. There may well be room for manoeuvre and negotiation by nursery and parents — about how policies work in practice, why they matter, how they can support or undermine them, and vice versa. Indeed, for many families their direct experience of discrimination will mean that their thinking may be very helpful to the development of equal opportunities practices in any early years setting.

In essence, each of the practical examples described above started by wanting to understand how parents saw a particular issue. This is in stark contrast to most of the examples which can be found in the literature where the nursery's or school's starting point is the desire to provide information or improve parenting. Yet these two aims are not incompatible. Indeed, parents usually welcome information and insights offered by the school, but these only make sense to parents if they are provided in a context and conceptual framework. And we cannot assume that we know parents' conceptual frameworks – particularly when parents have a culture, ethnic origin or language identity which is not shared with staff. Ways therefore need to be found of asking parents how they understand issues, and of building on and valuing their interest in and concern for their child.

CONCLUSIONS

Much of this chapter has hinged on the importance of workers' attitudes and values. Clearly, opportunities for staff development and training around work with parents is therefore of major importance. Workers need opportunities to reflect on their practice, to review their values, and to consider the impact of these on their work. More than this, they need to re-examine their professional role, and consider how work with parents could meet their aims. In summary, workers need staff development opportunities which will allow them to:

(1) explore their own attitudes and values about parenting and child-rearing;
(2) consider issues of class, ethnicity and culture and how these shape values about parenting and aspirations for children;
(3) develop skills in working with adults;
(4) examine how working with families fits with their own role, and with the role of their agency.

However, the way parents relate to a service is also influenced by how they got access to it in the first place. Where provision is on the basis of entitlement – or, perhaps more realistically in the current climate, on the basis of first come first served – they at least start off with the possibility of establishing an equal relationship with staff. Where a place is obtained because of a referral, or because they meet 'in need' criteria, parents may feel stigmatized at the outset. Yet parents freely acknowledge that 'prevention is better than cure', and welcome the support that all forms of pre-school provision can give. If a family has access to a service because they are identified as 'at risk' or 'in need', staff will have to work much harder to develop sound relationships with parents. In addition, providers need to think very carefully about how their service is available, and whether it might be possible to widen access using existing resources so as to avoid stigmatizing service users.

In conclusion, the following checklist for work with families is offered as a way of reviewing current practice and planning further developments.

A checklist for working with parents

(1) How do we relate to parents generally?
    (a) How do we induct children and parents?
    (b) How are they welcomed at the beginning of each session?
    (c) How do we say goodbye at the end of each session?
    (d) How do we tell children and parents about their progress?
    (e) How do we tell children and parents about events and activities we have planned?
    (f) How do we ask children and parents for their views and ideas about our work?
    (g) How do we recognize that 'parent' may be grandparent, childminder, other relative or friend?

(2) What opportunities do we provide for parents to get involved?
    (a) How do parents contribute to aspects of the work?
    (b) How do parents help with the work?
    (c) How do parents give and gain support in their role as parents?
    (d) How are parents asked to contribute to work being planned?
    (e) How do parents influence our thinking and our practice?

(3) Who gets involved in each type of activity?
    (a) Do they represent the local community/neighbourhood?
    (b) Are some in paid employment?
    (c) Do men and women get involved?
    (d) Do members of all ethnic groups in the community get involved?
    (e) Are other significant adults (e.g. childminders, grandparents) involved?
    (f) How many of the children's families are involved?

(4) What has changed as a result of working with parents?
    (a) For the workers?
    (b) For the institution/setting?
    (c) For the parents?
    (d) For the children?

Evaluating work with parents

It may also be helpful to look specifically at how you evaluate your work with parents. Defining some criteria for evaluation may seem daunting, but one very practical way is to ask 'Is it working? How do I know?' Combes (1990) makes some suggestions about evaluation of family education, and points out that criteria must evolve from the aims and values for work with parents in any setting. In nurseries the following questions might aid evaluation of work with parents:

(1) How many parents are we on first-name terms with? How representative are these of all the parents?
(2) What proportion of parents raise questions and make comments about their child?
(3) What proportion of parents make suggestions about how the nursery operates?
(4) What proportion of parents request specific provisions?
(5) Who makes use of the provisions we develop?
(6) What have we changed as a result of working with parents?

Finally, it is important to recognize that in many settings resources are very limited. This chapter has argued that informal relationships with parents are of vital importance. In many places with current limitations on resources it will be difficult to do anything over and above what is currently provided. This may not matter. Working with parents is as much about how we relate to parents when we see them, and how we communicate with them generally, as it is about developing specific projects and initiatives.

PART 3
TRAINING

11

TRAINING TO WORK IN THE EARLY YEARS

Audrey Curtis and Denise Hevey

INTRODUCTION

This chapter is divided into three parts. Part one examines the history and current issues in professional training for early years teachers. Part two looks at current developments in training for child care and education workers at vocational or sub-professional levels. Part three draws on both of these accounts to focus on the debate over what should constitute the ideal form of training and qualifications for 'professionals' in the early childhood field. Although parts one and two reveal very different approaches, there are at least four points which both accounts throw into relief.

Firstly, both agree that training for child care and education workers is at a crossroads. Decisions and events in the next few years are likely to have a profound effect on the nature of the early childhood professional or professionals for many years to come.

Secondly, there is a tension over existing notions of what a professional is and what this implicitly implies about other types of workers. Are others by definition non-professional or even unprofessional? Is the downside of traditional professionalism exclusiveness and élitism and can the advent of National Vocational Qualifications bring a new style of professionalism to all child care and education workers?

Thirdly, both raise issues about the extent to which a traditional, single-discipline based training, such as education, is adequate to meet the demands of changing services in the child care and education field. Is a multi-disciplinary approach with greater flexibility and transferability for workers the shape of things to come?

Finally, following on from the above, how special are the early years anyway? Should the continuity that all are looking for run across the age groups within a single-discipline based profession such as teaching (or social work or health visiting) or is it more important to have the basis in the training system of continuity across services and agencies within the early years age band?

DEVELOPMENTS IN TEACHER TRAINING

Since the nineteenth century there has been organized training of teachers in this country, set up originally by the voluntary bodies. In 1814 the British Society produced an outline for teacher training in primary schools which remained the model for courses until the early 1970s. It consisted of an academic entry qualification, a concurrent course of general education and professional training, a final examination and a probationary period of teaching, the whole culminating in the award of a teacher's certificate.

In 1960 all teacher training courses were extended from two to three years. Hitherto only the Froebel courses had offered courses of that length. This, and a sharp increase in the birth rate, led to a vast expansion in the number of teachers in training from 18,000 in 1958 to 114,000 by 1969. The next two decades were to see a drastic decline in the numbers, which fell to 46,500 in 1979 and 38,000 in 1989. These rapid changes in student numbers, plus the introduction of the B.Ed degree in the mid-1960s and its subsequent extension to a four-year course granting graduate status to all members of the teaching profession, were to have far-reaching effects upon the training of teachers and on early years courses in particular.

By the mid-1960s there were no longer courses specifically for those wishing to work with the three to five age range in nursery school or class. All early years students followed a course of training which covered the age ranges three to seven years or three to eight years.

The rapid increase in student numbers followed by an even more rapid decrease led to dramatic changes within teacher training institutions. Colleges were encouraged to broaden their teaching and offered degree courses in the arts and the sciences as well as their traditional education areas. The James Report (Committee of Enquiry, 1972) had recommended the ending of monotechnics and with this came the greater differentiation associated with present-day Institutes of Higher Education. In spite of their efforts, many colleges found themselves either overstaffed or with staff inappropriately qualified. However, excellent redundancy terms under the Crombie conditions encouraged many teacher trainers to apply for early retirement and among them were some of our finest trainers of early childhood educators. They were individuals who had been recruited into the colleges in the days when experience was considered more important than academic qualifications. Such tutors found themselves being overshadowed by young new entrants into teacher training, who had not necessarily been classroom teachers but who had the necessary academic status. This was to have an important effect upon early years training in the late 1970s and 1980s.

Having shed staff with early years expertise, colleges were forced either to run their training courses for the infant and nursery years with inappropriately trained staff, or to close their nursery courses. As a result, teachers professionally trained to work with young children were in short supply.

The shortage of early years teachers was further exacerbated by the introduction of the regulations laid down by the Council for the Accreditation of Teacher Education (CATE). The CATE requirement most likely to affect the number of courses offered for the training of early years teachers was the one which stated that all staff working on professional courses with students in initial training should have recent and relevant experience of the age range that they were teaching. Very properly, CATE rejected courses where the school experience of the lecturers was inappropriate and this led to a further decrease in the number of courses covering the three to five age range. Currently there are only eighteen Institutes of Higher Education training teachers to work with the three to eight age range. A further six prepare students for the four to eight age range and seven others offer 'options' in early years.

Although the institutions offering courses covering the three to eight age range offer students a substantial amount of preparation for working with the under fives, it is likely that the courses offering training for four to eight years will be concentrating upon infant education as most of the four-year-olds in educational establishments are in the primary classroom. If we also take into account the requirements of the National Curriculum and the criterion laid down by CATE that all teachers following a B.Ed course must have a subject specialism which accounts for 50 per cent of their study time as well as a specific number of hours for each of the foundation subjects of the National Curriculum (science, mathematics and English), then it is easy to understand why so many young teachers may feel inadequately prepared to cope with the needs of three- to five-year-old children.

During the period when comments were invited by the government over the CATE criteria, many early childhood specialists argued that an area of study like 'language and literacy' or 'aesthetic and creative' studies could be made rigorous enough to meet the regulations and yet would be more relevant to meet the needs of early years teachers (those preparing to work with three- to eight-year-olds). The government would not accept these arguments. Teachers preparing to work in the early years of schooling must have a subject discipline in the same way as those preparing to work with an older age range. The arguments for this approach are compelling and there is no doubt that we want teachers of the early years to be as well educated as those working with the older age range. The question is, should their training be the same?

There is no doubt that the introduction of the CATE requirements and the changing needs of the schools and early childhood centres have presented a problem to those educating the early childhood educators. How can they best prepare the teachers for the challenging work of the next century, when the needs of young children and their families may not be the same as they are today? Should there be a separate course for teachers working with the under fives or should we be advocating a situation as in Scotland where teachers working in the nurseries are expected to do a further course of training after gaining their qualifications in primary education?

The European dimension

Before we look at this crucial issue, let us consider another factor which may well affect the training of early childhood workers and teachers in particular, that is the situation relating to our joining the Common Market and the introduction of a common European system in 1992.

Although education is not seen as an integral part of the Treaty of Rome, there have been modifications during 1991 which will most probably have a bearing upon the training of teachers in the early years. The EC Directive which allowed equivalence in the recognition of qualifications has meant that teachers from the European countries can be employed within the English education sector. So far this has only been with primary aged children. There are, however, difficulties in accepting that there is equivalence with respect to the teaching of nursery-school-aged children since only in a few countries do teachers have the same level of training as we do in the UK. Furthermore, although the teachers may have the same length of training, in very few countries are they paid at the same level and nowhere else are teachers able to teach through the age range from three to eleven thus helping to ensure continuity and progression in children's education.

One of the strengths of our current teacher training programmes is that teachers are able to understand the development of children from three to eleven years or three to nine years and do not see starting statutory schooling as a cut-off point in this process. For example, although it is not standard practice in this country to teach children to read in the nursey school or class, in Europe generally this is frowned upon and is seen as a threat to natural development before the age of six. Consensus in the UK would suggest that the interest in print shown by many children as a result of the programmes offered should be, and is, encouraged and developed. Therefore, if the teacher has had no training in this aspect of education it could be very difficult for her to help the child appropriately.

In many parts of the EC there is a clearly defined distinction between care before six/seven years and education thereafter. This militates against the concept of continuity and progression, which is one of the strengths of our system, made possible by the nature of our training.

Although government responsibility for young children is split between the Department of Health and the Department of Education and Science, there is general agreement amongst professionals that there should be a greater educational input into all pre-school institutions. As a result, many local authorities are linking care and education in a positive way, or, indeed, placing total responsibility with the education committee (*see* Chapter 1).

What makes a good early years teacher?

The Rumbold Report (DES, 1990a) urged that there should be better quality in all early childhood provision. Before discussing further what constitutes a good early years training course to ensure this quality, it is important to consider what are the attributes we would like an early years teacher to possess.

Definitions of 'quality teaching' like those of 'good practice' are hard to find as most authors tend to be unwilling to commit themselves to state exactly what constitutes a 'good early years teacher'. However, it is essential to attempt this before considering how best to design the ideal training programme.

First of all, he/she is a professional, 'that is to say, professionals are persons who are able to carry out a complex and socially valued role for which defined expertise is required.' It is only teachers who are competent and qualified and mature who can be allowed 'the widest measure of professional autonomy' (Ward, 1986, p. 9).

Watts (1987) also had some appropriate comments to make on the topic of professionalism stating that

> whatever the future shape and nature of early childhood services, kindergarten teachers and other staff will continue to serve their clients well if they exemplify in their attitudes and behaviours the hallmarks of professionalism especially:
> − specific expertise and a specialized knowledge base;
> − commitment to continuing enquiry to advance the knowledge base;
> − altruism, service to a public good and assumptions of responsibility for their own continuing professional development.
>
> (Watts, 1987, p. 12)

Ebbeck, speaking at the OMEP World Congress in London in 1989, insisted that the hallmarks of professionalism are very important if we are to improve the status of early childhood educators.

What qualities does an early years teacher require?

These seem to fall naturally into three areas of skills which can be developed with sensitive training: personal/social skills, professional skills and practical skills. There is naturally some overlap between the areas.

Personal/social skills

The early years teacher should be:

(1) a well-adjusted person with a positive self-image;
(2) a well-educated person with wide interests in the arts and an awareness of the physical world;
(3) aware of and sensitive to the needs of others at all levels, regardless of cultural and social patterns;
(4) committed, non-judgemental;
(5) interested in and respectful of the autonomy of the child;
(6) of an enquiring mind and alert to the need for further personal professional development;
(7) able to *communicate* by all possible means with colleagues, parents, other agencies and above all with children, irrespective of their culture, religion or gender.

Professional skills
The early years teacher should have:

(1) a sound knowledge of child development and educational theory;
(2) the ability to develop strategies to transmit knowledge to others;
(3) a deep understanding of the subjects in the early years curriculum and the value of play;
(4) a knowledge of and respect for cultural and social similarities and differences;
(5) observational skills and ability to assess and evaluate not only the programmes they offer, and the children's progress, but also themselves.
(6) a knowledge of the laws relating to families;
(7) a knowledge of policies and the underlying philosophy;
(8) the ability to act as an advocate for children.

Practical skills
The early years teacher should be able to:

(1) plan programmes which ensure both continuity and progression;
(2) understand the point of view of others in order to manage the delivery of the programme in various settings with a range of people both professional and non-professional;
(3) encourage the team of workers to adopt common strategies, which will allow the aims of the pre-school to be met;
(4) encourage the personal development of team members.

To summarize the adult's role I think we can do no better than quote Parry and Archer who wrote:

A teacher of young children obviously needs to possess certain qualities if she is to face well her responsibilities which are complex in nature and highly demanding of excellence of many kinds. She needs to be someone who is essentially human; someone who likes people, especially children, and is not only full of warmth and goodwill toward them but determined to do right by them. To achieve such ends she needs to be perceptive, sensitive, sympathetic and imaginative. She needs to be highly educated personally and professionally in those areas of knowledge, understanding and skill which she will be conveying to children, albeit indirectly at their stage of development and in those spheres of learning which are essential to her understanding of children and adults and to her skill in dealing with them.

(Parry and Archer, 1974, p. 139)

How do we train teachers?

Are we meeting the training needs of these teachers whom we expect to function in a variety of pre-school settings, not just traditional nursery schools and classes?

The existing teacher training programmes preparing students to work with the three- to eight-year-old age range, if they have good selection procedures, should be able to select students with satisfactory personal/ social qualities. However, once we move into the areas of professional and practical skills it does not appear that we are offering an appropriate curriculum to achieve the high level of professionalism expected.

Many of the attributes and skills listed are covered in the current syllabi in training institutions but because of the pressures of the National Curriculum and the emphasis upon subject specialisms it is impossible to devote the amount of time to the study of child development and observational skills so vital to our understanding of the growth and development of young children. Few would argue against the need to reform the initial teacher training programmes and to introduce a more rigorous regime, but current research into the way young children's thinking develops should have resulted in a greater, not a lesser, study of child development. At least in former days those preparing to work with children in the early years of schooling were given an understanding of the development of children from birth to three years, just as they left college knowing something about the personal and curricular needs of children aged five to eight years. Furthermore, there was included in most early years courses a compulsory element in which students had to spend time with children of varying ages outside a school setting. For many students this was one of the most rewarding parts of their training. Looking at current syllabi it seems unlikely that this is now normal practice.

Just as schools are undergoing change so are many of the early childhood establishments where young teachers are finding work. The traditional role of the teacher in her own closed domain has to be abandoned in these settings as there is much greater emphasis upon team-work and co-operation. Students fortunate enough to have been trained in the institutes specializing in this age range will find it easier to cope, but even then it is unlikely, with the pressures of the rest of the course, that they will have a real understanding of the needs of workers in many of the family and community centres where teachers are now employed. In these settings where the emphasis is often upon the child *and* the family, teachers need not only management and leadership skills, but also skills to work with parents and professionals from other disciplines. Such a training is not well developed within the current initial training programmes.

In 1988 the government introduced two new school-based schemes for the training of teachers, the Articled Teacher Scheme and the Licensed Teacher Scheme. The success of these schemes will depend to a large extent upon the ability of existing overworked staff to give trainees the support they need to become competent early years teachers.

CURRENT DEVELOPMENTS IN TRAINING FOR CHILD CARE

Estimates vary between 200,000 and 400,000 individuals other than teachers currently involved in work with young children and their families throughout the UK. In England and Wales alone there are roughly 95,000 registered childminders, and probably as many playgroup leaders and assistants in 17,000 playgroups.

Workers with young children and their families are also found in nursery and primary education, crèches, parent and toddler groups, family centres, parent support and home visiting schemes, toy libraries, playbuses and many other types of provision. In fact, some eighty-five distinct job roles were identified by the occupational mapping survey of ten local authority areas undertaken as part of the Working with Under Sevens Project (Hevey and Windle, 1990). Further, provision for full day care, and hence the number of child care workers, is increasing. In a recent speech to the Women's National Commission (Bottomley, 1991), the Minister for Health reported that between 1988 and 1990 the number of places in registered day nurseries had increased by 60 per cent to 58,000 and that places in nurseries exempt from registration requirements (mainly on health authority premises) had increased by 80 per cent.

The vast majority (97 per cent) of this army of workers with young children are women (Hevey and Windle, 1990). Many work part time, some as unpaid volunteers, wages are low and turnover rates are high. According to a report by the European Childcare Network (European Commission, 1990), nannies earn just over half the average pay of women workers and childminders less than half. With the exception of full-time workers employed in the public sector, most do not hold any formally recognized qualifications related to their job role.

A small-scale survey in 1986 revealed that the pattern of training and qualifications for work with young children was both confused and confusing (Hevey, 1986). There was a burgeoning variety of training courses for child care, mainly aimed at sixteen- to nineteen-year-olds in full-time education or on training schemes, with no way of comparing their content or value for employment purposes. In contrast, the only training opportunities open to the majority of workers – mature women with family responsibilities – were likely to be informal, part-time and non-certificated. They varied in duration from as little as one evening a week for six weeks (the typical length of a childminder's pre-registration course) to one day a week for a year (the Foundation Course of the Pre-School Playgroups Association). However, only one-fifth of the respondents to the occupational mapping survey had not taken part in any form of training or induction for their job role, indicating a high degree of take-up of the limited training that was available.

Amazingly, considering the level of responsibility for children's well-being carried by most child care workers, training has never been a statutory requirement for employment in, or provision of, child care services. The Children Act 1989 for the first time empowers local authorities to provide training for those engaged in child care other than its own staff, but it does not require them to do so. The Guidance which accompanies the Act (DH, 1991) suggests the personal qualities and experience that might be looked for in child care personnel but it does not require qualifications nor specify the minimum amount of training and support necessary to enable workers to achieve acceptable standards of care. To have done so would have had large-scale resource implications. More significantly, however, the lack of insistence on qualifications for what are in reality highly responsible roles is underpinned by confused and outmoded public attitudes which deem training unnecessary. The care of young children is often not regarded a 'real' work but as an extension of the mothering role which is assumed to come naturally to women without the need for training. Such attitudes in turn reinforce the low status of child care work helping to keep pay low and turnover high.

Similar sentiments were expressed in the report of the National Child Care Staffing Study carried out in America in 1988:

> As a nation we are reluctant to acknowledge child care settings as a work environment for adults, let alone commit resources to improving them. Even though many Americans recognize that child care teachers are underpaid, outdated attitudes about women's work and the family obscure our view of teachers' economic needs and the demands of their work. If a job in child care is seen as an extension of women's familial role of rearing children, professional preparation and adequate resource compensation seem unnecessary.
>
> (Whitebook, 1990, p. 3)

It should be noted that the reference here to 'child care teachers' does not correspond to the British notion of qualified teacher status. In fact, only 31 per cent of the 'child care teachers' who were in charge of classes and centres had a degree or equivalent qualification and only 65 per cent of 'child care teachers' and 57 per cent of aides and assistants had some relevant training in child development. Nevertheless, the survey found that the level of formal education combined with specific training were key predictors of high quality care.

An additional problem both here and in the USA is that up until now, qualifications have not provided a basis for progression or access to higher education and professional training and there has been little incentive through pay or career opportunities for staff to pursue further training.

Radical changes in vocational education and training

In the early 1980s, concerned by low staying-on rates and unfavourable international comparisons of the level of qualifications in the UK work-force, the government commissioned a working group to review the state of vocational education and training across all sectors of industry (MSC and DES, 1986). This found a confusing mishmash of qualifications being awarded by a myriad of different awarding bodies with no way of comparing their value, few mechanisms for transferability of credit or credit exemption across related qualifications and no systematic framework through which workers could progress with increasing experience and expertise. Many existing qualifications were criticized for being out of touch with the reality of the work-place and for relying too heavily on knowledge-based assessment. Employers complained that students emerging at the end of training courses might know it all in theory but were ill equipped to do the jobs expected of them in practice and often required considerable on-the-job training before they could function at an acceptable level in the work-place.

The White Paper which followed (DE and DES, 1986) led to the setting up of the National Council for Vocational Qualifications in the autumn of 1986. The NCVQ was charged with producing a rationalized progressive framework of vocational qualifications across all sectors of industry by 1992.

These new qualifications were to meet certain basic criteria. National Vocational Qualifications (NVQs) were to be based on the notion of occupational competence − the ability to carry out work roles to the standards expected in employment − and assessed by evidence of what candidates could actually do in real work situations rather than on just what they knew (NCVQ, 1988, 1989). They were to be modular with provision for credit accumulation and transfer and all unnecessary barriers to access, such as rigid academic entry requirements or time serving, were to be removed. Ideally, candidates would be able to put themselves forward for assessment when they felt ready, regardless of how long or short a time it had taken them to become competent or what mode of study or preparation they had followed. What mattered in the new system was that candidates could actively demonstrate their competence to an assessor in real work settings. This represented a radical shift away from the specification of the 'inputs' of knowledge, skills and experience that a student should be given, and towards a focus on 'outcomes' in terms of the functions a competent worker should be able to perform.

Within the new NCVQ framework, all vocational qualifications were to be slotted into a four-staged ladder from the most basic competences carried out under constant supervision (Level I) to complex, technical and specialized activities carried out with a considerable degree of autonomy and including some managerial functions (Level IV). Each of these levels was to reflect nationally agreed, employment-led standards of occupational competence with agreed routes for progression including access to professional training. Part of the implicit agenda was to ensure that vocational qualifications would be equally valued alongside academic qualifications. Following the most recent White Paper, *Education and Training for the Twenty-First Century* (DES and DE, 1991), it is suggested that the parallel ladders can be bridged by the notion of 'core skills' and the introduction of General NVQs as a broad-based preparation for work roles.

The White Paper also expressed the government's commitment to the development of NVQs to cover 80 per cent of the work-force by 1992 and indicated the firm intention to extend the same radical approach to professional qualifications thereafter: 'Once that aim has been achieved, we must secure permanent arrangements to keep NVQs up to date, and to develop them for the remaining 20 per cent of employment, including professional levels' (DES and DE, 1991, p. 17).

Setting standards for work with young children

Because of these wider national reforms, it became imperative to establish a nationally agreed set of occupational standards cutting across the traditional divisions in the field of child care and education as the basis of new NVQs. This was the task of the 'Working with Under Sevens Project' operating under the auspices of the Care Sector Consortium — the industry lead body which represents all facets of employment interests for social and health care (Hevey, 1991a).

It is a basic requirement of the Employment Department, as major funders of development work in this field, that national occupational standards are developed according to a specified methodology and expressed according to strict conventions. Each standard consists of an element of competence describing the functions and activities that a competent worker should be able to do and performance criteria by which an assessor can judge whether the function is being carried out to a level acceptable in employment across a specified range of circumstances. These standards are then grouped together into units (areas of competence that have meaning and value in employment) for assessment purposes.

Applying standards development methodology and conventions to the field of child care and education was not an easy task because the former are reductionist and product/outcomes oriented whereas the latter is holistic and primarily concerned with process (Hevey, 1991b). The sheer diversity of roles and settings caused further problems when attempting to cover all types of workers with young children and their families, regardless of setting or responsible agency or employment status. However, every attempt was made to consult widely and to incorporate those values and principles which have broad-based acceptance in the early years field, such as the integral nature of both 'care' and 'education' functions to the work role, the importance of parent involvement and the need to value and meet the needs of each child as an individual. In fact, more than 3,000 practitioners and managers from across the spectrum of child care and education settings and from all parts of the UK were involved at some stage in the development of the national standards.

The first batch of National (and Scottish) Vocational Qualifications in Child Care and Education based on those standards were launched in February 1992. The structure of qualifications at Levels II and III is based on a core of units of competence covering the primary functions of promoting the welfare, learning and development of young children (Care Sector Consortium, 1991) combined with two or four option units respectively to give the necessary degree of specialization whilst avoiding job or setting specificity. For example, the first three 'endorsements' to be accredited at Level III cover 'Group Care and Education', 'Family Day Care' and 'Pre-school Provision' whilst in the following two to three years a further four endorsements are anticipated to cover the more specialist areas of 'Family Support', 'Primary Education', 'Special Needs' and 'Hospital Playwork'.

Implications for child care and education

The advent of National and Scottish Vocational Qualifications in Child Care and Education holds the potential to rationalize and revolutionize training and education and ultimately to improve vastly standards of provision (Messenger and Curtis, 1991) through:

(1) *improved access* to a nationally recognized, work-related qualification for thousands of women;
(2) *comparability* with other skilled occupations leading to increased status and recognition (and pay?) for child care work;
(3) *improved standards* of child care and education based on nationally agreed criteria for worker performance;
(4) *a framework for progression* within the work role or into higher education and professional training;
(5) *transferability* of workers across a wide variety of child care and education settings and into related occupations on the basis of generic or core competences;
(6) *a mechanism for specifying quality* of provision through graded levels of qualification as well as numbers of staff.

This potential has been widely acknowledged and endorsed. The report of the Rumbold Committee stated:

> We welcome the work of the National Council for Vocational Qualifications (NCVQ) towards establishing agreed standards for child care workers, including those in education settings. We believe that, given adequate resourcing, it could bring about significant rationalization of patterns of training. It should also improve the status of early years workers through recognition of the complex range and high level of the skills involved and by opening up prospects for further training.

> (DES, 1990a, para. 176, p. 24)

The EOC stated in their discussion paper and action plan, *The Key to Real Choice*:

> The need in the UK for a professional career structure for child care workers is acute. Work now being done in preparation for National and Scottish Vocational Qualifications in child care may represent an important first step, but will need to be systematically resourced and implemented.

> (EOC, 1990, para. 2.2.4, p. 4)

However, as these quotes highlight, whether implementation happens on a large enough scale to make a serious impact is dependent on the availability of resources to create and maintain the necessary training and assessment infrastructures.

Particular assumptions of the NCVQ model when combined with characteristics of the early years field make investment of central government resources an essential prerequisite of large-scale implementation. These assumptions stem from the fact that the whole NVQ system is employment based. 'The new model of education and training (or learning) assumes that companies and other employing organizations will become major providers of learning opportunities' (Jessup, 1991, p. 95).

Assessment of competence is assumed to take place largely in the work-place and to be undertaken by extension of the roles of existing line managers and supervisors to include the role of work-based assessor. In large organizations the first tier of standardization and verification is also operated 'in-house' and the awarding bodies merely approve work settings/ organizations as assessment centres and provide external verification of assessment. All of this conveniently hides the enormous costs of an individualized, criterion-referenced, competence-based assessment system compared with the traditional model of written examination of thirty or more candidates *en masse* in an examination hall.

The problems with applying this NVQ model to the field of child care and education are exacerbated by at least three factors. Firstly, with the exception of a hard-pressed public sector for whom services for the youngest children are entirely discretionary, large-scale organizations are notable by their absence. Who then is to provide the training and assessment infrastructures?

Secondly, child care workers tend to have a high degree of autonomy and responsibility. Roughly three-quarters of the work-force are not regularly observed and supervised in their work and half are not assessed in any way (Hevey and Windle, 1990). How is the competence of un-supervised workers (the majority) to be assessed?

Thirdly, even when a potential work-based assessor is present, on-going child care responsibilities within small-scale settings may make it unrealistic for him/her to carry out detailed observational assessments and questioning of candidates. Who then can fulfil this role?

The only practical solution for large-scale implementation of NVQs in child care and education would appear to be through the use of qualified and trained peripatetic assessors who visit and assess candidates in their individual work-places, but this will require the setting up of entirely new training and assessment infrastructures (Wedge, 1991) with considerable resource implications (Ross, 1990). Unlike other sectors of industry, there simply is no place to hide the costs.

The top of the ladder

Within the NCVQ framework it is assumed that entry into professional training can take place from a relevant 'advanced' NVQ at Level III as an alternative to the traditional A-level route. By implication, those who go on to achieve a 'higher' NVQ at Level IV should have some exemptions from professional training. Level IV, therefore, represents the interface between the vocational and what has traditionally been termed the professional. One problem for child care and education qualifications is that there are currently not one but at least three interfaces – with teaching, health visiting and social work, and indeed with community work as an additional contender in some cases. The areas of interface and overlap cannot be clearly defined until such time as each of these separate professions undertakes its own functional analysis giving a breakdown of their respective occupational roles in competence terms. However, even when this has been achieved we are left with something of a dilemma. The logical top rung or Level V for a multi-disciplinary ladder is not a single-discipline-based profession!

In this chapter and elsewhere it has been mentioned that dissatisfaction is growing with the existing discipline-based professional qualifications, such as teaching, as suitable preparation for the sorts of demands imposed by, for example, running a combined centre, a family centre or a community nursery (Calder, 1990). The managers of such provision need to be competent in the area of parent support and in the promotion of health and welfare for families with young children but they also critically need competence in curriculum design, evaluation and management if the educational needs of the children are not to take a back seat. The ultimate question then becomes, can existing professional qualifications be adapted to accommodate this range of competences or should we be talking about a new breed of multi-disciplinary early childhood professionals?

OPTIONS FOR CHANGE

Using the existing model of teacher training as a starting point, there are at least four different options for creating the sort of broader based professional who is needed to take on the emerging multi-disciplinary professional roles that are being demanded by developments in service provision and will be further encouraged by the Children Act 1989.

The first option would be to continue to improve and extend the existing early years initial teacher training to broaden the knowledge base and include a variety of placements, not just in nursery and primary schools, but in placements like family centres, combined centres, family support schemes and small-scale community-based provision. This would give the early years teacher the necessary knowledge, experience and competences to be able to function effectively in any type of setting. However, as we have already noted, the initial teacher training syllabus is already overcrowded and as long as the 50 per cent subject specialism remains, with no recognition of early learning as a subject specialism, there will be little scope for increasing the amount devoted to broader based components such as health promotion, counselling and advice giving, benefits entitlements, working with parents, team or centre management and liaison and support for community groups.

A second option, with some parallels to the Scottish model of training for nursery teachers, would be to require a multi-disciplinary post-qualifying diploma in addition to initial professional training for all those working in the early years field. Indeed, such diplomas have already been pioneered by institutes such as Roehampton and Derbyshire College of Higher Education. This would have the advantage of acceptability in posing the least threat to existing professional boundaries but it has the decided disadvantage of leaving a gap in the NCVQ ladder at Level V which would provide a barrier to access to those emerging through the multi-disciplinary vocational route. It also implies that professional work with young children and their families would demand a higher level of qualification than almost any other area of work which in turn would have implications for pay and conditions of service and would appear unrealistic in the current climate.

A third option would be to tackle the necessary broad-based multi-disciplinary components at the other end of training and to devise a new type of BA (Early Years) as is already being proposed by a number of institutions, with a common first two years for all types of early childhood professionals. This would not of itself count as a professional qualification but could be followed by a conventional PGCE to give qualified teacher status, or by a Dip. SW to give qualified social worker status. This option would still run foul of current CATE requirements for subject specialism but it could be made compatible with the NVQ framework if extensive provision was made for exemptions on the basis of their already acquired knowledge and competence.

Finally, the most radical option would be to create a new form of multi-disciplinary professional child care and education training on a par with, but distinct from, teaching, health visiting and social work. This would have the advantage of enabling the design of courses and qualifications from scratch to reflect the competences demanded by the emerging multi-disciplinary roles and to mesh in with the multi-disciplinary vocational ladder at Level IV instead of being a compromise between existing professional demands. Ideally modules would be designed to be common across the different professional trainings where functions overlap. It is interesting to note that in the consultation on the content and structure of National Vocational Qualifications in Child Care and Education (Hevey, 1991a) around 80 per cent support was found for the idea of a new form of multi-disciplinary child care and education professional at Level V. However, it would have a number of distinct disadvantages. The creation of an entirely new profession would lead to a head-on confrontation with existing professional interests and inevitable protectionisms and it might mean depriving the worker of participation in a wider well-established professional body — be it of social workers or teachers or nurses — with all the advantages that flow from that. In particular, professional 'educarers' would not meet the criteria for qualified teacher status which would enable them to teach any age group. There would be a danger of ghetto-ization of the early years staff as non-teachers, of being cut off from the mainstream of the education system and of downward drift of salaries back to what is normally associated with child care rather than teaching.

CONCLUSION

There is no doubt that at present we are at a crossroads in training and qualifications for workers in the early years field. There is a distinct shortage of personnel with a sufficient knowledge of the educational needs of young children or with the breadth of competence to fulfil emerging multi-disciplinary roles, yet demand is increasing for early years worker of all types.

If quality is to be maintained and there is to be a sound educational input to all types of early years provision, the issues raised in this chapter will have to be faced. The new NVQs in Child Care and Education have the potential to provide a framework for developing expertise at what have traditionally been termed vocational levels. This makes it all the more urgent that there is a radical rethink of the content and structure of training and qualifications for early years professionals.

REFERENCES

Ainsworth, M., Blehar, M., Walters, E. and Wall, S. (1990) *Patterns of Attachment*, Erlbaum, Hillsdale, New Jersey.

Alexander, R. (1988) Garden or jungle? Teacher development and informal primary education, in A. Blyth (ed.) *Informal Primary Education Today*, Falmer, Lewes.

Andersson, B. E. (1990) Intellectual and socio-emotional competence in Swedish school children related to early child care. Paper presented at the fourth European Conference on Developmental Psychology, Stirling, Scotland.

Anning, A. (1991) *The First Years at School: Education from Four to Eight*, Open University Press, Milton Keynes.

Association of Metropolitan Authorities (1991) *Children First*, AMA, London.

Athey, C. (1990) *Extending Thought in Young Children: A Parent-Teacher Partnership*, Paul Chapman, London.

Atkin, J., Bastiani, J. and Goode, J. (1988) *Listening to Parents*, Croom Helm, London.

Bain, A. and Barnett, L. (1980) *The Design of a Day Care System in a Nursery Setting for Children Under Five*, Tavistock Institute of Human Relations, London.

Ball, M. and Stone, J. (1991) *Setting Up an Early Years Forum: a Step by Step Guide*, VOLCUF, London.

Barrett, G. (1986) *Starting School: An Evaluation of the Experience*, AMMA, London.

Barrs, M. *et al*. (1988) *ILEA: The Primary Language Record*, now available from Centre for Language in Primary Education, London.

Bastiani, J. (1989) *Working with Parents: A Whole-School Approach*, NFER-Nelson, Windsor.

Bellman, M. and Cash, J. (1987) *The Schedule of Growing Skills in Practice*, NFER-Nelson, Windsor.

Belsky, J. (1988) The 'effects' of infant day care reconsidered, *Early Childhood Research Quarterly*, Vol. 3, pp. 235–72.

Bennett, N., Desforges, C., Cockburn, A. and Wilkinson, E. (1984) *The Quality of Pupil Learning Experiences*, Lawrence Erlbaum, London.

BIC (1991) *Employer's and Childcare*, Internal Note, London. March.

Bloom, B. S. (1964) *Stability and Change in Human Characteristics*, Wiley, New York.

Bottomley, V. (1991) Text of speech given at Women's National Commission: Seminar on Child Care, 12 June 1991.

Bower, T. G. R. (1977) *A Primer of Infant Development*, Freeman, San Francisco.

Bowlby, J. (1953) *Child Care and the Growth of Love*, Pelican, London.

Bradshaw, J. (1990) *Child Poverty and Deprivation in the UK*, National Children's Bureau, London.

Braun, D. (1987) *Spon Gate Mums' Group*, Community Education Development Centre, Coventry.

Braun, D. (1990) *Shared Care at Hillfields Nursery Centre*, Community Education Development Centre, Coventry.

Brown, B. (1990) *All Our Children*, BBC Education, London.

Brown, S. and Cleave, S. (1991) *Four-year-olds in School: Quality Matters*, NFER, Slough.

Browne, J. (1979) *Teachers of Teachers*, Hodder & Stoughton, Sevenoaks.

Bruce, T. (1987) *Early Childhood Education*, Hodder & Stoughton, Sevenoaks.

Bruce, T. (1991) *Time to Play in Early Childhood Education*, Hodder & Stoughton, Sevenoaks.

Burgess, R. G., Hughes, C. and Moxon, S. (1991) A curriculum for the under fives? Paper delivered at the Conference on Defining and Assessing Quality in the Education of Children from Four to Seven Years, University of Leuven, Belgium, 25–7 September 1991.

Calder, P. (1990) The training of nursery workers: the need for a new approach, *Children & Society*, Vol. 4, no. 3, pp. 251–60.

Caldera, Y., Huston, A. and O'Brien, M. (1989) Social interactions and play patterns of parents and toddlers with feminine, masculine and neutral toys, *Child Education*, Vol. 60, pp. 70–6.

Cambridgeshire Regional College (1990) Final report on Cambridgeshire NCVQ Nuce Project, unpublished.

Cameron, R. J. and Sturge-Moore, L. (1990) *Ordinary Everyday Families: Under Fives Project*, MENCAP London Division, 115 Golden Lane, London EC1Y OTJ.

Cameron, R. J. (1989) Teaching parents to teach children: the Portage approach to special needs, in N. Jones (ed.) *Special Educational Review*, Vol. (a), Falmer, Lewes.

Care Sector Consortium (1991) *National Occupational Standards for Work with Young Children and their Families*, available from National Children's Bureau.

Celestin, N. (1986) *A Guide to Anti-Racist Child Care Practice*, VOLCUF, London.

Central Advisory Council for Education (1967) *Children and Their Primary Schools* (Plowden Report), HMSO, London.

Clark, M. (1988) *Children under Five: Educational Research and Evidence*, Gordon & Breach, London.

Clark, M. (1989) *Understanding Research in Early Education*, Gordon & Breach, London.

Clarke-Stewart, A. (1991) Day care in the USA, in P. Moss and E. Melhuish (eds.) *Current Issues in Day Care for Young Children*, HMSO, London.

CNAF (1980) Consacre aux jeunes parents et la garde de leurs enfants, *Revue Informations Sociales*, no. 3/1980, CNAF, Paris.

Cole, M. (ed.) (1989) *Education for Equality: Some Guidelines for Good Practice*, Routledge, London.

Combes, G. (1990) Evaluating family education, *Journal of Community Education*, Vol. 8, no. 4, Community Education Development Centre, Coventry.

Combes, G. (1991) *You Can't Watch Them Twenty-Four Hours a Day: Parents' and Children's Perceptions, Understanding and Experiences of Accidents and Accident Prevention*, Child Accident Prevention Trust, London.

Combes, G. and Braun, D. (1989) *Everything gives you heart attacks these days...*, Community Education Development Centre, Coventry.

Commission for Racial Equality (1990) *From Cradle to School: A Practical Guide to Race Equality and Child Care* (2nd edn), CRE, London.

Commission for Racial Equality (1991) *From Cradle to School: A Practical Guide to Race Equality and Child Care* (3rd edn), CRE, London.

Committee of Enquiry (1972) *Teacher Education and Teacher Training*, a Report of a Committee of Enquiry under the Chairmanship of Lord James of Rusholme, HMSO, London.

Committee on Child Health Services (1976) *Fit for the Future* (Court Report), HMSO, London.

Council on Interracial Books for Children (1980) *Ten Quick Ways to Evaluate Children's Books for Racism and Sexism*, 1841 Broadway, New York 10023.

Cowley, L. (compiler) (1991) *Young Children in Group Day Care: Guidelines for Good Practice*, National Children's Bureau, London.

Curtis, A. (1986) *A Curriculum for the Pre-School Child: Learning to Learn*, NFER-Nelson, Windsor.

Curtis, A. (1991) *Early Childhood Explained: A Review of Provision in England and Wales*, OMEP (UK).

David, T. (1990) *Under Five — Under–educated?* Open University Press, Buckingham.

Davis, J. and Brember, I. (1991) The effects of gender and attendance period on children's adjustment to nursery classes, *British Educational Research Journal*, Vol. 17, no. 1.

Department of Education and Science (1978) *Report of the Committee of Inquiry into the Education of Handicapped Children and Young People* (Warnock Report), HMSO, London.

Department of Education and Science (1985a) *Curriculum Matters 2*, HMSO, London.

Department of Education and Science (1985b) *Better Schools* (Cmnd 9469), HMSO, London.

Department of Education and Science (1989a) *Aspects of Primary Education: The Education of Children Under Five*, HMSO, London.

Department of Education and Science (1989b) *Assessments and Statements of Special Educational Needs: Procedures Within the Education, Health and Social Services*, Circular 22/89, London.

Department of Education and Science (1989c) *Initial Teacher Training: Approval of Courses*, Circular 24/89, London.

Department of Education and Science (1990a) *Starting with Quality: Report of the Committee of Inquiry into the Educational Experiences Offered to Three- and*

Four-Year-Olds (Rumbold Report), HMSO, London.

Department of Education and Science (1990b) *Portage Projects: A Survey by HMI of Thirteen Projects Funded by Education Support Grants*, DES, London.

Department of Education and Science (1991a) *Interdisciplinary Support for Young Children with Special Educational Needs* (HMI Report), DES, London.

Department of Education and Science (1991b) *Students on Initial Teacher Training*, Statistical Bulletin 17/91, DES, London.

Department of Education and Science and Welsh Office (1989) *Science in the National Curriculum*, HMSO, London.

Department of Education and Science and Department of Employment (1991) *Education and Training for the Twenty-First Century* (Cmnd 1536), HMSO, London.

Department of Employment and Department of Education and Science (1986) *Working Together: Education and Training* (Cmnd 9823), HMSO, London.

Department of Health (1991) *The Children Act 1989 Guidance and Regulations, Vol. 2: Family Support, Day Care and Educational Provision for Young Children*, HMSO, London.

Department of Health and Social Security and Department of Education and Science (1976) *Co-ordination of Local Authority Services for Children Under Five* (LASSL (76)5) (S21 47 05), DHSS/DES, London.

Department of Health and Social Security and Department of Education and Science (1978) *Co-ordination of Services for Children Under Five* (LASSL (78)1) (HN(78)5), DHSS/DES, London.

Department of Health: Social Services Inspectorate (1991) *Inspecting for Quality: Guidance on Practice for Inspection Units in Social Services Departments and Other Agencies*, HMSO, London.

Derman-Sparks, D. (1989) *Anti-Bias Curriculum*, National Association for the Education of Young Children, Washington DC.

Development Education Centre (1991) *Us and the Kids: Activities and Resources for Parents' Groups*, DEC, Birmingham.

Dixon, B. (1989) *Playing them False: A Study of Children's Toys, Games and Puzzles*, Trentham, Stoke-on-Trent.

Dominelli, L. (1990) *Women and Community Action*, Venture Press, Birmingham.

Dowling, M. and Dauncey, E. (1984) *Teaching Three- to Nine-Year-Olds*, Ward Lock Educational, London.

Drummond, M. J., Lally, M. and Pugh, G. (eds.) (1989) *Working with Children: Developing a Curriculum for the Early Years*, National Children's Bureau, London.

Drummond, M. J. and Rouse, D. (eds.) (in preparation) *Making Assessment Work*, National Children's Bureau, London.

Early Years Curriculum Group (1989) *Early Childhood Education: The Early Years Curriculum and the National Curriculum*, Trentham, Stoke-on-Trent.

Ebbeck, M. (1990) Preparing early childhood personnel to be pro-active policy working professionals, *Early Child Development and Care*, Vol. 58, pp. 87–96.

Edwards, V. and Redfern, A. (1988) *At Home in School*, Routledge, London.

Elfer, P. and Beasley, G. (1991) *Registration of Childminding and Day Care: Using the Law to Raise Standards*, HMSO, London.

Elfer, P. and Gatiss, S. (1990) *Charting Child Health Services*, National Children's Bureau, London.

Epstein, D. and Sealey, A. (1990) *Where it Really Matters*, Development Education Centre, Birmingham.

Equal Opportunities Commission (1990) *The Key to Real Choice*, EOC, Manchester.

European Commission (1988) *Childcare and Equality of Opportunity*, European Commission, Brussels.

European Commission (1990) *Childcare in the European Communities, 1985–1990*, European Commission, Brussels.

European Commission Childcare Network (1991) *Quality in Childcare Services* (Report of an EC Childcare Network Technical Seminar, Barcelona, May 1990), European Commission Childcare Network, Brussels.

Farquhar, S.-E. (1990) Quality in early education and care: what do we mean? *Early Child Development and Care*, Vol. 64, pp. 71–83.

Faulkner, D., Miell, D., Oates, J., Robinson, A., Sheldon, M. and Walsh, M. (1991) *Working with Under Fives*, Open University Press, Milton Keynes.

Ferri, E. (in press) *What Makes Childminding Work?* National Children's Bureau, London.

Fish, D. (1989) *Learning through Practice in Initial Teacher Training*, Kogan Page, London.

Fox, M. (1990) Assessment of special needs: principles and process, *Support for Learning*, Vol. 5, no. 2, pp. 83–8.

Goldschmied, E. (1987) *Infants at Work*, available from the Early Childhood Unit, National Children's Bureau, London.

Goldschmied, E. (1991) What to do with the under twos. Heuristic play. Infants learning, in D. Rouse (ed.) (1991a) op. cit.

Hanney, M. (1991) *Under Fives in Wales: A New Look at Service Provision*, National Children's Bureau, Caerphilly.

Hannon, P., Weinberger, J. and Nutbrown, C. (1991) A study of work with parents to promote early literacy development, *Research Papers in Education*, Vol. 6, no. 2, pp. 77–97.

Harris, J. (1984) Early language intervention programmes: an update, *Newsletter of the Association for Child Psychology and Psychiatry*, Vol. 6, no. 2, April.

Her Majesty's Inspectorate of Schools (1989) *The Education of Children Under Five*, HMSO, London.

Hevey, D. (1986) *The Continuing Under Fives Training Muddle*, VOLCUF, London.

Hevey, D. (1991a) Final report of the Working with Under Sevens Project. Presented to the Care Sector Consortium, September.

Hevey, D. (1991b) Not child's play: developing occupational standards for workers with under sevens and their families, *Competence and Assessment*, Issue 15, pp. 11–14.

Hevey, D. and Windle, K. (1990) Unpublished Report of Working with Under Sevens Project Occupational Mapping Survey.

Hewitt, S. (ed.) (1971) *The Training of Teachers*, ULP, London.

High/Scope (1986) *Introduction to the High/Scope Preschool Curriculum: A Two-Day Workshop*, High Scope Educational Research Foundation, Ypsilanti, Michigan.

HMSO (1976) Race Relations Act.

HMSO (1988) Education Reform Act.

HMSO (1989) The Children Act.

Holtermann, S. (1992) *Investing in Young Children: costing an education and day care service*, National Children's Bureau, London.

Hopkins, D. (1985) *A Teacher's Guide to Classroom Research*, Open University Press, Buckingham.

Hornby, G. (1988) Launching parent-to-parent schemes, *British Journal of Special Education*, Vol. 15, no. 2, pp. 77–9.

House of Commons (1987) *Special Educational Needs: Implementation of the Education Act 1981* Education Science and Arts Committee, HMSO, London.

House of Commons (1989) *Educational Provision for the Under Fives*, Education, Science and Arts Committee, session 1988–9, first report, HMSO, London.

Howe, M. (1990) *Sense and Nonsense about Hothouse Children*, British Psychological Society, Leicester.

Hurst, V. (1991) *Planning for Early Learning: Education in the First Five Years*, Paul Chapman, London.

Hutt, C. (1979) *Play in the Under Fives: Form, Development and Function*, Brunner/Mazel, New York.

Hutt, S. J., Tyler, S., Hutt, C. and Christopherson, H. (1989) *Play, Exploration and Learning*, Routledge, London.

Isaacs, S. (1930) *Intellectual Growth in Young Children*, Routledge & Kegan Paul, London.

Jessup, G. (1991) *Outcomes: NVQs and the Emerging Model of Education and Training*, Falmer, Lewes.

Jordan, B. (1987) *Creative Social Work with Families*, BASW Publications, Birmingham.

Katz, L. (1987) Burnout by five, quoted in *The Times Educational Supplement*, 18 September 1987.

Kids Club Network (1989) *Guidelines of Good Practice for Out of School Care Schemes*, National Out of School Alliance (Now Kids Club Network), London.

Korner, A. (1989) Infant stimulation: the pros and cons in historical perspective, *Zero to Three*, Vol. X, no. 2, pp. 11–17.

Lally, M. (1991) *The Nursery Teacher in Action*, Paul Chapman, London.

Lane, J. (1990) Sticks and carrots: using the Race Relations Act to remove bad practice and the Children Act to promote good practice, *Local Government Policy Making*, Vol. 17, no. 3.

le Vine, R. A. (1989) Cultural environments in child development, in W. Damon (ed.) *Child Development Today and Tomorrow*, Jossey-Bass, San Francisco.

Lieberman, A. (1991) Attachment and exploration: the toddler's dilemma, *Zero to Three*, Vol. XI, no. 3, pp. 6–10.

Lubeck, S. (1986) *Sandbox Society*, Falmer, Lewes.

Manpower Services Commission and Department of Education and Science (1986) *Review of Vocational Qualifications in England and Wales*, HMSO, London.

Maximé, J. (1986) Some psychological models of black self-concept, in S. Ahmed, J. Cheetham and J. Small (eds.) *Social Work with Black Children and their Families*, Batsford, London.

Maximé, J. (1991) The importance of racial identity for the pyschological well-being of the young black child, in G. Pugh (ed.) *Quality and Equality for Under Fives Conference Report*, National Children's Bureau/NES.

Mayall, B. (1986) *Keeping Children Healthy*, Allen & Unwin, London.
Mayall, B. (1990) Childcare and childhood, *Children & Society*, Vol. 4, no. 4.
McConkey, R. (1985) *Working with Parents*, Croom Helm, London.
McLean, S. V. (1991) *The Human Encounter*, Falmer, Lewes.
Meadows, S. and Cashdan, A. (1988) *Helping Children Learn: Contributions to a Cognitive Curriculum*, David Fulton, London.
Melhuish, E. (1991) Research issues in day care, in P. Moss and E. Melhuish, op. cit.
Melhuish, E. and Moss, P. (eds.) (1990) *Day Care for Young Children: International Perspectives*, Routledge, London.
Meltzoff, A. and Moore, M. K. (1991) Cognitive foundations and social functions of imitation and intermodal representation in infancy, in M. Woodhead, R. Carr and P. Light (eds.) *Becoming a Person*, Open University Press, Buckingham.
Menter, I. (1989) They're too young to notice: young children and racism, in G. Barrett (ed.) *Disaffection from School: The Early Years*, Falmer, Lewes.
Messenger, K. and Curtis, C. (eds.) (1991) *NVQ: The Workplace Revolution*, Local Government Management Board, Luton.
Milner, D. (1983) *Children and Race: Ten Years On*, Ward Lock Educational, London.
Moore, M. K. (1975) Object permanence and object identity. Paper presented at conference of the Society for Research in Child Development, Denver, Colorado.
Moss, P. (1990) Work, family and the care of children: issues of equality and responsibility, *Children & Society*, Vol. 4, no. 2, pp. 145–66.
Moss, P. and Melhuish, E. (1991) (eds.) *Current Issues in Day Care for Young Children*, HMSO, London.
Moyles, J. (1989) *Just Playing? The Role and Status of Play in Early Childhood Education*, Open University Press, Milton Keynes.
National Childminding Association (1991) *Setting the Standards*, National Childminding Association, Bromley, Kent.
National Children's Bureau: Early Childhood Unit (1991) *Ensuring Standards in the Care of Young Children. Registering and Developing Quality Day Care* (A training pack for staff responsible for registration and inspection of childminding and day care under the Children Act 1989), National Children's Bureau, London.
National Children's Bureau: Under Fives Unit (1990) *A Policy for Young Children: A Framework for Action*, National Children's Bureau, London.
National Consumer Council (1986) *The Missing Links Between Home and School: a Consumer View*, NCC, London.
National Consumer Council (1991) *Daycare Services for Under Fives: A Consumer View*, NCC, London.
National Council for Vocational Qualifications (1988) *Assessment in National Vocational Qualifications*, NCVQ Information Note No. 4, NCVQ, London.
National Council for Vocational Qualifications (1989) *The NVQ Criteria and Related Guidance*, NCVQ, London.
National Curriculum Council (1989) *Special Educational Needs in the National Curriculum*, Curriculum Guidance 2, NCC, York.
National Foundation for Educational Research/Schools Curriculum Development Committee (1987) *Four-Year-Olds in School: Policy and Practice*, NFER, Windsor.

National Nursery Examination Board (1990) *The Diploma in Nursery Nursing.*

Nielsen, W. (1989) The longitudinal effects of Project Head Start on students' overall academic success: a review of the literature, *International Journal of Early Childhood*, Vol. 21, no. 1, pp. 35–42.

Norwich, B. (1990) *Reappraising Special Needs Education*, Cassell, London.

Nutbrown, C. (1987) A case study of the development and implementation of a nursery curriculum based on schematic theory. Unpublished B.Ed. dissertation, Sheffield City Polytechnic.

Nutbrown, C. (1991) *Early Literacy Development and Work with Parents: Putting the Theory into Practice*, OMEP (UK).

Osborn, A. and Milbank, J. (1987) *The Effects of Early Education*, Clarendon Press, Oxford.

Papousek, H. (1969) Individual variability in learned responses in human infants, in R. J. Robinson (ed.) *Brain and Early Behaviour*, Academic Press, London.

Parry, M. and Archer, H. (1974) *Pre-School Education*, Schools Council/Macmillan Educational, London.

Pascal, C. (1990) *Under Fives in Infant Classrooms*, Trentham, Stoke-on-Trent.

Penn, H. (in press) *The Rise of Private Nurseries*, Local Government Management Board, Luton.

Piaget, J. (1951) *Play, Dreams and Imitation*, Routledge & Kegan Paul, London.

Pre-School Playgroups Association (1990a) *PPA Guidelines: Good Practice for Sessional Playgroups*, Pre-School Playgroups Association, London.

Pre-School Playgroups Association (1990b) *PPA Guidelines. Good Practice for Full Daycare Playgroups*, Pre-School Playgroups Association, London.

Pringle, M. K. (1975) *The Needs of Children*, Hutchinson, London.

Prizant, B. and Wetherby, A. (1990) Assessing the communication of infants and toddlers: integrating a socioemotional perspective, *Zero to Three*, Vol. XI, no. 1, pp. 1–12.

Prosser, M. (1991) 'What makes me ME?' – children attempting to compile a model for self-assessment. Unpublished MA assignment, Cambridge Institute of Education.

Pugh, G. (1987) Early education and day care: in search of a policy, *Journal of Education Policy*, Vol. 2, no. 4, pp. 301–16.

Pugh, G. (1988) *Services for Under Fives: Developing a Coordinated Approach*, National Children's Bureau, London.

Pugh, G. (1989) Parents and professionals in preschool services: is partnership possible? in S. Wolfendale (ed.) *Parental Involvement: Developing Networks between School, Home and Community*, Cassell, London.

Pugh, G. (1990) Developing a policy for early childhood education: challenges and constraints, *Early Child Development and Care*, Vol. 58, pp. 3–13.

Pugh, G., Aplin, G., De'Ath, E. and Moxon, M. (1987) *Partnership in Action: Working with Parents in Pre-School Centres*, Vols. 1 and 2, National Children's Bureau, London.

Pugh, G. and De'Ath, E. (1989) *Working Towards Partnership in the Early Years*, National Children's Bureau, London.

Rieser, R. and Mason, M. (1990) *Disability, Equality in the Classroom: A Human Rights Issue*, Inner London Education Authority.

Roaf, C. and Bines, H. (eds.) (1989) *Needs, Rights and Opportunities*, Falmer, Lewes.

Robson, B. (1989) *Preschool Provision for Children with Special Needs*, Cassell, London.

Ross, D. (1990) *Costs of Implementing National Vocational Qualifications*. Papers 1, 2 and 3, CCETSW/Local Government Training Board in conjunction with the ADSS North West Regional Training Unit.

Rouse, D. (ed.) (1991a) *Babies and Toddlers: Carers and Educators. Quality for Under Threes*. National Children's Bureau, London.

Rouse, D. (1991b) *An Italian Experience*. Unpublished. Available for reference at the Early Childhood Unit, National Children's Bureau, London.

Ruddick, S. (1989) *Maternal Thinking Towards a Politics of Peace*, Ballantine, New York.

Russell, P. (1990) Policy and practice for young children with special educational needs: changes and challenges, *Support for Learning*, Vol. 5, no. 2, pp. 98–106.

Russell, P. and Gatiss, S. (1991) *Parental Involvement in the Assessment Procedures under 1981 Education Act*, DES-funded project based at National Children's Bureau, London.

Saffin, K. and McFarlane, A. (1988) Parent held child health and development records, *Journal of Family Medicine*, Vol. 13, no. 10, pp. 288–91.

Schaffer, H. and Emerson, P. (1964) The development of social attachments in infancy, *Child Development*, Vol. 29, no. 94.

Schools Council (1981) *The Practical Curriculum*, Schools Council, London.

Scott, G. (1989) *Families and Under Fives in Strathclyde*, Glasgow College and Strathclyde Regional Council.

SEAC (1990) *Records of Achievement in Primary Schools*.

Sheffield LEA (1986) *Nursery Education Guidelines for Curriculum, Organization, Assessment*, City of Sheffield Education Department.

Sheffield LEA (1991a) *Observation, Record Keeping and Classroom Management*. Course materials, City of Sheffield Education Department.

Sheffield LEA (1991b) *Record Keeping for Children Under Five in all Settings*, City of Sheffield Education Department.

Siraj-Blatchford, I. (1990) A positive role, *Child Education*, November.

Smail, D. (1984) *Taking Care: An Alternative to Therapy*, Dent, London.

Smith, P. K. (ed.) (1986) *Children's Play: Research, Development and Practical Applications*, Gordon & Breach, New York.

Smith, T. (1990) Services for the under fives: what children need and parents want? *Local Government Policy Making*, Vol. 17, no. 3, December.

Statham, J. (1991) *Under Fives in Sunderland: A Survey of Parents' Views of Pre-school Provision*, National Children's Bureau, London.

Statham, J., Lloyd, E. and Moss, P. (1989) *Playgroups in Three Countries*. TCRU Working and Occasional Paper No. 8, Thomas Coram Research Unit, London.

Statham, J., Lloyd, E., Moss, P., Melhuish, E. and Owen, C. (1990) *Playgroups in a Changing World*, HMSO, London.

Stephenson, S. (1990) Research supplement: promoting interaction among children, *British Journal of Special Education*, Vol. 17, no. 2, pp. 61–6, June.

Stewart, J. and Walsh, K. (1989) *The Search for Quality*, Local Government Training Board, Luton.

Stroh, K. and Robinson, T. (1991) Developmental delay in young children, *Child Language Teaching and Therapy*, Vol. 7, no. 1, p. 7.

Sylva, K., Campbell, R. J., Coates, E., David, T., Fitzgerald, J., Goodyear, R., Jowett, M., Lewis, A. and Neil, S. St. J. (1990) *Assessing Three- to Eight-Year-Olds*, NFER, Windsor.

Sylva, K. and David, T. (1990) 'Quality' education in preschool provision, *Local Government Policy Making*, Vol. 17, no. 3, pp. 61–7.

Sylva, K. and Lunt, I. (1982) *Child Development: A First Course*, Blackwell, Oxford.

Sylva, K., Roy, C. and Painter, M. (1980) *Childwatching at Playgroup and Nursery School*, Grant McIntyre, London.

Thoburn, J. (1986) Quality control in child care, *British Journal of Social Work*, Vol. 16, no. 5, pp. 543–56.

Tizard, B. and Hughes, M. (1984) *Young Children Learning*, Fontana, London.

Tizard, B., Mortimore, J. and Burchell, B. (1981) *Involving Parents in Nursery and Infant Schools*, Grant McIntyre, London.

Tobin, J., Wu, D. and Davidson, D. (1989) *Preschool in Three Cultures: Japan, China and the United States*, Yale University Press.

Tomlinson, J. (1986) The co-ordinator of services for under fives, *TACTYC*, Vol. 7, no. 1, Autumn 1986.

Tomlinson, J. (1991) Attitudes to children: are children valued? *Early Years*, Vol. 11, no. 2, Spring 1991.

Trevarthen, C. (1990) Early parent-child interaction, in *Portage at Pontins*. Conference Proceedings, National Portage Association, London.

Unicef (1989) *The Draft Convention on the Rights of the Child*.

Unicef-UK (1990) *Convention on the Rights of the Child*, 55 Lincoln's Inn Fields, London WC2 3NB.

Vygotsky, L. S. (1978) *Mind in Society: The Development of Higher Level Psychological Processes*, Harvard University Press.

Walker, R. (1985) *Doing Research*, Methuen, London.

Walkerdine, V. and Lucey, H. (1989) *Democracy in the Kitchen: Regulating Mothers and Socialising Daughters*, Virago, London.

Ward, E. (1986) Sound policies promote effective programmes for young children, in *Children are worth the Effort: Today, Tomorrow and Beyond: A Memorial to Evangeline Ward 1920–85*, Australian Early Childhood Association, Canberra.

Watt, J. (1990) *Early Education: The Current Debate*, Scottish Academic Press, Edinburgh.

Watts, B. N. (1987) Changing families: changing children's services, *Australian Journal of Early Childhood Education*, Vol. 12, no. 3, pp. 4–12.

Webster, B. (1990) Reviewing services for under fives and their families in Gloucestershire, *Local Government Policy Making*, Vol. 17, no. 3, December.

Wedge, D. (1991) Building a consortium, in K. Messenger and C. Curtis (eds.) op. cit.

Weinberger, J., Hannon, P. and Nutbrown, C. (1990) *Ways of Working with Parents to Promote Early Literacy Development*. USDE Papers in Education No. 14, University of Sheffield Division of Education.

Wells, G. (1985) *Language Development in the Preschool Years*, Cambridge University Press.

Wells, I. (1989) Parents and education for severe learning difficulties, research supplement, *British Journal of Special Education*, Vol. 16, no. 4, pp. 151–61.

Whitebook, M., Howes, C. and Phillips (1990) *Who Cares? Child Care Teachers and the Quality of Care in America*. Executive summary of the National Child Care Staffing Study, Berkeley, Child Care Employee Project.

Wolfendale, S. (1983) *Parental Participation in Children's Development and Education*, Gordon & Breach, London.

Wolfendale, S. (1987a) Development services to meet the special needs of children under five, *Children and Society*, Vol. 3, Autumn, pp. 224–39.

Wolfendale, S. (1987b) The evaluation and revision of the ALL ABOUT ME preschool parent-completed scales, *Early Child Development and Care*, Vol. 29, pp. 473–558.

Wolfendale, S. (1988) *The Parental Contribution to Assessment*, Developing Horizons No. 10, National Council for Special Education, Coventry.

Wolfendale, S. (1989a) Parental involvement and power sharing in special needs, in S. Wolfendale (ed.) *Parental Involvement: Developing Networks between School, Home and Community*, Cassell, London.

Wolfendale, S. (1989b) Special needs in early education, in C. Desforges (ed.) *Early Childhood Education*, Scottish Academic Press, Edinburgh.

Wolfendale, S. (1990) *All about Me*, NES Arnold, Nottingham.

Wood, D., McMahon, L. and Cranstoun, Y. (1980) *Working with Under Fives*, Grant McIntyre, London.

Woodhead, M. (1976) *Intervening in Disadvantage*, NFER-Nelson, Windsor.

Woodhead, M. (1985) Pre-school education has long-term effects: but can they be generalized? *Oxford Review Education*, Vol. 11, no. 2, pp. 133–55.

Woodhead, M. (1987) Some lessons from research into preschool effectiveness, *Concern*, Summer, National Children's Bureau, London.

Woodhead, M. (1991) Psychology and the cultural construction of children's needs, in M. Woodhead, M. Light and R. Carr (eds.) *Growing up in a Changing Society*, Routledge, London.

Woodruffe, C. and Kurtz, Z. (1989) *Working for Children? Children's Services and the NHS Review*, National Children's Bureau, London.

Working Group Against Racism in Children's Resources (1990) *Guidelines: For the Evaluation and Selection of Toys and other Resources for Children*, 460 Wandsworth Road, London SW8 3LX.

Zigler, E. F. (1987) Formal schooling for four-year-olds? No, *American Psychologist*, Vol. 42, no. 3, pp. 254–60.

AUTHOR INDEX

SUBJECT INDEX

access: to services 13–14, 28, 91,
   128–9, 136; to qualifications 206
accident prevention 184
accountability 100
admission to primary school 35
adult: education 67, 181, 183; roles
   and relationships 84–5; role in
   children's learning 26, 72, 80,
   81–5, 89
advertising 106
advisers, social services day care 51,
   60, 111, 121; see also inspectors
aesthetic development 81, 148,
   196
Africa 105, 108, 115
Afro-Caribbean 105, 119
anti-racist education 41, 136; see also
   equal opportunities, racism
Asia, Asian 105, 116, 117, 119
assertiveness 157, 163
assessment: instruments 96–7, 128,
   136; of children 5, 13, 16, 27, 65,
   73, 83, 87 ff, 125, 129–135, 136, 149,
   154, 163, 171, 199; of practitioners
   65, 205, 207; of quality 53; of
   teacher assessment 98; see also
   SATs
Association of County Councils 16
Association of Metropolitan
   Authorities 18, 19, 28
attachment 140–2, 144
audiology 131
autism 134–5
autonomy 142, 144–7, 198

B.Ed (Batchelor of Education) 194,
   195
B.A. (Batchelor of Arts) (early
   years) 209
babies 93, 99, 138 ff
behaviour 65, 94, 134–5, 148, 150,
   173–4; see also racist behaviour
Belgium 30, 31–2, 33, 36
beliefs see values
bilingualism 85, 99, 116, 120
Black people 105 ff

books 116–7, 120
braille 115
Britain 34–5, 39, 41; see also United
   Kingdom

CATE (Council for the Accreditation
   of Teacher Education) 195–6, 209
CQSW (Certificate of Qualification in
   Social Work) 160, 162
Cambridgeshire 50, 61, 63–7
Camden 113
Care Sector Consortium 2, 204–5
caring for staff see support
case conference 161
Caribbean 105, 117
child: abuse 167, 172, 173–4;
   care 2, 46, 205; development 65,
   163, 176, 199, 200; Development
   Centre 130–5; guidance 162;
   protection 14, 21, 123, 163;
   psychology 163; rearing 121, 147,
   185
Childcare Links 25, 33
childminders 11, 13, 21, 22, 23, 36,
   49, 58, 111, 112, 115, 120, 121, 138,
   139–40, 144, 177, 189, 201, 205
Children Act 2, 4, 14–17, 18, 24, 25,
   41, 50, 54, 57–63, 83, 89, 105,
   110–111, 124, 125, 136–140, 163,
   181, 202, 208; Guidance 2, 15, 16,
   25, 50, 53, 59–60, 110–111, 140, 202
children: 'at risk' 177; 'in need' 15,
   21–2, 58, 62, 124, 188; interests of
   103; needs of 2, 10, 51–2; rights of
   2, 123, 140, 150; with disabilities
   15, 22, 27, 122 ff, 146, 147; with
   special educational needs 5, 13, 15,
   21, 122 ff, 205
China, Chinese 114, 117, 141, 142–3
cliques 183
choice: for children 76; for
   parents 40
cognitive development 115–6, 128,
   148, 151
collaboration 62–3, 83, 137, 168; see
   also multidisciplinary collaboration

ASSESSMENT IN EARLY CHILDHOOD EDUCATION

Edited by Geva M. Blenkin and A.V. Kelly

Assessment has always been a major feature of education in the early years. This book has three objectives: to identify the essential features of forms of assessment which will be genuinely supportive of education in the early years; to help teachers in their search for such forms; and to evaluate the likely impact of the system of external assessment currently being imposed.

1 85396 153 1 Paper 1992 200pp

CHILDREN AND DAY CARE

Lessons from Research

Eilis Hennessy, Sue Martin, Peter Moss and Edward Melhuish

A number of questions relevant to child development are being asked now that more children spend some of their pre-school years in day care. These questions include: Are there differences in the development of children in different types of day care? How do children in day care fare when they go to school? This book looks at these and other questions and at the research relevant to the development of these children.

1 85396 184 1 Paper 1992 128pp

THE NURSERY TEACHER IN ACTION

Margaret Lally

This book provides a detailed discussion of the responsibilities and achievements of the skilled nursery teacher.

The issues and concerns outlined are ones all nursery teachers must address in their work. The practical suggestions in the book highlight many of the ways effective nursery teachers are translating principles into practice.

1 85396 131 0 Paper 1991 208pp

EDUCATION 3–5 *SECOND EDITION*

Marion Dowling

The Second Edition of this widely used book blends a practical approach to nursery work with a consideration of research which highlights the best practices. It will be of great benefit to everyone in pre-school education.

1 85396 166 3 Paper 1992 240pp

EXPLORING LEARNING
Young Children and Blockplay

**Edited by Pat Gura with the Froebel Blockplay
Research Group directed by Tina Bruce**

This book shows how blockplay illustrates, at the
micro-level, the development of the child's
understanding of and competence in controlling
three-dimensional space.

1 85396 171 X Paper 1992 240pp

EXTENDING THOUGHT IN YOUNG CHILDREN
A Parent–Teacher Partnership

Chris Athey

This book documents invariant 'forms of thought'
used by young children, which are currently
unrecorded in the literature on children's thinking.

Throughout the book, illustrations focus on the
positive achievements of children, parents and
teachers. The book draws on a wide range of
research and advances educational theory in the
early years.

1 85396 182 6 Paper 1990 256pp

PLANNING FOR EARLY LEARNING
Education in the First Five Years

Victoria Hurst

In this book for parents and practitioners the author explores what a good start for the under-fives looks like, and how it can be built into the provision we make for them.

1 85396 129 9 Paper 1991 176pp

BEGINNING TEACHING
An Introduction to Early Years Education

Anne D Cockburn, University of East Anglia, with Cathy Whalen, Vivienne Gray and Peter Gibley

Beginning Teaching is about educating young children in their early years of schooling and is essential reading for all those planning a career teaching 4–8 year olds. It assumes no prior knowledge.

Easy-to-read, the book contains many practical examples gained from the authors' 15 years as a teacher and researcher in first school classrooms, and provides real insight into the lives of pupils, students and early years teachers. Beginning Teaching covers a wide range of issues including an introduction to young children's thinking, knowledge and behaviour.

1 85396 162 0 Paper March 1992 128pp

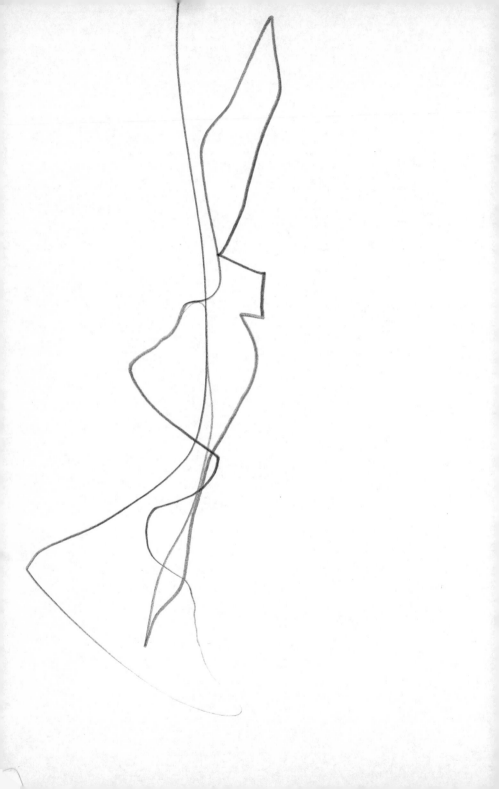